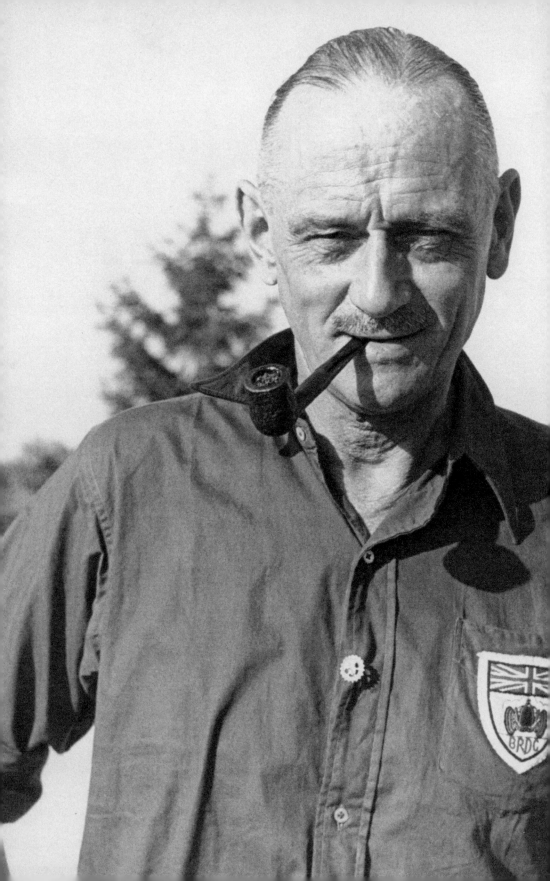

GOLDIE

JOHN MAYHEAD

NATIONAL MOTOR MUSEUM PUBLISHING

Published by National Motor Museum Publishing
www.nationalmotormuseum.org.uk

First published 2023
Third issue

ISBN 978-1-7396297-3-1

A CIP catalogue record for this book is available from the British Library.

Typeset in 11/16 pt Baskerville.
Design and typesetting by James Bristow at Beanwave.
Printed in Great Britain by Biddles Books Ltd, King's Lynn, Norfolk.
All materials have been sourced from sustainably managed forests.

MICHAEL SEDGWICK
MEMORIAL TRUST

Goldie is published with the financial assistance of the Michael Sedgwick Memorial
Trust. The M.S.M.T. was founded in memory of the motoring historian and author
Michael C. Sedgwick (1926–1983) to encourage the publication of new motoring
research, and the recording of Road Transport History. Support by the Trust does
not imply any involvement in the editorial process, which remains the responsibility
of the editor and publisher. The Trust is a Registered Charity, No 290841, and a full
list of the Trustees and an overview of the functions of the M.S.M.T. can be found
on: www.michaelsedgwicktrust.co.uk

For Johanna

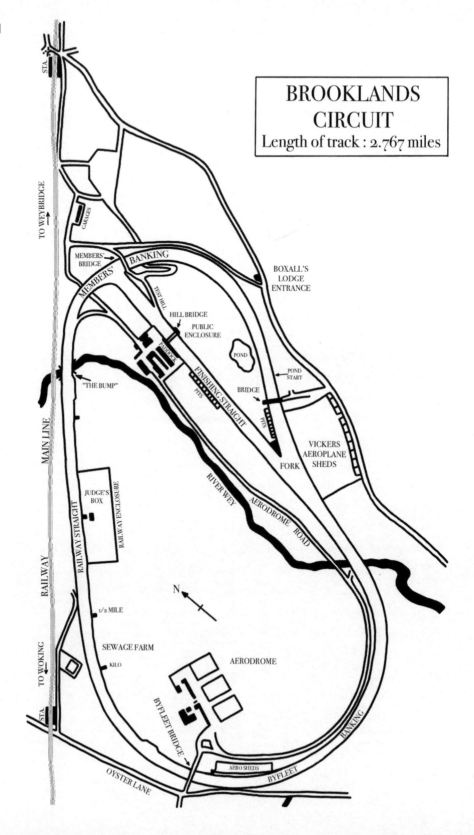

BROOKLANDS CIRCUIT
Length of track : 2.767 miles

Contents		Page
	Maps	vi & viii
	Foreword	1
	Introduction	4
1	Gunfire	7
2	The Greatest Thrill	12
3	The Flight	24
4	Racing	34
5	Death and Success	49
6	Catching Breath	56
7	Kimber	71
8	Battered About	84
9	Daytona	100
10	Faster & Faster	108
11	The First Records	117
12	The Streamlined Job	132
13	The Double Ton	144
14	A Return to the Colours	154
15	Back to Work	166
16	Jabbeke	178
17	10,000 Miles in 10,000 Minutes	189
18	Speed on the Salt	200
19	The Final Run	212
20	Sickness	219
21	Legacy	225
	Epilogue	235
	Acknowledgements	240
	List of races	244
	List of records	253
	List of cars	263
	Bibliography	268
	Index	273

CONTENTS

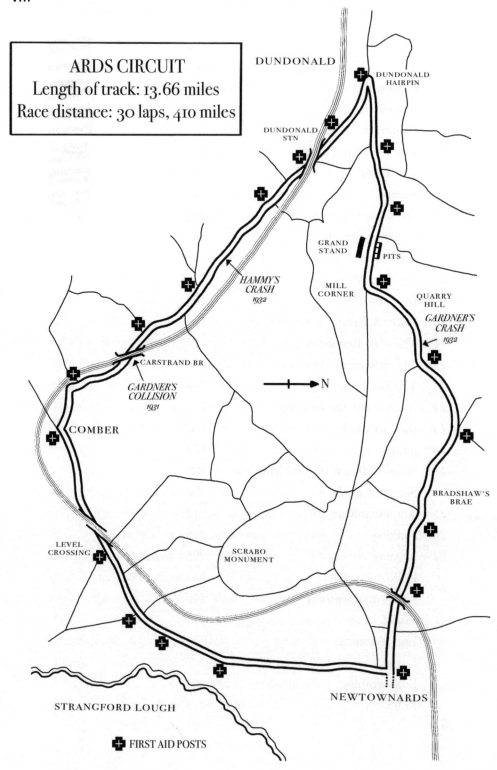

ARDS CIRCUIT
Length of track: 13.66 miles
Race distance: 30 laps, 410 miles

DUNDONALD

DUNDONALD
HAIRPIN

DUNDONALD
STN

HAMMY'S
CRASH
1932

GRAND
STAND

PITS

MILL
CORNER

QUARRY
HILL

GARDNER'S
CRASH
1932

CARSTRAND BR

GARDNER'S
COLLISION
1931

N

COMBER

BRADSHAW'S
BRAE

LEVEL
CROSSING

SCRABO
MONUMENT

STRANGFORD LOUGH

NEWTOWNARDS

FIRST AID POSTS

FOREWORD

BY HIS GRACE THE DUKE OF RICHMOND AND GORDON

The friendship between my grandfather, Freddie Richmond and Goldie Gardner was forged on the unforgiving concrete of the Brooklands banking in the mid-1920s. It lasted for over thirty years until Gardner's death in 1958. Although my grandfather was fourteen years younger than the wounded Great War veteran, they found a great deal in common, not least of which was a pure love of motor racing.

From the very start, both men bonded over their attraction to the tiny racing cars created by Cecil Kimber under the new MG brand. Freddie's first ever competitive outing was in a MG M-Type Midget in the July 1929 Junior Car Club (JCC) High Speed Trial. A couple of years later, when the new C-Type Midget was unveiled, he and Gardner were among the very first recipients of the new model and they were each given one with great fanfare at the Brooklands track. The cars were light, fast and nimble, making them extremely competitive against the huge aero-engined behemoths that also graced the racing circuits of the day, but at a fraction of the cost.

For the next few years, there was a keen rivalry between the two friends, each of whom ran a team of three Midgets. Beyond Brooklands, the teams competed in the gruelling road races of the Ulster Tourist Trophy and the Irish Grand Prix in Dublin, their cars often duelling for the lead to the delight of Cecil Kimber, who could not have bought the publicity this brought.

By the late 1930s, the two men had moved in different directions in their motoring careers. Goldie Gardner had become very well known

STEWARDS OF THE MEETING

His Grace the Duke of Richmond and Gordon

T. Blackburn

Capt. G. E. T. Eyston, O.B.E., M.C.

Lt.-Col. A. T. Goldie Gardner, O.B.E., M.C.

OFFICIALS

Held under the International Sporting Code of the Federation Internationale de l'Automobile, the General Competition Rules of the Royal Automobile Club and Supplementary Regulations issued by the British Racing Drivers' Club.

STEWARDS

His Grace the Duke of Richmond and Gordon (for the R.A.C.).
T. Blackburn.   Capt. G. E. T. Eyston, O.B.E., M.C.
Lt.-Col. A. T. Goldie Gardner, O.B.E., M.C.

JUDGES

F. E. Clifford.   The Rt. Hon. Lord E...   ...ughes.
H. J. Morgan.

OBSERVERS

Chief Observer : H. D. Parker.

Assisted by :   A. Daunt Bateman, O.B.E.
N. E. Bracey.   P. C. T. Clark.
L. P. Driscoll.   C. G. H. Dunham.
A. B. Gilbert.   C. L. Goodacre.
F. W. Kennington. F. J. Monkhouse.
I. H. Nickols.   G. P. Harvey Noble.
W. D. Phillips. V. L. Seyd. J. L. Stableford.
ford. W. L. Thompson. R. E. Tongue.

Chief

Assist

Assi
Maj
for
C.
Ga
D
T
J

B·A·R·C
INTERNATIONAL CAR RACE MEETING
GOODWOOD
Near Chichester, Sussex
By arrangement with the Goodwood Road Racing Co., Ltd.
MONDAY, 6th APRIL, 1953

The Meeting is held under the International Sporting Code of the Federation Internationale de l'Automobile (hereinafter called the F.I.A.), the General Competition Rules of the Royal Automobile Club, the General Competition Rules of the British Automobile Racing Club, and such Supplementary Regulations and Instructions as the Club may issue for the Meeting. R.A.C. Permit No. 0/41.

PATRONS OF THE MEETING:
His Grace the Duke of Richmond and Gordon
(President of the British Automobile Racing Club)
D. M. Glover

Stewards of the Meeting   OFFICIALS
The Rt. Hon. Earl Howe (representing the R.A.C.)
F. H. Bale, O.B.E., M.I.Mech.E.
Professor A. M. Low, D.Sc., A.C.G.I., etc.   A. Logette
Judges   Major L. H. White
J. Duncan Ferguson, F.C.A.   Lieut.-Col. A. T. G. Gardner, O.B.E., M.C.
Stanley Sedgwick, A.C.A. H. R. Godfrey, M.I.Mech.E
Chief Observer
J. Gordon Offord   Incident Officer   Chief Marshal
Observers   Geo. Roberts   S. M. Lawry
Cmdr. B. V. Alcock
A. I. Geikie Cobb   Lieut.-Col A
P. J. M...

for his record-breaking achievements and my grandfather became more and more involved in the leadership of the JCC, taking over as President after the war. With Brooklands having closed for good, the club merged with the old BARC, changing its name to the British Automobile Racing Club, Gardner being voted in straight away as an honorary life member. The club needed a new home and when my grandfather, who was by then Duke of Richmond, decided to convert the perimeter track of the old RAF Westhampnett aerodrome on the Goodwood estate into a motor racing circuit, it was only right that his old friend was invited along. Gardner's daughter Ros has very clear memories of standing at the start/finish straight at Goodwood as a young girl watching her father and my grandfather standing together as the cars roared past. Right through the early 1950s until his health deteriorated, Goldie was a regular official at Goodwood race meetings. In the autumn of 1958, Goldie finally succumbed to the head injury sustained on the salt flats of Bonneville and on 18th September, my grandfather led the mourners at his memorial service in London.

That Goldie Gardner is not more well known today is a great shame. Unlike many of the other great record breakers and racing drivers of that era, neither Gardner nor my grandfather were showmen. Both had deeply formative experiences in their early lives: Gardner in the trenches at the Somme and my grandfather losing his older brother and hero, Charlie, before taking up an apprenticeship on the shop floor at Bentley. As a result, neither man felt the need to make a fuss about their love of motor racing - they just got on and did it. Both, for very different reasons, have extraordinary legacies.

INTRODUCTION

My relationship with Goldie Gardner started entirely by accident. A few years ago, on my way to a friend's wedding in the Netherlands and on the verge of testing my wife's patience to its limit, I decided to stop off and try to find a particular strip of dead-straight Belgian motorway. Following instructions that I found on an online forum, I pulled up in a service station and, leaving my bemused spouse in the car, climbed over the barrier and waded through tall grass as lorries thundered by. Soon, I found what I was looking for: a ribbon of obsolete tarmac now separated from the main carriageway, its crumbling edges skirted with weeds.

This was the place that in the late forties and early fifties resonated to the sound of the fastest cars of the day being pushed to their limits, setting speed records to the delight of the press who were desperate to report on something that diverted their readers from the drab austerity of the post-war world. The nearby town of Jabbeke was suddenly a place of glamour and excitement, attracting the most famous drivers of the day like Stirling Moss and the charismatic Sheila Van Damm, driving sleek new cars like the Jaguar XK120 and Rover's futuristic gas turbine-powered Jet 1.

But amongst the familiar names, one unknown man stood out: a 56-year-old, injured war veteran who could only walk with a stick and at 6'3" was so tall he could only just prise himself into his car. This man, Alfred Goldie Gardner, was the first to attempt a record run at Jabbeke and, try as I might, I could not find much written about him online other than a scant Wikipedia page and a few old newspaper articles. Then, I discovered that the National Motor Museum has 35 boxes of his papers and paid them a visit. Over three years later, after a wonderful journey of discovery that combined dusty museum archives, scores of out-of-print books, access to personal collections that had lain hidden in attics for decades and getting to know a lovely group of people who are connected to Goldie Gardner, here we are.

Rediscovering Goldie's story was a fascinating journey. The Boy's Own elements were expected: the moustache-wearing hero who pushed himself to the limit both in search of race wins and record titles, who triumphed with a home-built 'special' car to the astonishment of his Nazi hosts before the war and later took part in secret wartime missions. But other elements came as a surprise: the deeper subtext of what drove him and the other drivers to risk their lives for honour and country, his turbulent relationships and the obsession that almost destroyed his family.

I'm very fortunate that my day job is also one of my life's passions: I write about classic cars. That means that although I could never know the fear of taking the big 'bump' at Brooklands at over a ton or the exhilaration of pushing to over 200 miles-per-hour with just a small set of drum brakes to slow you if anything went wrong, I do know what it feels like to drive old cars both on the road and on the track. Since the Goodwood Revival started, I've been present in the paddock and on the pit wall, seeing the work the unsung mechanics put in behind the scenes, watching the drivers push the envelope of what is possible and experiencing the sights and sounds of pre-war cars firing up on a cold and misty dawn. As Goldie did, I have raced up the hill at Shelsley Walsh and I've even driven a couple of his cars. I also have the dubious honour of having experienced someone trying to kill me with rockets, mortar shells and rifle bullets, thanks to my service as a younger man in the British Army that included deployments to Northern Ireland, Iraq, and Afghanistan.

In my day job, I'm used to writing for an audience of knowledge-able, well-informed motoring enthusiasts. I have written this book for them, but also for people who just love a good story that includes love, obsession, bravery, and intrigue. For the former, I have included de-tailed notes and annexes. For the latter, I have hopefully woven enough of a tale so that all my readers are entertained and enthralled by the account of this exceptional man. I believe it is a story that deserves to be heard.

The author, in his 1946 MG TC.
Photo: Jonathan Fleetwood/Octane.

1

GUNFIRE

26.8.16 At 11.15am to 12.30pm Batteries very heavily shelled with 5.9s and 8",
about 50 rounds per minute. B72 1 gun knocked out, 1 man slightly wounded. D72
1 man killed. C72 3 wounded. In the evening, enemy shelled again.[1]

The Adjutant's entry in the war diary was typically short, typically devoid of emotion. His job was to channel the carnage and chaos of war
into a few sentences, recording the tally as if it were a cricket score-
book: shots fired, shots received; our wounded and killed versus theirs.

He didn't have time to explain that the identification of the incoming German artillery shells was hard-won information. For over eighteen months now, the troops of the 72nd Brigade of the Royal Field
Artillery had experienced what the British Army blandly calls 'indirect
fire', cowering in their trenches, knees clamped to their chests, helmets
pulled down, eyelids squeezed as tightly as they would go, like children
cloaking themselves under a blanket to escape a monster. They'd all
learnt by now that none of it mattered; if you were lucky, you felt the

---

1   72 Bde Royal Field Artillery, *Regimental Diary*, 1917 (IWM).

round explode, the pressure gripping your chest, ripping the air from your lungs and leaving you gasping for breath. If you were lucky, you saw the fizzing shards of shrapnel arc away like the fiery petals of a white-hot flower. If you were lucky, you started to recognise the different noises the shells made: the whizz that gave you a microsecond warning before the bang of the 105mm round; the ominous thud of the gas shell that had you scrabbling for your M2 gas mask, and the ground-shaking smash of the heavy artillery that tore huge clods of earth skywards, taking men, horses and equipment with them. If you were unlucky, your helmet, your trench, your rank, your training, your closed eyes… nothing would matter.

On that late summer's morning in August 1916, Captain Alfred Thomas Goldie Gardner took cover like the rest of the men in B Battery. He was more fortunate than most; as the Officer Commanding of 'B72' he had had a bunker dug for him when they had moved into position a few days earlier, next to the shattered remains of what had been the Martinpuich to High Wood Road in the heart of the Somme valley.[2] After the rains at the beginning of the month, the last few weeks had been mercifully dry and the ground was hard, but the men had managed to dig a hole big enough for Gardner, his signaller, and a runner. The sides had been revetted with anything they could find: splintered logs, wooden duckboards and the carcasses of ammunition boxes had been dragged over the top and around three feet of soil shovelled back into place. It was enough to prevent the odd fragment, but Gardner knew that it wouldn't provide any meaningful protection against a direct hit.

The first shells to arrive were the Five-Nines; huge, 15cm-diameter shells that delivered 93lbs of high explosive and left a trademark trail of black smoke. The troops called these the 'Jack Johnsons' after the American heavyweight boxer: black, deadly, always ready to deliver a knockout punch. As the deafening barrage crept closer to the bunker,

---

2   Air photographs, IWM, and Trevor Pidgeon, *The Tanks at Flers*, (Fairmile Books, 1995).

the runner looked up at his commander. Gunner Watson[3] was a junior soldier, originally from Tottenham in London, one of the recent replacements sent from England and as such hadn't yet earned the right to be considered anything other than expendable. His job was to run messages from the Battery Commander to the guns, amid the battle if so required, and he was terrified. Gardner looked at him, gave a brief smile, and then started tapping his cane against his boot, as if irritated by the time it was taking to conclude. The young Watson, caught off guard by his officer's nonchalance, forgot the shells for a moment and felt reassured: if Captain Gardner was calm, maybe it wasn't so bad after all.

It *was* that bad, but Gardner had learnt to control his emotions. Inside he was as scared as the young man opposite him, and probably more so. He had experienced counter-battery fire many times before, the deadly game the opposing artillery played with each other: track down your foe and send some of his bitter medicine back down his own throat. He had seen the results: some men survived at first, despite their bodies being shredded into vivid scarlet by shrapnel or reduced to a blackened, limbless torso by a close-proximity burst. Others died easily, hit in just the wrong place by a tiny fragment that hardly left a trace of its destructive path. Unlike the young lad, he also knew the reality: that this preliminary bombardment by Five-Nines was leading up to something else, something worse: maybe the deafening roar of the eight-inch howitzer shells or the bitter stench of mustard gas as they'd suffered a few days previously. But for his whole life, Gardner had been prepared to hide his true feelings: from the stiff, formal attire of his nursery and the cold showers and strict discipline of Uppingham School to the brutality of the rugby pitch, he had learnt that he was of the class that did not fuss, ignored the pain, and *led by example*. As a gentleman and as an officer, it was his duty.

---

3   Watson later wrote to Gardner (letter dated 25 July 1950, NMM Archive).

'Heavily shelled… about 50 rounds per minute,' the Adjutant had written, but that didn't start to capture the horror of the next hour-and-a-quarter. A few days previously, B72 had supported the attack of the 2nd Munster Fusiliers as they tried to take High Wood. They had fired 38 rounds *per hour* at the German trenches to keep their infantry's head down whilst the Munsters advanced. This was something else altogether: a concerted effort to kill the British gunners and destroy their weapons. Second after nerve-jangling second, the explosions kept coming, each picking its own random place to detonate.

Finally, the explosions ceased. The runner went to leave the bunker, but Gardner held him back. They sat in silence for a few minutes longer, just in case the Germans had decided to fire one last salvo to catch them as they emerged. Then they heard shouting, and Gardner knew it was over. Carefully, he led the two soldiers out into the sunlight and looked around them at the chaos that had engulfed the detachment.

The voice he had heard belonged to Sergeant Ernie Hewitt, the most capable of his non-commissioned officers.[4] He was yapping at the men like a snarling terrier, rousing them from their petrified state and forcing them back into the world of soldiery. Some way off along one of the trenches a man was screaming, and Hewitt physically grabbed two passing men by their webbing straps and launched them off to help their stricken colleague. Other stunned men were given simple but necessary tasks: cleaning the mud off the guns, repairing the trenches, and checking to see if the twisted, smouldering artillery piece that had received a direct hit could be salvaged.

Gardner knew better than to interfere. There was a time and a place for an officer to lead, and this was not it. In the aftermath of combat, it was a non-commissioned officer's war: men who had started at the bottom and worked their way up through competence, good fortune and often a fair amount of physicality. He stood back, lit a cigarette, and watched as Hewitt and the other NCOs went about their task of

---

4   Later promoted to Warrant Officer (Forces-war-records.co.uk).

re-establishing order to a landscape of abject chaos. In the two years he had been in uniform, Gardner had grown to like the men he served with. Although none of them would ever cross over the boundary of rank into informality, he considered some of them to be like friends. He looked at Hewitt harrying the troops, took another drag of his cigarette, and caught himself thinking that sometimes it wasn't too bad after all. Then, the Gunner who would later be described as 'slightly wounded' was carried past him still writhing in agony, his face wrapped in a puffy, marshmallow pad of field dressings, a vivid red stain of blood starting to seep through the bright white linen. Captain Gardner looked away, straightened his tunic, and went to find his Second-in-Command. Now that the enemy had their location, in all likelihood they would be moving again soon.

'That the damage was not heavier was in great measure due to Captain Gardner's energy in preparing dug-outs and withdrawing his men under cover at the critical moment,' wrote his commanding officer, Colonel James Stirling.[5] 'For his gallantry and coolness on this and on other occasions, he was awarded a Military Cross.'

That was Goldie Gardner all over: cool, determined and seemingly fearless. These traits were to see him dominate the deadly motor racing circuits of the 1920s and '30s, to throw himself almost obsessively into capturing speed records for himself and his country and ultimately to his death after pushing his luck once too many times. And, although he didn't know it on that warm summer's day in 1916, he had just a year to go before he would receive a terrible wound, the dark secret of which would define his life.

---

5   Stirling and Richie, *A Short History of 72ⁿᵈ Brigade RFA 1914-1919*, (RAA, 1920).

2

THE GREATEST THRILL

At Woodford Green, Essex on 31st May 1890, in the midst of a notably cold summer that led on to a bitter winter, twenty-one-year-old Isabella McIntosh Gardner gave birth to a son. The wife of Alfred Gardner, a well-to-do colonial broker some 15 years her senior, the family were the epitome of the Victorian middle class success story, very comfortably off with a large house, cook and two servants. Despite her Italian-sounding name, Isabella was from strong Scottish stock, hailing from Airdrie on the outskirts of Glasgow and Alfred, having decided that his first-born son should be named after him, then agreed that her family name of Goldie should be retained. Accordingly, three weeks later at St Ann's church in Tottenham, some nine miles from their home in Charteris Road, Woodford, their son was christened Alfred Thomas Goldie Gardner.

Alfred junior was a cheerful child, but photographs from his youth show a look of determination on his face that was to become his calling card. After two years, he was joined by a brother, Edgar, but 'Goldie' (as he was often called even then)[6] had a wild streak that his brother didn't have and before he was ten his father had packed him off to the exclusive Pelham House preparatory school in Sandgate, on the outskirts of Folkestone in Kent. In May 1904, just days before his 14th birthday, his father moved him to Uppingham, the historic private school near the town of Corby, founded in 1584. Alfred senior hoped that Uppingham's focus on daily cold showers and physical fitness – it was the first school in the country to have a gymnasium and swimming pool – would give Goldie an outlet for his energies.

The ploy partially worked. Gardner quickly settled into his boarding house, The Hall, and threw himself into an active sporting life. Morning runs through the muddy Rutland fields around the school, games of 'fives', the arcane public school game played on a court built to look like the side of a chapel, and regular riding lessons were all taken eagerly by Goldie who excelled at them all. Tall, even then, with a reputation for being seemingly immune to pain, it was on the rugby pitch where he became best known as a powerful second-row forward.

But within months, another brand-new sport turned his eye, one that offered exhilaration, danger, and romance. Motoring was in its infancy, but after the maximum speed limit on British roads had been lifted in 1903 to a heady 20 miles-per-hour, motor vehicles were starting to become things of wonder, especially to adolescent boys. Although most cars were still box-shaped, hissing beasts, motorcycles were sleek, fast, and often shrouded in glinting polished aluminium. It was to these sirens that Goldie Gardner was drawn, but he needed money. Still within his first term at Uppingham he decided to act, penning a long letter to his father, asking for the funds to buy a motorcycle. A few days later, his father's blunt reply came: although Alfred senior admired his eldest son's literary style and his proactivity in this matter, any consideration would have to be made *after* his end-of-term school report had been received.

---

6   Photographic archive, (NMM).

The pressure was on, but Goldie Gardner was already a very determined young man. He worked hard, impressed the teachers and, to his father's delight, represented the school at various sports.[7] That summer, a glowing report having been received, his persistence paid off and his father gave him 30 shillings (around £200 today). With it, Gardner junior purchased his first ever motorised vehicle, a second-hand 1¾ horsepower Excelsior motorcycle.

The Excelsior was a rudimentary design, built of welded steel pipes and swept-back handlebars with a sprung leather saddle the only concession to comfort, but Gardner loved it with a passion. He didn't even mind the extraordinary effort required to start the machine, pedalling the bike furiously on its stand, then quickly pushing it off when the engine showed a sign of firing. 'With this particular machine I am sure I covered a greater imaginary distance pedalling on its stand than I covered on the actual high road,' he later wrote.[8]

Gardner would roar along the lanes around Uppingham, feeling the wind in his hair and the adrenaline surge as he built up speed. It thrilled him and quickly became like a drug; the more he had, the more he needed. Soon, the two-speed Excelsior felt too slow and when a friend offered him the chance to purchase a 3½ horsepower Kerry motorcycle *with greatly improved petrol tank which will be appreciated by the more experienced motor-cyclists.*[9] Gardner knew he had to have it. Again, he asked his father. Unexpectedly, he quickly agreed, seeing it as a good investment to keep his son occupied and possibly even starting to appreciate the machines. Gardner bought it and had it shipped promptly to Uppingham where it was stripped down, overhauled, and tuned up in the school workshop.

---

7   Gardner represented his house at Fives and the school in the running VIII and rugby VX. (Uppingham School Archive)
8   ATG Gardner, *Magic MPH* (Motor Racing Publications, 1951).
9   Advertisement for the 1910 Olympia Motorcycle Exhibition. https://cybermotorcycle.com/articles/olympia-show-1910.htm

'As far back as I can recall, speed was my greatest thrill,' Gardner wrote, but even the Kerry didn't give him enough of the heady intoxicant he desired. In the early summer of 1908 during his final term at Uppingham, out for drive through tiny local villages, he stumbled across an exotic beauty: a wonderful twin-cylinder, 5 horsepower motorcycle with 'all-aluminium paint finish,' built by the *Rex* company of Coventry, famous for their innovation of creating telescopic front forks. It was the bike everyone wanted, and he quickly enquired whether the motorcycle was for sale, offered a fair sum and rode away the new owner. He didn't know it then, but he was in a very select group: W.O. Bentley, Malcolm Campbell and Cecil Kimber, great men who would help shape the emerging years of the British motor industry, all owned the same model. Like them, Gardner had an innate feel for the machine that would give him the most power and was quickly developing the skill to extract every last mile-per-hour from the bike, but for now his time at Uppingham was coming to an end. Now, it was time to enter the real world.

Through his father's connections, it was relatively easy for Goldie Gardner to secure a job at Lloyd's of London, starting work in their Registry of Shipping and to try to satisfy his urge for adventure he joined the Honourable Artillery Company, the ancient militia organisation that had just become part of Britain's 'Territorial' (reserve) forces. Despite the distraction of his part-time service career, he was not enjoying office life and, when given the opportunity to take a job as a tea broker in Ceylon, he jumped at the chance. He resigned from the HAC on 12 June 1911 and promptly reenlisted in the Ceylon Mounted Rifles.[10]

Ceylon was everything he was looking for. The country was a booming outpost of the British Empire, and the ex-pat community was a thriving mix of middle-class traders, Ceylon Defence Force officers and local government officials. The Colombo Hockey and Football Club (CH&FC), Ceylon Polo Club and Ceylon Mounted Rifles offered the

---

10   HAC attestation paperwork (Royal Artillery Archives).

same physical challenges he'd experienced at school plus a ready-made social network of friends, but for Goldie, the country offered one other attraction above all others: a network of long, winding metalled roads constructed through the jungle to bring the spoils of Empire back to the capital. With little else to spend his wage on and ample time on his hands, he quickly imported a state-of-the-art 5-horsepower twin-cylinder *Indian* motorcycle with long, swept-back handlebars and attracted a group of other young men who also lived for speed. The main protagonists were E.M. Ley, a planter and Second Lieutenant in the Ceylon Volunteers who later served at Gallipoli, Eric Wardrop of the Colombo Commercial Company, tea plantation owner Frederick Denham Till who later went on to be a pilot in the Fleet Air Arm[11] before working for the British intelligence services and Henry Kirton, an accountant whose main claim to fame within the group was that he owned a 'well-meaning but rather weak $3\frac{1}{2}$-horsepower *Premier.*'[12]

'England could not have held him had she tried' wrote a journalist of Goldie Gardner, and he was right.[13] He was the de facto leader of this linen-suited and pith helmet-wearing group of young men, leading them on whatever machine they could lay their hands on along the jungle roads, pushing their motorcycles as fast as they would go to the alarm of local pedestrians and livestock who were used to a much more sedate pace of life. The mountain routes between Colombo and Kandi were their favourite playground, establishing the winding track up through the green-shrouded Kadugannawa Pass as an ad hoc hill-climb course, then pausing for lunch at Balumgala Mountain to look back across the verdant forest vista towards the sea. After one day's fun in the mountains, having left it until the very last moment, Gardner set off at 2am giving himself just a few hours to ride 130 miles back to his office in Colombo to start work the next day. Under a brilliant moon,

---

11　National Archive, ADM 273/6/263.
12　*In the Early Days*, (*Ceylon Times*, December 1938) NMM Archive.
13　*Autocar*, 28 July 1939.

the road dappled in pools of light, with his dim acetylene headlamp only faintly helping his straining eyes, he rode back through the night. Every shape emerging from the gloom he imagined was a buffalo or elephant, every shriek in the dark jungle a predator ready to pounce, but on he rode, faster and faster through the humid darkness until finally, the lights of Colombo welcomed him just as the dawn started to break. He arrived, slightly dishevelled but otherwise still buzzing with adrenaline, ready for the workday to start at 7am. The following weekend there were more motorcycle trips, more polo, more rugby, and more gin. It was an idyllic life.

But finally, in the late spring of 1913, Goldie Gardner's contract came to an end. With a handful of other passengers and with a heavy heart, he boarded the *RMS Orama* as she arrived from Australia and sailed back slowly to the port of Tilbury in the Thames Estuary, arriving on 24th May.[14] Back in the leafy London suburb of Reigate where the Gardner family had moved from Woodford, Goldie quickly became very bored indeed. Only one place entranced him: the motoring mecca of Brooklands, the purpose-built motor racing track built by Hugh Fortescue Locke King, epitome of the landed gentry, on a previously scrubby part of his estate near Weybridge in Surrey, some 20 miles from central London and less than half-an-hour from Gardner's home. Its construction was an epic undertaking that almost finished Locke King, his wife Ethel having to take over leadership of the build when it all became too much for her husband. The $2^{3}/_{4}$- mile circuit, banked at both ends with a diagonal start-finish straight and purpose-built pits, clubhouse, grandstands, and airstrip was unlike anything else in the world when it opened in 1907. The vast expanse of concrete, wider than a six-lane motorway and without any of the crash barriers, run-off zones or chicanes of today's motor racing circuits was designed for one purpose only: to allow cars and motorcycles to race at their maximum possible speed. It drew Goldie Gardner like a moth to a flame.

---

14   Tilbury immigration records (www.ancestry.com).

He avidly attended every race of the season and looked on in awe as the Vauxhalls, Mercedes and Sunbeams raced, their oil-spattered drivers dicing with one another around the huge concrete walls, pushing their rudimentary cars to the edge of oblivion and receiving the adulation of the crowd for simply *surviving*, let alone winning. Another type of machine fascinated him there, too: the flimsy aircraft that stuttered into the air but then swooped gracefully over the circuit, delighting the onlookers. On 25th September, he made a special trip to Brooklands along with thousands of others to watch in awe as the French ace pilot Adolph Pegoud performed the first ever loop-the-loop above Britain in his Bleriot monoplane. Gardner was hooked; he wanted to try this for himself.

But that had to wait. After a few months at home, his boredom got the better of him and when he was offered a five-year contract in Burma, he jumped at the chance. In late 1913, he sailed to Rangoon then made the long overland journey up country through the seemingly endless jungles to a forestry department in the Katha region, some 350km north of the relative civilisation of Mandalay on the mosquito-blown Irrawaddy River. In charge of around 50 locals and 25 elephants, his job was to oversee the felling of valuable teak trees which were then pulled to the river and floated downstream to the sawmills. Katha's remoteness was stifling as was the heat, with average temperatures reaching over 30 degrees Celsius every month of the year. Then there were the rains: torrential downpours between June and October that turned the rivers into raging torrents. Katha was the town that George Orwell later served in as a police officer and which he used as the setting to his book *Burmese Days,* a dark tale of colonial exploitation, and for Gardner it was far from being the adventurous location he'd been expecting. There weren't any roads, let alone linen-suited hunting jaunts on two wheels, just ochre-red dirt tracks that either choked with dust or engulfed with mud depending on the season. There was no rugby, no polo and very rarely did he see another European; to bide his time, Gardner started to learn Burmese, but it wasn't enough to keep him from longing to go home. Then, less than a year after he'd arrived, deliverance came from an unlikely source. 'Luckily,' he wrote, 'I went down... with a really bad attack of typhoid, with malaria for full measure, which resulted in my being sent home on six months' sick leave.'[15]

Within weeks, he had disembarked again back in England, ready to start his convalescence. Again, he quickly became bored, and once he was well enough made frequent trips to Brooklands to watch whatever was going on that day. One morning he saw a rider testing a bike to its limits around the track. After a few laps, he pulled into the pits in front of Gardner who instantly recognised both man and machine. The motorcycle was a 5-horsepower Rex, similar to the one Gardner had owned at Uppingham, and riding it was Frank Applebee, winner of the previous year's Isle of Man Senior TT, the blue riband event for motorcycle road racing. Once he'd climbed off, Gardner went over and started a conversation, telling Applebee that he had once owned a bike very similar to this one. Somehow, he managed to persuade Applebee to let him take the Rex for a spin and had very nearly completed a full lap when an irate course official waved him in. Gardner's beaming smile as he handed the bike back to Applebee was proof that it was worth the ticking off. 'By this time,' Gardner later wrote, 'I really was determined by hook or crook to race a motorcycle at Brooklands.'[16]

But it was not to be. Just as he would not return to Burma, he would never ride a motorcycle around the Brooklands circuit again. Soon after, on 28th June 1914, Archduke Franz Ferdinand of the Austro-Hungarian Empire was assassinated in Sarajevo. The following month, Austria-Hungary declared war on Serbia and in the coming days, country after country joined what would develop into the Great War. On 4th August 1914, Great Britain declared war and within weeks, Alfred Goldie Gardner, still officially on sick leave, visited a doctor who did not know him. Omitting to mention his typhoid/malaria mix, the

15 *Magic MPH* (ibid) p12.
16 *Magic MPH* (ibid) p12.

unwitting doctor passed him fit for military service. On 11th October
he was commissioned as a Second Lieutenant, an officer in the Royal
Field Artillery,[17] and told to report to Louisburg Barracks at Bordon
in Hampshire.

Gardner's first experience of Army life was one of abject chaos.
Some 3,000 volunteer soldiers had arrived for duty at the sprawling
Bordon Garrison during the first half of October, none of whom had
any prior military experience. The barrack rooms, designed for a much
smaller peacetime detachment, had to be stripped of furniture to fit
them all in and the men slept shoulder to shoulder on the floor every
night with just a single blanket each to wrap around themselves. On
22nd October, 59-year-old Colonel James Stirling returned from retirement to command 600 troops in what was now designated 72nd Brigade
of the Royal Field Artillery and, aided by a handful of other ex-regular
officers and the veteran Regimental Sergeant Major Day, he started to
build the raw recruits into something resembling an operational unit.

It was a challenging prospect, even for these old soldiers. At first,
they were trained as one under the watchful eye of the wonderfully
named Captain Heaven but equipment was in short supply with little in the way of artillery guns, horses or even military clothing; the
non-commissioned officers were given cast-off breeches provided by a
local hunt so that they could at least start their riding lessons, critical for
a unit that still had to pull its guns into place behind teams of horses.
Equestrian skills were rare, even amongst the officers, but one stood
out: with his experience in Ceylon, Lieutenant Gardner was a capable
and confident rider. Along with three brothers named Pierce who were
competent horsemen, he led the Brigade's transition into a mounted
formation using thirty mangy animals that the regular artillery unit had
left behind when they'd deployed to France a few weeks previously, re-
garding them as unfit for service. Even saddles were in short supply and

---

17   Commissioning scroll (NMM).

Goldie sent out messages to his civilian friends asking for second-hand items to be sent through. Slowly, these started to arrive. They were old, but they were better than nothing.

When they weren't discovering the delights of military riding, the soldiers' waking hours were filled with other forms of education. Foot and rifle drill featured very heavily, as did the terrific screeching of the Sergeant Major when things invariably went wrong. Despite their role, gun drills were rare as they had just a single 15lb howitzer to train on, the rest having to improvise with dummy 'artillery' built from scaffolding poles. When His Majesty the King visited to inspect his new troops, the artillerymen stood as infantry, their embarrassing lack of armament hidden from their Colonel-in-Chief.[18]

On a cold day in February 1915, the Brigade left the barracks that had by then become their home and moved to Bulford Camp in Wiltshire on the edge of Salisbury Plain, the largest British Army training area in the south of England. This was where the serious training for battle was to take place: digging, signalling and finally, live firing of artillery. While the men travelled in trucks Gardner rode down on his motorbike, an impressive Zenith *Gradua*, and parked it next to the draughty wooden hut that was to be his home for the next few weeks before they deployed to France. Lieutenant Gardner had quickly made a name for himself within the Brigade and not just because of his expertise with the horses. His experiences on the rugby pitches of Uppingham and Colombo had helped him become a competent leader and he had an easy-going style that instilled confidence in both his soldiers and those above him in the chain of command. He gained a reputation as one who was firm but fair, and this was respected by his soldiers.[19] Importantly, he also looked the part: tall, strong, and immaculately dressed in the uniforms he'd had made on Savile Row, Gardner would ride

---

18   A detailed record of the 72nd Brigade's training was written by its commanding officer, Colonel JW Stirling. *A Short History of 72nd Brigade RFA 1914-1919* (1920, RAA).
19   Letter, W.G.Watson to Gardner dated 25/7/50 (NMM Archive).

out across the Plain on horseback to oversee the drills. When the time came for Colonel Stirling to choose officers to lead each of his three detachments, Lieutenant Gardner was an obvious choice. He was given command of 'B' Battery and promoted to Captain, the others selected being Majors with prior military experience. For someone who a few months previously had been a teak trader, it was a stratospheric transformation but a natural one: Gardner thrived in this environment and couldn't wait to face the challenge of battle. But, like so many men in his position, the reality of the trenches proved to have little of the romance that he had expected. War, he soon found out, was by turns a stultifyingly dull, abjectly terrifying, and brutally gruesome experience. Like so many men of his generation, he made this discovery on the rolling chalk plains of the Somme valley in northern France. In early July the Brigade had moved by train to Southampton, then by troop ship to Le Havre after which they were transported north, not far from Calais. From here, the Brigade shackled up the guns and made their own way behind the British lines, the officers like Gardner on their horses, the men taking their turn on the gun carriages and then marching behind the column. Even for an experienced horseman like Gardner, it was a brutal experience. The horses they had been issued were of American and Canadian stock, long backed and always demanding fodder that just wasn't available in the quantities they needed. It was a constant struggle to prevent both animals and men from going lame, as none of them were used to marching so far, some days up to 25 miles in a stretch. Gardner did what he could, guiding his men to rest themselves and their horses when possible and motivating them when it was time to move. Finally, and with an ironic sense of relief, they arrived in a tented concentration area on 17th July near the village of Lapugnoy close to the remains of the town of Béthune. Here, Gardner received his orders: B Battery was to be quickly brought into the line to get experience of hostile fire as there was something being planned, something big. He didn't know it then, but he was just days away from his first major battle, one in which he would first distinguish himself for gallantry.

But for now, he left the orders group, lit a cigarette, and made his way back to his tent to brief his men.

3

THE FLIGHT

The doctor scrawled his signature on the paper before passing it to his patient. Major Gardner glanced at the letter, then quietly folded it, and placed it in the breast pocket of his service dress jacket. He had known it was coming, of course, but that didn't take away the shock that he felt reading those words: *Medically unfit for further military service.*[20] In pain but determined not to show it, he placed his weight on his stick and rose, nodding to the doctor before walking as purposefully as he could muster from the surgery.

Back in his room, he removed his uniform for the final time. Seven years had passed since that perfect summer of 1914 when, like tens of thousands of other young British men, he had answered Kitchener's call to take up arms against the foe. So much had changed since then. His extraordinary self-confidence and youthful optimism had been the first casualties, battered out of him within weeks of arriving at the front line. The awful reality of industrialised conflict shocked him as much as any other who experienced it: the random brutality of bullets, shells,

20 Discharge papers, (IWM).

and gas; the terrible wounds of those who survived; the total destruction of nearly everything. Soon though, these became a strange sort of normal; he seemed to lack any sense of shock when faced with the latest carnage, accepting all the death and destruction as one might accept an unpleasant aspect of any normal occupation.

The next change was a more insidious one. The relentless stress of war weighed on him, as it did for most of those who experienced it. This wasn't caused by the heart-thumping, adrenaline-charged vignettes of combat but the months of background noise that surrounded those relatively rare events, a combination of monotony, underlying fear, and the need to be permanently ready for action. Nobody even acknowledged this at first, unaware of the slow change that was taking place, unable to recognise that the need to be hyper-vigilant at all times was wearing them down. Gardner noticed the physical symptoms first: by the spring of 1917 his once well-fitting uniform hung on him like a bag[21] and every time he shaved, he noticed his sunken eyes and empty cheeks. Then he became aware of other consequences: smarting instinctively to the slightest noise and never sleeping more than an hour-or-so at a time.

But war service had also given him a sense of purpose that he had never felt before. At first, this was fuelled by the pride in his country that his education and upbringing had instilled in him. Back in 1915, it was easy for him to perceive the great conflict he was involved in as a struggle of good versus evil, the British Empire defending the Belgians and French against German oppression. But a few months in the trenches subtly changed the opinion of many who served there, realising that war is never a black and white proposition, and the real purpose he found was from his sense of identity as an officer. Surrounded by the chaos of the battlefield, he found leadership came easily and was undeniably brave: after this very first experience of battle at Loos in September 1915 he was personally mentioned in dispatches by Field

---

21   Photographic archive, (NMM).

Marshal Sir John French,[22] commander of all British troops on the western front and in January 1917 he received the Military Cross,[23] the country's third-highest gallantry award. He was well-respected by his peers and promoted accordingly, even standing in as commander of the entire 72nd Brigade when his commanding officer, Colonel James Stirling, was absent in January 1917. Gardner felt that he was an indispensable part of a professional team, and despite the death and destruction, he thrived. Then, having survived the battles of Loos, Poziers, Martinpuich and Flers-Courcelette relatively unscathed, suddenly everything changed.

For the rest of his life, Goldie Gardner refused to talk in detail about the incident that had a defining effect on it. Most of those who knew him thought that he was just being the old soldier who didn't want to dwell on difficult times past. In his autobiography, he covered the whole of the First World War in two sentences and simply referred to being 'wounded' in late August 1917. The only other person who certainly knew his story was his wife, Una. She lived until 2008 and told a few, trusted people what happened. There was also a report found in an *SO Book 130* official military notebook, composed in handwriting that was not Goldie Gardner's, that gave an account of the incident.[24] This is the tale it told.

As a senior Major, he shouldn't have been anywhere near the Royal Aircraft Factory RE 8 artillery reconnaissance aircraft on that sunny summer's day in August 1917.[25] The observers were almost without exception young officers, Lieutenants in their early 20s, and for good reason: it was an extremely dangerous place to be. The RE 8 was a relatively new addition to the Royal Flying Corps, having arrived at the front in late 1916. Already, the aircraft had built up a reputation for

---

22   MID scroll, (NMM).
23   *London Gazette*, 1 Jan 1917.
24   Reported by Steve Holter (interview, May 2023). It now cannot be found but was believed to have been donated, then recovered from the NMM Archive back to Una Gardner's possession.
25   Magic MPH (ibid) P12.

being tricky to fly even in ideal conditions,[26] stalling without warning and then bursting into flames if it came down hard, some pilots even resorting to filling the reserve fuel tank with fire extinguisher fluid to try to give themselves some sort of protection should the worst happen. The rear 'spotter' seat had also become something of a misnomer, the crews having realised by now that the pilot was in a much better position to correct artillery fire than someone in the back, the latter now generally reduced to manning the Lewis gun and keeping a lookout for enemy aircraft.

But for Goldie Gardner, the attraction of these aerial machines was too much to resist. Powered flight was a novel and quite extraordinary concept, and for someone so enthralled with the feeling of speed, he knew he had to experience it. The dangers... well, there were dangers everywhere on the battlefield. He knew it probably wouldn't happen to him. He set about the process of persuading his commanding officer that it was an operational necessity for him to conduct an aerial reconnaissance[27] of a planned position and grudgingly, he agreed. A few hours later, Major Gardner arrived at the airfield some way back from the front line where a young pilot wearily introduced himself and showed him around the cockpit. The interior was sparse: a tiny leather seat surrounded by the exposed wooden fuselage frame braced with wire, slots containing spare .303-inch Lewis gun magazines, a box containing the camera apparatus and the machine gun mounted on a rotating pintle. Gardner was kitted out in a flying suit, leather helmet and goggles then with some difficulty squeezed his 6'3" frame into the circular cockpit. With his knees squeezed up to his chest it was less than comfortable, but he managed to brace himself into a position that was bearable. Moments later, he heard a bang as the engine fired into life and was quickly engulfed in a plume of grey, oily smoke. For a split second the motor laboured but then roared up to full speed, the wash

---

26   https://www.key.aero/article/royal-aircraft-factory-re8
27   *The Autocar,* 28 Jul 1939.

from the propeller ripping at his face and reminding him to drop his goggles into place. The pilot turned and gave him a thumbs-up, which he returned. The aircraft trundled off to the end of the runway, paused, then he heard the engine pick up the revs as they started to accelerate down the grass strip.

It took moments for the tiny biplane to wobble into the air, then a few minutes more for the pilot to climb in a spiral until he was out of small-arms range. Only then did he set a course towards the front line. Gardner looked down. Robbed of any sense of elevation, the ground was extremely hard to read; although he intimately knew every shredded copse and battered village from the trench maps that he pored over daily, it took him a while to spot even one point of reference. But then, by following the meanderings of the rivers, he suddenly recognised the scratch of a familiar trench line. Quickly, he mentally traced the route back through the battlefield that he had taken hundreds of times, and there it was: his unit, a few black dots littering a brown smudge of dislocated earth.

They flew on. Although the front was quiet that day, the odd puff of smoke burst like silent fireworks below them as the opposing artillery continued to remind their opposition to keep their heads down. From this altitude, it seemed serene, almost unreal.

Gardner felt a tap on his shoulder, and turned towards the pilot, who pointed two gloved fingers towards his eyes. Gardner nodded and scanned the cloud-dotted sky around them for signs of other aircraft. They were crossing into enemy territory now, and the German fighters would have been alerted to their presence by their network of watchers on the ground. They had to be quick; in, take a look at the target, then slip out before the enemy had time to react.

Five minutes later, they were there. Gardner received another tap on the shoulder and looked at where the pilot was pointing. He looked down, fiddling with the camera settings then, satisfied it was all correct, pressed the switch to expose the film. He had become quite adept at using this relatively new portable photographic technology and took pride in the results he obtained. He wound on the *rollfilm*, then clicked the shutter again.

Suddenly, the aircraft lurched violently to the right. Gardner was thrown onto the floor of the cockpit, instinctively dropped the camera which clattered into a corner and grabbed onto the gun rail. He looked up and saw what the pilot had mercifully spotted first: the ominous black outline of another biplane silhouetted against the bright white of the clouds. Even to Gardner's untrained eye it was obvious that the other pilot was lining up for a shot, and he quickly grabbed the Lewis gun, lining up the circular sight with the German aircraft, and squeezed the trigger. After a millisecond delay, the machine gun spat its first .303-inch round towards the enemy, then settled into a reassuring rhythm: 'thud, thud, thud'.

Instantly, the German reacted, kinking his aircraft left and right, and loosing his own volley of shots. Gardner saw the muzzle flashes first, followed almost instantly with a set of ear-piercing cracks as the bullets zipped past them. They had missed, but the fragile British plane had been lucky, and the pilot knew they didn't have much time left. Just as Gardner squeezed off his second burst, the pilot snapped the stick forwards, dropping the nose towards the ground and spiralling away from the enemy fighter, urgently trying to reach a line of low, fluffy clouds that lay temptingly below them. Gardner felt himself lifting away from his seat and clung to the gun, pushing his legs out against the wood frame of the fuselage to stop himself falling out. As the dive continued, Gardner tried to line the sights up again and fired off another salvo, but the German kept coming. More flashes; more cracks, this time closer. Suddenly, the British aircraft jinked as one of the German bullets smashed into a wing spar leaving a trail of ripped canvas flapping in the wind. They were nearly at the cloud, and the pilot pulled up hard, throwing Gardner once again onto the floor, the G-force pummelling him like a boxer on the ropes. He tried to lift his head and line up the sights again, but the German had gone. Two seconds later, he felt his goggles mist as the cloud enveloped them.

The British pilot flew on, often changing direction to throw their pursuer off the scent. Gardner, feeling quite sick from the strong combination of aerobatics and adrenaline, slipped his hand through the leather loop on the Lewis gun's magazine and fumbled through his thick leather gloves with the release catch. Once disconnected, he dropped the half-empty cartridge into the aircraft, unclipped another from its holder and clicked it into place on top of the gun. He rubbed his goggles clear and spun the gun around, searching for his foe.

This time, the British pilot didn't have time to react. As they emerged from a patch of cloud, suddenly German bullets were everywhere, lancing through the paper-thin body of the aircraft, smashing wood, ripping steel, and tearing canvas. The enemy pilot had anticipated their exit from the cloud perfectly and strafed the length of the British aircraft with a scything run from his twin nose-mounted machine guns. Gardner felt great thumps on his back as parts of the airframe disintegrated, and he retched as a choking swathe of black smoke engulfed him. As the pilot dropped the nose, desperately seeking the safety of the ground, Gardner pulled the trigger again, wildly blasting as many bullets as he could in the general direction of where he felt their enemy must be. As the hot, empty .303 cases fell like a brass torrent into the cockpit, even in this moment of utter desperation, he felt strangely reassured by the rhythm of the gun as it chattered away. Finally, it clicked empty just as they emerged from the bottom of the cloud and in the now-clear sky, Gardner saw a heartening sight: the German aircraft, a thin trail of smoke leading like a silk scarf from its damaged engine, limping away from them back towards its own lines.

Although the immediate danger from their foe was gone, the British aircraft was in a bad way. Oil was seeping from the battered engine and starved of lubrication, the motor started to labour and the noise of its dry pistons melting themselves into the crankcase became deafening. Moments later, as the pilot guided the aircraft on a lazy descent back towards the British lines, the engine clattered to a halt. The utter silence that followed, punctuated only by the whistling of air dancing through the wing struts, was as terrifying as the cacophony of combat the two men had experienced just minutes before.

The pilot tried to glide the plane as far as he could, searching for a relatively flat area in which to land. But too quickly, they descended; the outlines of buildings, streams and roads suddenly jumping into clear focus as they raced towards them. At around fifty feet from the ground, the pilot spun round, shouting to Gardner to brace himself. He did so, pushing himself as far into the cockpit as he could, pressing his legs up against the bulkhead and wrapping his arms around his head. He closed his eyes and waited for the inevitable impact.

There was a bump, and the aircraft began to slide along the ground. For an instant, Gardner let himself believe that they had made it down in one piece but then the fuselage caught on an unseen obtrusion, and he was flung forwards as the aircraft began to tumble. Everything became blurred as the aircraft somersaulted, his body thrashed around inside like a dog shakes a captured toy until mercifully, he blacked out.

Gardner slowly came round to the strange sound of fizzing, and for a moment he wondered where he was. Then, he remembered. Upside down, smothered by broken pieces of aircraft, spent bullet cases and other detritus, he was suddenly very aware of a strong smell of fuel. A gap in the ripped canvas of the plane's body offered him a glimpse of daylight, and a route to freedom. Frantically, he tore at the canvas, pulled snapped wood spars out of the way, and dragged himself out through the hole. Now free of the wreckage, he went to stand but groggily realised that his right leg wouldn't work as it should, and quickly fell back to the floor. He pulled himself to the shattered remains of the front cockpit and there found the pilot, dazed but alive. Together, the pair crawled away to the relative safety of a ditch some twenty yards from the aircraft. Utterly spent, Gardner lapsed again into the black.

This time, it was the pain that woke him up: crippling, searing agony that shot through his right leg, hip and back. He pulled himself up onto his elbows and looked down; his right leg was twisted at an extraordinary angle and there was a dark patch sodden with blood above his knee. He knew instantly that it was very badly broken. He also realised that they were in no-man's land, and if he was to make it back to the British lines, he'd have to stabilise the leg. The pilot went back to the crumpled aircraft that miraculously had not caught fire and searched until he found what he was looking for: three wooden fuselage struts and a large flap of canvas that he tore into strips. Carefully, he broke the struts to length and bound two of them each side of his broken leg with the canvas. Then, using the longer strut as a crutch, he helped Gardner gingerly pull himself up onto his good leg. It was excruciatingly painful, but Major Alfred Goldie Gardner MC of the Royal Field Artillery was made of extremely strong stuff. He grimaced in pain, but did not falter, instead forcing himself to drag his broken limb forwards, one small, painful step at a time.

Hours turned to days. Hobbling, crawling; mud, blood. The pair hid in shell holes during the day and dragged themselves back towards their own lines at night as swinging flares lit the sky. Eventually, they picked their way through the British wire and, waving some of the canvas they'd taken from the aircraft, were seen by a sentry. A few minutes later they were safe, and Gardner lay still in the bottom of a trench as an infantrymen tied a first field dressing around his leg and a sergeant listened incredulously to the officers' story of survival. A few days later, on the 26th August 1917, Gardner was back in London, taken on strength as a patient at the Queen Alexandra's Military Hospital, Millbank.[28] There, he started along his very long road to recovery, a journey that included two years in the Esperance Hospital in Eastbourne,[29] 20 operations to try to rebuild his shattered hip and terribly damaged leg over the next four years and ended in the ignominy of a medical discharge.

28   Hospital records show that Gardner was in QAMH Millbank from 26th Aug to 7th Nov 1917 (www.fold3.com).
29   Interview Steve Holter, May 2023.

***

It wasn't meant to end like this, Gardner thought as he looked down at his service dress jacket laid out on the bed, the hard-won splash of medal ribbons above the left breast pocket in bright contrast to the drab brown of the twill they were sewn on to. His head dipped for a second, but he pulled himself as upright as he could, grasped his stick firmly in his hand, and hobbled out of an Officers' Mess for the final time. Or so he thought.

4

RACING

———————⟍————————

Adjusting to life after the Army, after the war, was hard. His previous life had been one of exercise and excitement: breakneck motorcycle rides through the jungles of Ceylon, the physical exertion of rugby tournaments and long summer days watching the motoring gladiators at Brooklands with the sure belief that one day he'd join them. Then, the trenches: horror, it's true, but also camaraderie and personal growth. Even in hospital, he'd built strong friendships with his fellow 'inmates' as they called themselves, making black jokes with each other and railing against the strict rule of the matrons. Now, all of it was gone. He had no idea what to do.

He wasn't alone; the streets of Great Britain were filled with damaged and disfigured men, all trying to make sense of what had happened and work out what to do with the rest of their lives. Very few people had escaped the conflict without being fundamentally changed, from the families torn apart by death to the women now used to working long factory shifts. But for the men who served on the front line, especially those physically or mentally wounded, returning to what other people liked to call 'normal' life was almost impossible.

The reaction of civilians didn't help. At first, there had been an understandable sense of national celebration. Returning units were cheered as they disembarked trains and Union Flags were waved as parish councils unveiled memorials on nearly every village green. Well-meaning gentlefolk established charities to help those injured and wrote to the newspapers, urging more to be done for our brave veterans. But ever so gradually the goodwill dissipated, the letters dried up, and the concern for those who had fought was replaced in the public consciousness by the mundane priorities of peacetime life. And, so the story went, everyone had suffered. Everyone now needed to move on.

But many veterans couldn't move on. They had experienced the opposite of mundanity: excruciating terror, stultifying boredom, life being snuffed out in an instant or clinging on despite the odds. They sought each other's company, either to talk to those who truly understood, or just to sit in silence, sipping a pint of bitter in the knowledge that their comrade had been there too. Gardner, like millions of others, joined his official regimental club when the Royal Artillery Association was formed in May 1920.[30] It helped, a little, as did retaining his title of Major, which gave him an excuse for his limp, but in reality, he was as adrift as the majority of his soldiers.

Work was a large part of the problem. Many men who had served had not expected to live beyond the conflict, and so future career planning was not high on their agenda. Now returned, issued a demob suit, and thrust into the job market, many found that their priorities had changed. Some volunteered to return with tens of thousands of men from the Chinese Labour Corps to clear the Western Front battlefield as best they could, back to a regimented life that they understood. Others completely changed careers; some previously white-collar workers couldn't bear to work inside and took up outdoor, physical roles like bricklaying or roofing, simple jobs that showed progress at the end of every day. Others decided to follow their passions, becom-

---

30   Badge and membership details, (NMM).

ing artists, writers, or teachers, or travelling the world if their circum-
stances allowed.

Gardner knew that his options were limited by his disability. Other
than an interest in photography,[31] he had just one passion – that of
speed – but as an 'invalid' he knew that he would never be able to
ride his beloved motorcycles again. But, when in early 1921 it was announced that the first major Grand Prix race since the war would take
place that summer, he decided to put off his more immediate concerns
and allow himself the pleasure of watching motor racing once again.
In late July, in the midst of a sweltering heatwave that saw temperatures
reach 32 degrees Celsius, he crossed the channel and made his way to
the Circuit de la Sarthe at Le Mans.

Mixing with the crowd in their suits and straw boaters, Gardner
soaked up the atmosphere. For the first time in years, he felt elated:
he was back in the bustling paddock watching the mechanics working
feverishly on an engine or bashing a wheel spinner home with a copper
hammer. He had the smell of burnt castor oil in his nostrils and the
fearsome sound of unsilenced engines blatting themselves awake and
ready for the off. He watched as the seemingly fearless drivers prepared
themselves for their mechanical duel: no Germans yet, but plenty of
French and Americans, plus a few Italians whose cars failed to arrive in
time for the start, and who hung around the paddock, cigarettes droop-
ing from their sullen lips as they gesticulated at each other.

Gardner, new camera in hand, toured the pits. He cheered on the
home nations drivers, Kenelm Lee Guinness of the famous brewing
dynasty and newcomer Henry Segrave who was taking part in his first
Grand Prix, both driving Talbot-badged *STD* racing cars, and watched
the local heroes, French drivers Andre Boillot and René Thomas. Gardner spent a little time photographing Boillot's blue machine, but spent
the most with Segrave, whose car was wearing number ten. He had a
lot in common with his compatriot: Segrave had also curtailed his own

---

31 *Magic MPH* and photographic archive NMM including albums of his photos from Le Mans, Strasbourg.

military career after the aircraft he was piloting was shot down over the Somme in July 1916, badly damaging his ankle. Gardner pored over his car, looking longingly at the tight twin bucket seats of the interior and the huge steering wheel protected by a rudimentary flyscreen to the front. The final result – Segrave finished ninth, his car struggling with road holding, the chequered flag being taken by American Jimmy Murphy in a Duesenberg – was almost irrelevant. Gardner was happy again for the first time in many months.

Gardner had to wait until the following year for the next Grand Prix. This one was further afield, in the French city of Strasbourg on the banks of the Rhine, but he saw no alternative: he must be there. Once again, he made his way to the racetrack and watched Segrave and Guinness, this time each driving a two-litre, four-cylinder Sunbeam. Although the engine was phenomenally advanced for its time, the car wasn't competitive, losing around 7 or 8 miles-per-hour to the winning Fiat 804s, and was also fragile; all the Sunbeams eventually retired with engine problems.

Nobody seemed to care that much. The horrors of the war were starting to fade a little from the country's memory and the sense of relief having just emerged from the Spanish influenza pandemic was palpable. The roaring twenties were beginning, and hampers of *Ayala & Co* champagne were cracked open, Hartford shock absorber canisters being used as impromptu ice buckets; everyone was just happy to be alive. The unseasonably dull weather and even a late-on crash that killed one of the leading Fiat drivers failed to dampen the spirits of most of the spectators. After the race, Gardner and Segrave chatted until finally, as the evening light started to dull, Segrave took himself off to the back seat of a car, pulled his goggles down over his eyes, wrapped his driving coat around himself, succumbed to post-race exhaustion and fell into a deep sleep.[32] Smiling to himself, Gardner snapped a photo of Segrave then hobbled back to the party. As his drink was topped

---

32   Photo by Gardner, (NMM).

up and he lit another cigarette, he felt a sense of warmth flood over him. He realised that this was what he had been searching for: here was a group of men, bound together by death and danger, but living with all the urgency they could muster. From all walks of life, they came; mechanics from the back streets of soot-bound cities, aristocratic drivers from their landed estates and university-educated engineers. Here, they all had their place. And here, Gardner realised, was where he needed to be. His wound could be damned, and the small matter of the money it would take… he'd find a way.

Fate gave him a way, and far sooner that he expected. The next morning, the bellhop at his hotel rushed in with an urgent telegram from his brother: he was to travel back immediately to the family home on Raglan Road in Reigate, Surrey, as his father was seriously ill. Gardner hurriedly packed, then rushed back to England as quickly as he could, but it was too late; by the time he arrived, his father was already dead.

It took four months for his father's executors to finalise his estate. On a cold, dank day in January 1923, the family met at home for their solicitor to read the will. It was a sad and sombre affair, and Gardner barely registered the legal jargon that was read out, itemising his father's life, reducing the houses they had lived in and loved to anonymous assets. At the end, he noted just one fact: that Alfred Gardner had left £9,745[33] to his wife Isabella and his sons, the majority kept in a trust until his widow died or remarried. This wasn't a king's ransom, but still a very significant amount of money – today it would be worth around £600,000 – and even with the majority tied up in the trust, the remainder was just about enough for him to buy a car. Gardner knew that it would allow him to race.

It took Gardner just six weeks to find his car. He had been drawn like a moth to a flame back to Brooklands, the coliseum of British motor racing now finding its feet again and holding regular meetings. Ear-

---

33   Alfred Gardner will (1898) and probate statement (1923) (www.gov.uk).

ly on Easter Monday, 2nd April 1923, he eagerly walked through the paddock, soaking up the atmosphere and relishing the sound of engines being revved into life. All the talk was of a new car, being driven for the first time that day on track by Captain Arthur Waite, the son-in-law of the founder of the company that made it. His father-in-law was Herbert Austin, and the tiny car he drove was the Austin Seven, designed to be a car for the masses. It had a tiny, 6'3" wheelbase, weighed just 794lbs and was designed by Herbert Austin working with a young draughtsman called Stanley Edge, the pair of them laying out drawings on a billiard table. Despite being very similar to the standard road model except for a streamlined body and altered gear ratios, Waite's car was perfect for racing, its light weight making it extremely quick. Gardner applauded when Waite easily won,[34] then as the crowds dispersed, took a good look at the Seven. It was ideal for him: easier to handle than the big racing Bentleys and other specials, quick, but also not ruinously expensive. But what type of Seven to buy?

A few months later, Gardner watched as another racer took one of the new Austins and put his own stamp on it. Eric Gordon England, a driver, pioneering pilot and competent engineer, emerged on to the Brooklands track in a spectacular car. The doorless body clad in polished aluminium finished in a beautifully pointed tail, and the frame was so narrow that a bulge had to be added to accommodate the driver's right foot. The highly tuned engine throbbed under the bonnet, its exhaust running along the side of the car and deafeningly firing sparks rearwards on every drop of the accelerator. The car sat low and purposefully on Hartford shock absorbers, cranked up to their stiffest settings.[35]

The vehicle was a phenomenon. At the Brooklands Junior Car Club 200-Mile Race, Gordon England pushed it up to 85 miles-per-hour,[36]

---

34   William Boddy *Brooklands*, (Grenville, 1957).
35   *Motor Sport* magazine, October 1968.
36   Brooklands (ibid) p212.

and in a field of enormous cars finished in an unlikely second place, beaten only by the much larger-engined Salmson of Spanish Grand-Prix racer Ramon Bueno. By the end of the 1923 season, Gordon England held all 22 of the Brooklands 750cc speed records in the Austin and a few weeks later, he announced that he would be selling replicas of his racing Seven to discerning racing motorists. The demand for the new car was instantaneous, with Sir Francis Samuelson, later noted as probably the only person to have raced competitively before the Great War and after the Second World War, announcing himself as the first customer. Following very shortly afterwards another order arrived at Gordon England's Oxford showroom, from a certain Major ATG Gardner MC. Goldie had decided to go racing.

Compared to the standard car, the Gordon England 'Brooklands' model was expensive – its £265 price tag was more than double the list price for the Austin Seven chassis alone – but as this was to be his only car, Gardner paid £10/10/- extra for cycle-style wings to keep the mud at bay, £5/5/- for a windscreen and asked that headlamps be fitted. He didn't bother with the optional hood but – given that he still wasn't sure how easy the car would be to drive with his injury – he specified hand controls[37].

A few weeks later, the car was delivered to Raglan Road. Gardner carefully inspected his gleaming new car, its 'RK1020' number plate proudly affixed to the front fairing, and a number roundel painted on the rear flank in readiness for the track. He quickly fitted his brass Automobile Association member's badge then stepped back and looked at Gordon England's handiwork. It was an impressive machine and despite his height and his disability, he managed to climb in and settle himself comfortably into the cabin with little fuss. On the seat lay the paperwork; Gardner was amused to see that it included a signed certificate from Gordon England stating that he had tested the car up

---

37 *Motor Sport* magazine, October 1968.

to 75 miles-per-hour on the Brooklands track. With cigarillo gripped purposefully between his lips he posed for a photograph, a determined look on his face. In the family album, he simply entitled this picture 'My first racing car.'[38] The following day, he sent a letter to the Clerk of the Course at Brooklands, enclosing his entry form for the Easter Meeting, to be held on Monday, 21st April 1924. There was now no turning back.

The days leading up to the event were far from ideal. Heavy rain lashed the south of England from Good Friday until Easter Sunday, leaving torrents pouring off the concrete Brooklands track. But as Easter Monday dawned, the clouds had moved off towards the continent and the ground began to dry. Nevertheless, there was a weight in the air as the 25,000 spectators and those racing converged on the circuit. Tensions were running high between the Brooklands Committee and local residents, many of whom had complained bitterly about the noise of the racing. The Committee had reached an agreement: all racing cars would be fitted with 'fantail' exhaust pipes, designed to reduce the noise to an acceptable level. It was a compromise that satisfied nobody; residents felt it made little difference and the racers were outraged when it was rumoured that the new exhaust would take 4 miles-per-hour off a top speed. To add further insult to injury, the Committee had decided that the cars had become too fast for the start/finish straight and were experimenting with moving the grid to the 'Pond Start', just after the Fork[39] where the straight split from the outer circuit, an act that was met with uproar from regulars who had become extremely comfortable sipping drinks around the clubhouse as the cars lined up.

Gardner heard a great deal of grumbling as he readied himself for his first race. His mechanic had pushed his Seven into the paddock and now sat fiddling with the carburettor settings and checking the wheel nuts were tight. The tiny Austin was lined up with the other two Sevens

---

38   Photographic archive, (NMM).
39   *Brooklands* (ibid).

that had also been entered into the Private Competitors' Handicap, by tradition the first race of the season and open to all, regardless of engine capacity. Gardner's tiny car was dwarfed by some of the others in the seventeen-car field, the largest of which was an enormous, red Lorraine-Dietrich built to complete in the 1912 Dieppe Grand Prix, its engine containing four vast pistons displacing over 15 litres, twenty times that of the Austin, that drove the rear wheels through a danger-ously exposed chain.[40]

There were other behemoths, too: a pair of seven-litre Leylands, an exotic side-valve Aston Martin and a Vauxhall OE 30/98 known as the 'Silver Arrow'[41] that glinted in the sunlight were all impressive machines, but it was a Bugatti Type 30 racing car that Gardner recog-nised from the Strasbourg Grand Prix that caught his eye. Now owned by the fabulously wealthy Count Louis Zborowski who had bought it to run in the previous season's Indianapolis 500, the streamlined blue car was a very quick indeed.[42] Suddenly, Gardner felt very small and very insignificant in his little Austin.

As the 1pm start ticked closer, the mechanics carried out their last checks. With the sleeves of their oil-stained white overalls rolled back, flat caps pushed to the back of their heads and the ubiquitous cigarettes hanging from their mouths, the men readied the vehicles, checking tyre pressures, chain tension and oil levels. A mistake here could mean more than just an unsuccessful race, it could end in horrendous injury or even death for the driver. Then suddenly, the tannoy blasted: *All com-petitors to the start line.*

Every driver had their own pre-race ritual. Some prayed. Some carefully cleaned their already sparkling goggles. Others followed ex-

---

40   'Vieux Charles III' owned and driven by Mr A. Ellison. (Race programme, Brooklands archive).
41   The two modified Leyland Eights were driven by brothers Jack (white car with black wheels) and Dick Howey (grey car) the latter who was to die in an horrific crash in it two years later in Boulogne. Dick Summers drove the Aston Martin with a two-seater body by Atcherley of Birmingham and Major Leonard Ropner the Vauxhall OE 30/98 'Silver Arrow.' (*Brooklands*, ibid).
42   Chassis 4004 was run at Strasbourg as a works entry, driven by the Marquis de Casa Maury who finished 5th but bearing failure led to its retirement from the Indianapolis 500.

actly the same process as they had done many times before, fitting gloves, wind-hat and goggles in the specific order that had kept them safe on every previous race. Gardner reverted to how he'd been in the trenches: with a slight smile, and keeping his cigarette firmly clamped between his lips, he quickly donned his protective gear and nodded to his mechanic, as if he'd done this a thousand times before. The mechanic nodded back as Gardner heaved himself onto the back of the Austin and lifted his injured leg over the car's side before sliding down into the cockpit. Inside, he could feel his heart racing.

In quick succession, the cars around him fired their engines. Most just needed a quick crank of a starting handle, others required a short push. Alive now, the cars surged into life, the revs dancing as the engines were coaxed up to race-ready temperature. Sparks flew from exhausts and the spectators pressed against the surrounding picket fence, some pushing their fingers in their ears as the noise rose to a crescendo. Finally, the cars started to roll out: led by one of the big Leylands they pulled onto the track, turning right then snaking along in single file, warming brakes and tyres as best they could. Gardner sat, awaiting his turn, keeping the engine revs rising and falling and feeling comforted by the rhythm it created. Fourteenth of sixteen cars, he finally pulled away, following a primrose Austin[43] out past the crowds, up to the Fork, turning left onto the straight and pulling up at the start line. Ahead of him was a small pedestrian bridge crossing the track; to his right, the vast edifice of the Vickers factory; to his left, the pits, and various buildings housing officials and those with the best tickets. Every inch of the trackside verge was filled with spectators, all watching, waiting for this, the start of another season's racing. Then, it was time. The last of the cars[44] had just pulled into line when the official timer, Mr. Ebblewhite –

---

43   Belonging to Sir Francis Samuelson.
44   A Talbot belonging to Mr C.J. Randall.

known to all as 'Ebby' – strode on to the track, stood to the right of the first car, and raised his small Union Flag in the air.[45]

The sense of anticipation was palpable. The drivers were all staring at Ebby, and the revs had built to a crescendo, the cars like a pack of frenzied dogs baying to start the hunt. With no ceremony, Ebby dropped the flag and the first car was off, its tyres squealing as it shot towards the first corner. Ebby instantly moved back past the three Austins and raised his flag again, staring at the timing box in his hand. Eighteen seconds after the first car had departed, Gardner saw Ebby's flag twitch, dropped the clutch and floored the accelerator. In a fog of noise and tyre smoke, the three Austins shot away from the line and launched themselves towards the first corner, where the leader had just disappeared out of view.

Behind them, the rest of the starters, their handicaps having been previously set by Ebby based on their car's potential and their own driving ability were set off in ones and twos until finally, nearly two minutes after the first car, the big black wheels of the vast Leyland spun and its driver set out in pursuit of the rest of the field.

For Gardner, all sense of nervousness had evaporated as the flag dropped, replaced by a huge sense of exhilaration. For the first few yards the three Austins kept pace with one another, but Gardner quickly realised that brown car on his inside[46] held a performance advantage over the other two and watched as it started to pull away. Gardner tucked in behind him, keeping to the inside of the track as the pine trees and cheering spectators flashed by, just a few feet to his left. Up into top gear now, he crouched down in the cockpit, willing his little car forwards towards the Members' Banking. As he turned into the corner, he allowed the car to run up the slope to make the most of the incline. A one hundred feet-wide expanse of concrete, so steep that a person

---

45   Numerous books and articles tell the story of 'Ebby' who, Union flag in hand and bowler hat on head, would decide handicaps, start the races and be the final arbiter of race timing. Boddy, Lydon, et al.

46   Driven by J.P. Dingle.

could not walk up it unaided and enclosed in a man-made valley with the 'mountain' on the left and the Members' Enclosure on the right, the track was simultaneously both vast and claustrophobic. A few seconds later, the brown Austin still heading off into the distance in front of him, Gardner shot under the Members' Bridge, past the exit to the start/finish straight, then hit the 'big bump' where the track crossed the River Wey, and for a split second became airborne. Although his conscious brain knew it was coming, the lurch in his stomach caught him by surprise and he felt the adrenaline surge as the tyres crashed back onto the rough concrete and he wrestled with the vast, black steering wheel to bring the car back into line. Beyond the bend now, he let the car drift over to the inside of the Railway Straight, willing himself faster. The rusting corrugated-iron fencing running along the right of the circuit flashed by as did the dark forest of pine trees behind, ready to catch any driver who strayed from the track, dashing them into pieces. On the inside, the crowd: suited men with overcoats and Homburgs or flat caps depending on their class, the women almost all in fashionable cloche hats, no barrier separating them from the cars racing past. Then, the track started to rise again for the Byfleet Banking, a longer curve than the bank at the other end of the track but with a narrower surface, dotted with numerous vast patches where the concrete had been repaired over the years and as he rose up the bank, Gardner instinctively backed off slightly, the short, black telegraph poles carrying the wires linking the white timing boxes flashing past slightly less frequently as before. As he did, the first of the chasing cars thundered past on his outside.[47]

Until now, Gardner had convinced himself that he had a chance of a podium finish. He had been running happily in third place, but as the first of the large-engined cars roared past, running a good thirty

---

47   The description of racing at Brooklands has come from a variety of sources. The place itself still gives a sense of what it must have been like, with sections of the course including Members' Banking, start/finish straight and elements of the Byfleet Banking remaining open to the public. For contemporary reports, Barré Lydon's (pseudonym of Alfred Edgar) book *Combat* (1933) gives a great first-person view of the experience, as does *Brooklands: Behind The Scenes* by Charles Mortimer (although focusing on motorcycles). YouTube is also a fascinating archive of old news reports showing cars racing, and the movie *Death Drives Through* (1935) although a challenging watch, has a great deal of archive footage. At the time of writing, it is available on Amazon Prime in the UK.

miles an hour faster than his own, it was obvious that racing was not to be this easy a challenge to master. The race was to be one full lap followed by one that branched off left at the Fork, ending before the grandstands, and by the time he reached the Members' Banking for the second time, half a dozen cars had already passed him. Expecting the big bump now, he skipped over it without any problem and once settled, pushed himself faster again. Hunched down, he rose again up the Byfleet Banking, his tiny tyres skittering across the ragged track at the edge of their grip as he pushed as hard as he could. A few other cars overtook him on the turn, not so quickly now, but edging past all the same, the little Austin unable to answer the challenge it had been set. Finally, the slope subsided, the track widened, and Gardner saw the Fork ahead. The car that had started first – a Talbot – was just a few lengths ahead of him now, and Gardner could feel the spatter of hot, oily exhaust gas as the two cars hugged the inside of the circuit, tyres clipping the ragged grass that grew there. With just yards to go, both drivers pulled themselves as low as they could in the cockpit, willing the cars on as they crossed the line and passed the waved flag marking the end of the race.

The two drivers backed off, slowed to a walking pace and turned into the parc fermé. As the revs dropped and his engine quietened to a gentle splutter, Gardner was suddenly aware of the noise that replaced the screaming exhaust note that had left his ears ringing: a wall of cheering and applause for the victors who now sat on their bonnets, laurel clad and covered in a mist of oil, soaking up the atmosphere. The smiling Count Zborowski in his glorious blue Bugatti was the winner,[48] with the 'Silver Arrow' Vauxhall second and one of the other Austin Sevens third.[49]

---

48   Zborowski won with average speed of 98.75 miles-per-hour and a fastest lap averaging
       107.57 miles-per-hour. (Brooklands Museum).
49   Driven by J.P. Dingle.

As he climbed out of the Austin, still panting from the exertion and feeling his fingers tingle from the vibrations of the car, a broad smile spread across his face. He had not troubled the leaders and obviously needed more experience to improve as a racer, but the exhilaration he felt was extraordinary. He realised the crowd were cheering him too, acknowledging his bravery, applauding his skill. His wound meant that he had missed the homecoming parades that followed the Armistice, when crowds had cheered the returning soldiers, so this public adulation was a new experience for him. Although it was cloaked in his usual carefully guarded expressions, he realised that he liked it, a lot.

He didn't have long to appreciate this novel emotion. The Private Competitors' Handicap had taken just a few minutes to complete and very soon after finishing he was called back to the start line for the next race, scheduled to start at 1.25pm.[50] Following the same route but finishing at a slightly later line, the Easter Small Car Handicap was less intensive than the first race: just seven competitors, each in a small car with engine size limited to 1,100cc. This time, he tried to settle into the rhythm of the race, sometimes pushing his car higher up the banking to see if it improved his speed, trying to learn the subtle lumps and bumps of the ragged concrete and watching the fast drivers to see where they made up time. At the finish, although he was not near the front of the pack, he once again found himself cheered into the parc fermé, allowed his mask of control to slip, and smiled heartily back at the crowd.[51] His racing over for the day, he generously tipped his mechanic, changed out of his racing clothes and made his way to the Members' Banking to watch the rest of the races, where he was surprised to be met with many handshakes and pats on the back. He later realised he could not recall any results from the later races, but as he drove the

---

50   Race programme, Brooklands archive.
51   The race was won by Owen Wilson-Jones in a Salmson, with Dingle moving up one place from the previous race to finish in second. Eric Gordon England, in his original Austin 'Brooklands' Seven, came third with Gardner and Sir Francis Samuelson following, their Austins noted as being noticeably slower than Gordon England's 'works' car. *Brooklands* (ibid).

Austin out of the track and back to Reigate that evening, the still-cold night air biting at his face and the dim headlamps guiding him along, the smile returned once again to his face. He was hooked.

5

DEATH AND SUCCESS

In the days following his competitive debut at Brooklands, Gardner felt a buzz of adrenaline that he'd not felt for a long time, and immediately desired more. He quickly sent in his entry fees and secured his places in the next few spring meetings.

Every time he drove there, he felt the same surge of elation. Each race, he felt himself becoming more confident in the car, able to push it a little further towards its limits. He thrived in the practical challenge of mastering this new skill and felt another emotion that had lain dormant for a long time: personal pride in overcoming the fear that enveloped his body as he took to the track. Not since the trenches had he felt like this.

His ability to control his emotions, push harder than most and seemingly ignore the risks quickly led him to gaining a reputation as a courageous and competent driver. In the drivers' bar after each race meeting, he would be clapped on the back and bought a drink by another racer, and discovered he felt very comfortable in their presence. Many were men like him: officers who had served in the Great War, a

surprising number of whom had been wounded in action, and a fair
few whose war hadn't ended the way they had envisaged.

Some he warmed to straight away, like the charismatic Malcolm
Campbell, who had also been at school at Uppingham. Five years older
than Gardner, Campbell immediately made a huge impression on him.
They found that they had a great deal in common, swapping stories of
brutish school masters and even discovering they had both been lured
into motorsport through first ownership of the same model of Rex motorcycle.[52] Campbell came from a similar background to Gardner, his
father making his money through a family business, although Campbell senior left a rather more substantial legacy of around £250,000
(£11.7M at 2023 values[53]) for his son to finance his racing. Charismatic and undoubtedly brave, and having raced at Brooklands before the
war, it is not hard to see how Gardner quickly came to regard Campbell as a mentor. For his part, Campbell took Gardner under his wing
and regaled him not just with stories of his racing exploits, but also
with his newfound passion for land speed record attempts. Campbell
was convinced he had been cheated out of beating Kenelm Lee Guinness's speed record the previous year when he'd recorded an average of
137.72 miles-per-hour at the international speed trials at Fanoe in Denmark. Driving the same Sunbeam car in which Guinness had set the
previous record at Brooklands back in 1922, Campbell's time was disallowed by the International Sporting Commission because the electrical
timing equipment used by the Danish Automobile Club was not of the
officially approved type. Campbell was livid, but not deterred. He told
Gardner of his plans: a return to Fanoe in August, this time with a new,
streamlined body fitted to the car and Ebby the Brooklands timekeeper
being shipped over to officiate. Gardner hung on every word.

---

52   Malcolm Campbell, *My Thirty Years of Speed*, (Hutchinson & Co, 1935), p21.
53   Phil Drackett's 1969 book *Like Father Like Son* is strongly recommended for those who want to read
     more about the Campbells' records.

Other drivers, even ex-military, proved harder for Gardner to get to know such as Captain James 'Jack' Toop, a 41-year-old who he had met briefly during his first few races at Brooklands. Although he had served on the Eastern front during the war, Toop wasn't quite like most of the others. He'd fought in the London Regiment as a young officer, a unit with a reputation as dependable line infantry, but quickly transferred to the Royal Army Ordnance Corps. Rather unfairly nicknamed 'The Blanket Stackers' by the rest of the Army, they carried out the essential, although not very glamorous role of supplying and maintaining equipment, ammunition, and stores. Surrounded by decorated officers from more prestigious regiments, Toop gained a reputation for having a reserved personality and tended to keep himself to himself, socialising only really with Charles Brocklebank, another 'Corps' man who had served in the Royal Engineers. The fact that Toop had chosen to retain his military rank of Captain after the war – traditionally the preserve of field officers of the rank of Major and above – was enough to make others perceive him with a touch of suspicion.

The Whitsun Meeting on 9th June 1924 was Gardner's third competitive outing, and in front of a crowd of 15,000 he took part in the first and fourth races. He'd spent time watching the faster drivers, looking at the lines they took into the corners and trying to understand how they coped with traffic. During the races, he tried to put what he'd learned into practice and found that it worked; although he still wasn't on the podium, he was closing the gap. His confidence was booming and as he pulled up at the end of his last race, he was feeling fantastic. He quickly changed and rushed back to watch the next race, the 100 miles-per-hour Long Handicap.

Jack Toop had secured his place in the race, his first since the war, and persuaded his friend Brocklebank to lend him his Peugeot[54] for the duration. Having already won the Lightning Handicap, Brock-

---

54   4.5-Litre 1913 Grand Prix Type Peugeot L45.

lebank agreed,[55] and suggested he vacate the passenger's seat to give Toop a lighter load and a shot at the win. All went well until the final lap of the 8½-mile race. In second place and charging to catch the leader,[56] Toop caught up with him and entered his slipstream just as the two cars reached the Byfleet Banking. The car in front was throwing up a lot of grit, spattering Toop's eyes, and as the cars skittered at the very edge of their grip, Toop's wheels began to wobble. Whether it was his unfamiliarity with the car, his lack of recent race experience or, as a witness suggested at the inquest, he fainted, Toop lost control and the car shot up and over the top of the banking.[57] The Peugeot pirouetted as it crashed through the trees at 100 miles-per-hour, broken parts being strewn over the track and the wrecked chassis engulfed in flame as it finally came to a halt with the driver's body pinned underneath. Racegoers climbed over the embankment, but nothing could be done for Toop, whose semi-dismembered head proved that death at least came quickly. According to the inquest, Toop had just bought a black cat charm for luck.[58] It was found still attached to his racing jacket after his body was recovered.

The death was a shock for everyone in the paddock. Despite the very rudimentary safety equipment, lack of barriers and tyres that had an alarming habit of disintegrating at high speed, Toop's had been just the sixth death recorded at Brooklands since it opened in 1907. As both drivers and spectators stood around in groups following the accident, the mood was very sombre and by common consent it was decided that the rest of the meeting should be abandoned. Not all agreed: one woman harangued driver John Parry-Thomas who had finished second, demanding that he confirm whether she would lose her winnings, to which it was reported he showed 'praiseworthy self-control'.[59]

55   *Motor Sport*, July 1924.
56   Clive Gallop in his 5-Litre Ballot.
57   *Yorkshire Post*, 13 June 1924.
58   *The Times*, 13 June 1924.
59   *The Times* (ibid).

Although he knew his sport was a dangerous one and he had previously experienced death at very close quarters, the circuit's carnival
atmosphere of betting, drinking and society entertaining had lulled
Goldie into a false sense of security. Toop's death so early in his racing
career was a harsh lesson, but not one that was going to put him off.
He chose not to compete in the next Brooklands meeting in early July
– an event dominated by Parry-Thomas, Campbell and Irish driver
Kaye Don – but booked himself an entry at the August Bank Holiday meeting.

Gardner's summer was not devoid of the elixir of speed. Numerous
other drivers took to the Brooklands track to attempt to break various records, and many were successful. Parry-Thomas took the most,
breaking everything from the flying start half-mile to the 100 Kilometre
records, but it was another racer – REO Hall – who fascinated Gardner most. Driving another Gordon England Austin Seven, Hall set a
host of records in Class L for the light car. Both drivers received hearty
congratulations from the rest of the paddock, and Parry-Thomas's
achievement even gained a column inch-or-so on page three of *The
Daily Herald.*[60]

Goldie looked on in fascination, and it only fuelled his desire to return to the track. On 4th August, he lined up in the race that proved to
be the final one in his debut Brooklands season, and it was a bruising
experience. He set off well, and for the first time took a sizeable lead.
'I had visions of cups, bags of gold, etc,' he wrote, but then 'I heard
a "sizzling" followed by a "bump". I cruised to a standstill… very ap-
prehensively opened the bonnet and shut it down again very quickly
– horrible sight, a gaping hole in the side of the crankcase!'[61]

The significant cost of an engine rebuild (complete with new block)
wasn't something he'd bargained for. The price of entry – three sov-
ereigns for a short race and five for a longer one – added to costs of

---

60   *Daily Herald*, 26 May 1924.
61   *Magic MPH* (ibid) p13.

BARC membership, a mechanic, a set of tyres nearly every meeting and routine maintenance items like spark plugs, oil and replacing the odd burnt valve, meant that this was becoming a very expensive pastime. An article in *The Motor* that year suggested that it cost around £200 to run a car through a Brooklands season and that was based on the assumption of around £125 in winnings - something Gardner had so far failed to achieve. So, round that up to £325, add probably another £100 for the engine rebuild, and you have a cost that would be over £20,000 in 2023. This sort of outlay didn't bother his fellow racers like Campbell with his thousands in the bank or Count Louis Zborowski who owned acres of Manhattan real estate, but for Gardner, it hurt.

As a result, Gardner sat out the rest of the season but watched as the brutality of the sport was reiterated time and again. His friend Campbell did as he had promised and returned to Fanoe in Denmark with his Sunbeam to attempt the land speed record.[62] Storms had swept the beach on the days before the trial, leaving debris strewn across the sand. A narrow path was cleared, but it was in poor condition and spectators were allowed to crowd too close to the edge. Warnings were given, but no action taken, and as Campbell pushed his car past 150 miles-per-hour, a wheel became detached and bounded into the crowd. It struck a boy spectator, who died later of his injuries. Campbell was said to be distraught but determined to continue and the following month, on 25th September 1924, he took his car to Pendine Sands in Wales where he finally achieved his aim, setting an average speed of 146.16 miles-per-hour, beating the existing record by less than half a mile-per-hour.

Other record attempts were less successful but equally as tragic as Campbell's Fanoe attempt. On 3rd September, Dario 'Dolly' Resta, the winner of the 1916 Indianapolis 500 drove a 2-litre, supercharged Sunbeam at Brooklands in a bid to beat the Class B records. After setting some shorter times he went back out on track to attempt the longer records, but at top speed on the Railway Straight a snapped belt shred-

---

62   Phil Drackett, *Like Father Like Son*, (Clifton Books, 1969), p39.

ded a tyre, causing the car to smash through the fence bordering the track, burst into flames and instantly kill Resta.[63] Then, on 19th October, news reached Gardner of the death of another driver he admired: Count Zborowski had left the track at the Lesmo curve on lap 44 of the Italian Grand Prix at Monza, struck a tree and died later despite being rushed to hospital.[64]

Gardner finished the year with conflicting emotions. For the first time since the War, he had built up a network of friends, a group in which he was liked and recognised as a brave driver who was improving rapidly. But the risks involved had been starkly displayed to him, and moreover, his beloved Austin Seven had not shown itself to be the giant killer he had envisioned. Gardner didn't just want to take part, he wanted to win, and he knew that if he was to continue racing, he needed a new, competitive car, and the serious money to pay for it. And that presented a problem.

---

63   Boddy, *Brooklands* (ibid) p235.
64   He had been invited to drive the Mercedes-Benz 2-litre M72/94 car.
     His mechanic, Len Martin, survived.

6

CATCHING BREATH

———————

After the phenomenal surge of excitement that he felt during the 1924 racing season, the months that followed were a strange time for Gardner. His first priority was the repair of his car, and quickly entrusted the engine rebuild to his local Austin dealer, Milne & Russell Ltd, on the Brighton Road in Crawley, where their competent works manager Herbert Polson took charge. He imagined it would be repaired quickly, but delay after expensive delay beset the refurbishment. By the time the 1925 Brooklands season began on 13th April, Gardner was still a long way off being in a position to compete.

Frustrated and stung by the relentless bills that arrived monthly, Gardner was determined not to lose his passion for the sport and returned as a spectator. At the first meeting, he watched with some envy from the grandstands as his friend Malcolm Campbell stormed to victory but it was 'Bentley Boy' Dudley Benjafield's car that caught his eye: a sleek, new 'San Sebastien' Salmson, emblazoned with the manufacturer's distinctive diagonal spars enveloping the smooth-cowled radiator in the shape of a St. Andrew's cross.[65] The racing was entertaining and it was good to see his fellow drivers again, but he needed an outlet for the energy that still burned within him, and desperately missed the challenge of the track.

As the days became longer, the Brooklands season rolled on as it had done every year since the war. At Easter, Whitsun, August and in the autumn, the crowds surged to the circuit eager to watch the duelling, the drivers raced, and the bookies took their cut. Somehow though, there was a feeling in the paddock that the allure was a little tarnished, that the magic was maybe slipping away. Maybe it was the inevitability of the same old names with the same old money winning the same old races. Maybe it was a lack of excitement: once you'd seen the cars thunder around the outer circuit a few times, the sense of achievement wasn't quite as acute as it had once been. Maybe it was the drivers themselves: once they'd mastered driving on the huge, banked track they yearned for more.

The Brooklands authorities tried to give them more, by adapting the old races to inject a sense of challenge. The Junior Car Club 200-Mile event was run over a course dotted with artificial hazards that created two new hairpin turns per lap, and the High-Speed Trial now required drivers to negotiate a course including the paddock entrance road, the tunnel, and a descent down Test Hill. At the Whitsun Meeting, another novel approach was tried, with a race created just for drivers of the ever-popular Austin Seven model. For those watching, it seemed to work: the season was filled with the usual adventures, from close-won races to the inevitable spills and near-misses that some went to experience. But for some of the drivers, these tinkered-with rules removed the very thing that had drawn them to Brooklands in the first place: the surge of adrenaline that comes from pure, unadulterated speed.

---

65   Campbell's victory was in the 90 Long race driving a 2.8-Litre Itala of the type that his company, Malcolm Campbell (London) Ltd, was importing and Benjafield came third in the 75 Short race. Boddy *Brooklands* ibid.

John Parry-Thomas was one such man. He did not fit the usual
gentleman driver mould, being the son of a Welsh parson who drove
an omnibus during the general strike, but what he lacked in financial
support he made up for with his exceptional engineering talent. Hired
by Leyland to the role of chief engineer after the Great War, he already
had various motoring patents to his name when, in 1920, he decided to
leave his job and dedicated his life to motor racing. Success came quickly through a combination of competent driving and by meticulously
rebuilding his cars to eke out the maximum performance possible. By
1925, he had more than fifty Brooklands podium finishes under his
belt and a team of six engineers who worked on his and other drivers'
cars in a building next to his home, a bungalow known as *The Hermitage*
that he rented from the circuit's owners. One car dominated his efforts:
an immense, aero-engined monster that Parry-Thomas had bought
from the estate of his racing colleague Count Zborowski,[66] a car that
he hoped would help him achieve his ambition of securing the world
land speed record. He'd been enthused by the recent establishment of
formal record categories based on engine size and distance, catego-
rised by Colonel Lindsay Lloyd, the Clerk of the Course at Brooklands.
Parry-Thomas saw these as personal challenges and set about creating
the vehicles in which he could secure as many as possible. Various cars
emerged from his stable, all clad in his white and blue colours[67] and he
picked up various speed and distance records on the track, but for the
serious drivers there was only one crown that mattered: the outright
title of being the fastest man on earth. He'd watched a few months previously as Malcolm Campbell had returned from his successful run at
Pendine Sands and been feted by both the other racers and the general
public in a way that dwarfed the recognition they received for winning

---

66   Powered by a huge 27-Litre Liberty V12 engine, this car had been destined to become one of the
     Count's famous 'Chitty' cars but was sold unfinished as the *Higham Special*, named after Zborowski's
     Higham Park home, following his death.
67   These included a stubby four-cylinder 1.8-Litre Thomas Special, sometimes fitted with an experimental
     pointed tail, a 1.5-litre straight-eight 'Flat Iron' special, and the monstrous 'Leyland-Thomas Number 1'
     in which he set the 1925 lap record at an eye-watering 129.36 miles-per-hour.

at Brooklands. Parry-Thomas knew that the word in the paddock was that Campbell was preparing his car for another attempt to aim for the 150 miles-per-hour barrier, and that another old racing rival, Henry Segrave, was hot on his heels. Segrave had thrown money at the problem and commissioned the Sunbeam company to create a car that would smash Campbell's record.

The rumours were correct. In July 1925, Campbell returned to Wales with his Sunbeam 350hp *Bluebird* record car. Longer exhaust pipes now protruded from the polished silver bonnet and the windscreen had been removed since his last run, and this time the weather at Pendine was much better. "For once, everything went without a hitch," Campbell said after the run, in which he averaged 150.87 miles-per-hour, the first person to break the 150 miles-per-hour barrier in a car. He returned triumphant, to the delight of the motoring public.[68]

The record stood for another eight months before Segrave's Sunbeam *Tiger* was rolled out on the seven-mile Ainsdale beach at Southport in Merseyside. The 4-Litre car was very different to both Campbell and Parry-Thomas's huge-engined beasts, trading engine size for lightweight, aerodynamic design developed from Sunbeam's Grand Prix cars. Despite suffering from a series of supercharger failures that stopped Segrave from pushing the car as much as he wished and a 60-foot leap thanks to an impact with an undulation in the sand on the return run, his speed over the measured kilometre was 152.33 miles-per-hour, making him the new fastest man on the planet.

Back at Brooklands, Parry-Thomas was quietly confident when he heard the news. Even before his full rebuild, he'd pushed the Higham Special up to 126 miles per hour on the track. Now, rechristened 'Babs', the meticulously re-engineered car clad in a sleek body was capable of smashing Segrave's record, or so Parry-Thomas thought. He didn't have too long to wait to find out: a little over a month after

---

68   This car, still in this configuration and running well, is on display at the
      National Motor Museum, Beaulieu.

Segrave's record, on 27th April 1926, Parry-Thomas arrived at Pendine Sands with *Babs*.

Gardner had travelled with Parry-Thomas, and as his engineers finished fuelling the car, he linked arms with the others in the party to keep the press of onlookers at a safe distance. Clad in a sensible tweed suit complete with plus fours, Gardner looked the part of the gentleman racer. Parry-Thomas, in his typical oil-stained Fair Isle sweater,[69] open-collar white shirt, leather wind helmet and cigarette clasped between his blackened fingers, looked rather more relaxed. With very little fanfare, Parry-Thomas cracked the huge engine into life, sparks leaping from the twelve stub exhausts that fired straight out of the side of the engine and tappets dancing as he revved it into life. Then, after the engine was warm, he encouraged some of the men to give him a push off the line. Forgetting his damaged leg for a moment in the excitement, Gardner eagerly added his weight to the maul and was engulfed with a wall of noise as the huge white and blue car thundered off along the sand. He recovered his footing then watched as Parry-Thomas turned *Babs* around in a lazy arc, pointed the car along the beach and dropped the accelerator to the floor.

It was an astonishing sight. Gardner had seen fast cars before at Brooklands, but nothing like this. *Babs'* wheels spun, shooting arcs of sand into the air as the car charged off. The engine screamed as Parry-Thomas fought with the big steering wheel, hunched over as if willing the car to go faster. Within seconds, it shot past the flag marking where Colonel Lindsay Lloyd, who attended as the official Royal Automobile Club timekeeper, was standing with his equipment. Off into the distance, Parry-Thomas pushed *Babs* hard until, the car now just a spec on the horizon, he turned again and pointed back towards the start. Time and again Parry-Thomas thundered up and down the beach, each time pushing closer and closer to the limit of what was possible.

---

69 Drackett, *Like Father Like Son* (ibid) p43 et al. Parry-Thomas's achievements are well documented, and newsreel footage of his runs are on YouTube.

Finally, excited word came from the timer and the men waved frantically at Parry-Thomas to tell him that the record was his.[70] With the sand
becoming waterlogged, Parry-Thomas knew he'd pushed his luck as far
as it would stretch this time and decided to make his way home with
his new record. This time, it wasn't just the regional press who were interested in the speed records. Parry-Thomas was celebrated across the
headlines of national newspapers, and he received the ultimate media
accolade of the day: a camera crew had been dispatched to Pendine
to record a movie of his record-breaking attempt which was shown
between films at picture houses around the country.

Back at Brooklands, Parry-Thomas was a sensation. When he entered *Babs* in three races in the Whitsun meeting, the crowds had to
be held back as they surged to see this now world-famous car and its
fearless driver. Gardner watched, and was enthralled, his determination to get back on track rejuvenated once more, and the glimmer of
an idea forming in his head. But money was still a problem, given that
his mother was still unwilling to spend his trust fund on racing cars. He
knew that he needed a job.

Within weeks, one fell into his lap. Visiting Milne & Russell to discuss
the progress on his Austin, Polson mentioned that they were looking to
expand the business. Quickly, a plan formed, and Gardner returned
home to suggest an investment to his mother. Persuading herself that
this could provide her eldest son with a respectable job that would keep
him out of the Brooklands paddock, Isabella agreed, and bought him
into the company as a partner.[71] For the first couple of years, it seemed
to work. Other than a single race in a borrowed Salmson in 1926,
Gardner focused on the business and not on his own racing. Sure, he
still attended the Brooklands meetings, taking his camera whenever he

---

70   Colonel Lloyd confirmed that Parry-Thomas had increased the world record by nearly 17 miles per hour,
      and by the second day he had set a new level of 171.02 miles-per-hour. At the end of his last run, *Babs*
      was driven off to a roped-off enclosure to be inspected. Both front shock absorber bolts had worked loose,
      the engineers finding that one was held on by a nut with a single thread keeping it in place.
71   NMM archive.

could and keeping in touch with his friends, but he didn't act on his growing urge to return to racing.

Not until 1928, that is, when the urge to get back on track became unbearable. Memories of his last race filled his mind, as did the emotions generated by the Salmson he had borrowed. It was a fast car, but Salmson had just unveiled a model that was even quicker – the supercharged Grand Sport,[72] sold 'for racing only' – and were dominating their class, including wins in the notorious Targa Florio in 1926 and '27, an epic endurance competition through the rocky mountain roads of Sicily. Sales at Milne & Russell were going very well, and Gardner benefitted from a fair salary which he had been saving, but buying a Salmson to race was a big step, especially having already discovered with the Austin that cars can cost a lot of money to fix if they go wrong. Knowing he was interested, the British Salmson importer offered to lend him one for the Essex Motor Club Six Hour race at Brooklands in early May 1928 and Gardner jumped at the chance.

The outing was far from uneventful. Having just reached half-distance and just before leaving the Byfleet Banking, he received what he described as 'a real wallop' on his right shoulder. 'For the moment I did not know what had happened,' he wrote. 'But looking down at my right offside wheel, I noted the tyre was bare of all signs of rubber and that I was running on the canvas! I was luckily very close to our pit so coasted in to change the wheel.'[73]

'The word "imperturbable" is much used in connection with racing drivers,' a journalist wrote in the wonderfully-titled *Chloride Chronicle and Exide News,*[74] 'but to sit in an office and hear Major Gardner tell of having a back wheel torn off whilst racing is to realise that the word is not inapplicable to the man… you ordinary chaps who, like the writer,

---

72   Sold as the 'Grand Prix' in Great Britain, it was fitted with the San Sebastian double-overhead camshaft engine with Cozette No. 8 Supercharger and twin-spark plug ignition, producing up to 85 brake horsepower. It lapped Montlhéry, the banked, French equivalent of Brooklands on the outskirts of Paris, at 97 miles-per-hour.
73   Gardner, *Magic MPH,* (ibid), p13.
74   NMM Archive.

get a thrill out of driving your cars along [at] 65 or 70 will understand to some extent the feelings of a racing driver who is pounding along at 100 miles-per-hour or more and realises that one of his rear tyres is shredding its tread! – yet the Major calmly assures me that it is not so bad with the rear tyres, but deuced awkward with the front ones!' Despite the tyre problems, Gardner achieved a respectable 10th place overall and earned himself a coveted gold medal. When, a few days later, Salmson offered him the chance to buy a gleaming new *Grand Sport* model, complete with tricolour-painted tail and 2ft horn, it was too much to resist. In the firm belief that it would give him the success he had been yearning for, he bought it, road-registered it as 'VB3080' and immediately entered it in various Brooklands races throughout the summer with some success, winning various awards including a first place in the August novice race. His confidence raised, he took part in the Boulogne Speed Trials, racing overseas for the first time, winning the 1,100cc class of the 3-kilometre speed trials and the Wimille Hill Climb. At Le Touquet he entered his final event of the week, the 900m speed trial. With headlamps removed to minimise weight, Gardner was successful again, although his late afternoon start meant his return run through the pitch-black night back to the casino in Boulogne to collect his prize was, by his own admission, 'plenty of fun'.

Gardner finished the season a transformed man. He was now racing with confidence and gaining a reputation as a brave and capable driver. He loved the respect he was given, enjoyed the company of the other drivers and thrived in the racing environment, working with his mechanics to get the best result in every competitive outing. Wins at Brooklands and Boulogne had felt wonderful but now he wanted even more; when he heard that a Grand Prix was to be held in Dublin the following summer, he immediately sent in his entry and then started looking for a new, more powerful car.

Unsurprisingly, he found his new car at Brooklands. He watched as his friend Vernon Balls, the importer of French *Amilcar* models, drove one of their sleek, supercharged C6 racing cars around the track at an average speed of 103.76 miles-per-hour, a phenomenal speed for an 1,100cc car.[75] Gardner loved not just the outright pace of the machine, but also its looks – bright red, low to the ground, poised and purposeful – as well as the way the engine screamed as it revved to over 6,500rpm. Balls had imported just seven of these cars into the UK but one was for sale: a year-old model registered 'YV91' that belonged to Beris Harcourt-Wood, one of the 'Bentley Boys', who had run it in the 1928 Junior Car Club 200 Mile race at Brooklands. Despite the cost, Gardner couldn't resist.[76]

The Irish Grand Prix was a big deal. The four-mile clockwise course passed through Phoenix Park in Dublin in the shape of a flattened 'D', with a huge straight, nearly two miles long,

passing the grandstand with a corner at each end: Mountjoy at the northwest end and Gough at the southeast. Organised by the Royal Irish Automobile Club (RIAC), preparations for the race had included the requirement to move the Phoenix Monument, a 30-foot-high column of Portland stone, from the middle of the main straight. Ireland was now a Free State, and the race was seen as a statement of its capability to hold such a prestigious international event which was to be held over two days, cars under 1,500cc competing for the Saorstát Cup on Friday 12th July 1929 and those above racing for the Éireann Cup the following day. A very healthy £1,000 prize for each race – more than double the average value of a semi-detached house – drew a big field of well-known international drivers.[77]

Gardner arrived in Dublin the week before the race, and on Monday 8th July, duly presented himself to the RIAC headquarters in Dawson Street to collect his paperwork and to meet his co-driver, the 22-year-old Robert 'Pippin' Murton-Neale, the son of another of his Brooklands racing friends.[78] They were given arm bands, a sheaf of pa-

75   Mick Walsh, *Classic & Sports Car*, April 2022.
76   The list price new was £750.
77   Bob Montgomery, *The Irish International Grand Prix* (Dreolin, 2019), p51.
78   Alfred Murton-Neale.

pers including Free State driving licences, and told when they needed to report for scrutineering and practice. Excitement for this new race spread through the city, encouraged by press reports that included the ultimate compliment that it was, 'one of the finest courses for a motor race which it is possible to imagine.'[79]

The car performed very well during nearly three days of practice. Both Gardner and Murton-Neale took a turn at the wheel as the regulations required, and by the end of the session Gardner was quietly confident in this poised French machine despite being surrounded by some of the most famous cars and drivers of the time. The pits were a who's who of the motoring world, from the dominant Bentley and elegant Alfa Romeo racing teams to arguably the most famous driver in England, the charismatic Malcolm Campbell who let his eight-year-old son Donald accompany him during practice.[80]

The day of the race dawned to glorious weather and by the time the cars started to form up at 11.30am, the sun was dancing off the corrugated iron roof of the imposing grandstand and the heat shimmering off the gleaming bonnets of the cars lined up on the opposite side of the road. The final preparations complete and the track cleared, the drivers and passengers walked across to the fence by the grandstand, ready to run across the road, jump in their cars and roar off in a *Le Mans*-style start. All except one: as the result of his war wound, Gardner had been excused from the run and now sat on the pit wall next to his car, a lonely figure dressed in his white overalls and black helmet, waiting for Murton-Neale to join him. 'Ebby', the Brooklands timekeeper, had been invited over to start the race. Briskly, he raised a white flag then dropped it, and the sprint began. Murton-Neale dashed over and climbed in, followed by Gardner, whose leg still needed some persuasion to squeeze into the car. Then, with the other cars roaring out of the pits around them, they were off.

---

79   *The Motor* magazine, 1929.
80   Montgomery, *The Irish International Grand Prix* (ibid), p57.

The race was unlike anything Gardner had experienced before. The sheer number of cars on the track, the high-speed long straight and the two sharp corners were all very different to what he had become used to at Brooklands, but he loved the challenge. Lap after lap he drove in the searing heat, keeping a steady pace as those around him skidded wide onto the verges or were forced to retire with mechanical problems. By his half-distance pit stop, with over 70 laps under his belt, he was feeling confident; if he maintained this speed, he had the potential of a very strong finish. But as he pulled up for his scheduled stop, things immediately started to go wrong. He overshot his pit board and had to stamp on the brakes, slewing to a halt as the neighbouring pit crews jumped out of his way. Backed up to his correct stop, he switched off the engine and was suddenly hit by the acrid stench of burning followed by a worried glance from Murton-Neale, who had seen the red paint on the Amilcar's bonnet blistering in the heat. Fuelled and ready to go, Gardner pressed the starter… and nothing happened. Frantic activity followed: The bonnet was lifted, fuel feed checked and ignition wires tightened, but to no avail. Finally, after a painful fifteen minutes of effort, the pair gave up and Gardner was forced to announce the car's retirement. It was an extremely frustrating way to finish their first Grand Prix, and the pair watched the rest of the race from the pit wall in dejected silence. After the finish, as the pit crews cleared up, Gardner tried the car again. It started first time.

The race had been a formative experience for Gardner. He had loved the challenge of the race itself, but also enjoyed being part of a group that felt very special: the prize-giving in Dublin's opulent Metropole Hotel was attended by almost all ministers of state and the trophies awarded by the Irish Free State president himself. He loved being part of this elite group and wanted more. Returning to Brooklands for the August Bank Holiday Meeting the following month felt like an anti-climax, and even a race win there in September did not satisfy his competitive urges.[81] Over the winter, he invested in having the car properly set up and, with the confidence provided by having one Grand Prix entry under his belt, he felt the 1930 season was to be a watershed, the point at which he went from being a part-time gentleman driver to a serious and successful racer.

Despite his efforts to prepare the car and his confidence, the first race of the 1930 season was inauspicious, failing to finish at the Brooklands Easter Meeting on the 'mountain' course. Then came another important race and one of the jewels in the Brooklands crown, the Double Twelve on 9th and 10th May. Meant to be the British answer to the 24 Hours of Le Mans, vocal Surrey residents prevented the race from being run in one stint so two back-to-back twelve-hour endurance races sufficed with the cars locked away overnight between sessions.

This was to be another racing first for Gardner, and he partnered with Miss D.M. Burnett in her imposing 1.5-litre Aston Martin.[82] Although Brooklands soon became very egalitarian, allowing women equal racing rights as men, in 1930 the old rule still applied that stated, '*Every driver or mechanic taking part in any race shall be a male person, unless the race proposition expressly states otherwise.*'[83]

Fortunately for Miss Burnett, the Junior Car Club who organised the Double Twelve were happy to let female drivers enter, and a healthy contingent of ladies took part. During practice, Gardner and Burnett posed for photographs in the Aston Martin, her in full race attire including helmet and visor (although underneath still wearing a shoe with a small heel), him in a driving coat and black beret pulled down low on his head. The looks on their faces speak volumes: it was not a happy arrangement. [84] Nevertheless, when the start came and the 59 drivers jumped into their cars and roared off down the start/finish

---

81   At the Autumn Meeting, he won the 100 miles-per-hour Short Handicap, lapping at a brisk
     91.72 miles-per-hour.
82   Aston Martin International chassis S31 'VB7976'.
83   Brooklands Museum.
84   NMM Archive.

straight towards the first corner, the big Aston gave them a chance. All they had to do was keep going and maintain consistency, but on a race of that length, neither was easy to achieve. Others fell by the wayside or spent hours in the pits: in an epic feat, one Austin Seven driver,[85] having lost all his oil, completed a full engine rebuild mid-race including having his conrods re-metalled, and duly finished the race. Team Gardner/Burnett were not so fortunate, and mid-way through the race a valve spring failed, seemingly a less dramatic problem than losing oil, but the result was still catastrophic. The now-unsprung valve remained in the path of the thrashing piston below; the result a mash of oil and metal that quickly led to their retirement. Both Gardner and Burnett watched the rest of the race from the stands and applauded as Frank Clement and Woolf Barnato won the race in their big Bentley Speed Six[86] but it was the performance of the smaller cars that, as ever, caught Gardner's eye: no fewer than five MG Midgets had finished in the top twenty, winning the team prize. A few days later, *Motor Sport* magazine published a five-page race report[87] but Goldie Gardner and Miss Burnett were not even mentioned.

Then, as the summer weather improved, so did Gardner's fortunes. On 8th June 1930, during the BARC Whitsun Meeting, he won again at Brooklands, this time taking first place in the Devon Junior Long Handicap and his spirits were once again raised before it was back to Dublin for the second Irish Grand Prix in July. This time, with his knowledge of the track from the previous year and more confidence in the mechanical condition of his car, he went into the race with high expectations. During practice, he managed a fair 9th place in class but in the main Saorstát Cup event set off very strongly. His half-way pit-stop passed without incident and he was just allowing himself thoughts of glory when suddenly the car's exhaust pipe split. Gardner and his

---

85   Eric Burt took his conrods over to Thompson and Taylor.
86   They completed a total of 2080.34 miles at a blistering average speed of 86.68 miles-per-hour.
87   *Motor Sport*, June 1930.

co-driver, this time another young man called Martin Jameson, looked at one another, then to the pipe that skirted along the left-hand side of the car. Already loud enough, the hole now emitted an almost deafening roar and, to the delight of the crowd, also produced huge sheets of flame every time Gardner dropped down a gear. Jameson quickly rummaged through the emergency toolkit packed down by his feet and emerged clutching a hammer; as Gardner continued to drive, Jameson hung over the side of the car, and tried to hammer the broken exhaust into some sort of shape that would allow them to continue. Against all expectations, he succeeded, and at the finish of the race the pair had achieved a masterful second place in the 1,100cc category. It was a grand result.[88]

Back at Brooklands the following month, his next race was just as dramatic. Following fellow racer Victor Gillow off the Members' Banking, he saw Gillow's offside front wheel collapse then watched in horror as the front axle dug into the concrete, flipping the car over in a full somersault and crashing back down on its remaining wheels with the limp body of the driver motionless inside. Goldie pulled up and ran over to help his friend who had taken the force of the blow on his head and was covered in blood. He stayed with him until an ambulance arrived and took Gillow to hospital. Miraculously, he survived.[89]

Despite this experience, Gardner was driving well, managing to take a third place during that meeting and gaining three more podium finishes in his next outing at Brooklands.[90] His achievements impressed Amilcar importer Vernon Balls who asked Gardner to partner with him as a 'factory' team for the British Racing Drivers' Club (BRDC) 500 Miles at Brooklands in October, along with the Double Twelve, the most important race in the calendar. But out of his own comfortable Amilcar and driving one set up for Balls who was some inches short-

---

88 *Magic MPH* (ibid) p15.
89 *Lancashire Evening Post* 4 Aug 1930 and *Motor Sport*, September 1930.
90 His record for the year was one win, three second places and three third. See annex listing races for more details.

er than him, Gardner was relieved when mechanical problems caused him to withdraw shortly after his stint began.

It was the end of the season, and Gardner was more than content. He'd not only achieved a good finish in the Irish Grand Prix and taken some excellent results at Brooklands but he'd also been invited to take part in both the two major British endurance races, the Double Twelve and the BRDC 500. But that winter, he decided that his Amilcar was old and slightly too unwieldy for the racing that he wanted to try next: the winding roads of the Ulster TT around the Ards Circuit near Belfast. One nimble little car had caught his eye that season, and he intended to buy one. For 1931, Major Goldie Gardner MC would, for the first time, be driving an MG.

7

KIMBER

It was only a matter of time before Gardner crossed paths with Cecil Kimber, the force behind The MG Car Company. In mid-1930, Kimber had been appointed the company's Managing Director, and Milne & Russell was on the list of large dealerships that he intended to contact. Gardner immediately warmed to the passionate and determined Kimber and found they had much in common: Kimber had also badly damaged his right leg and hip that left him with a limp, and they shared a passion for photography. 'A real enthusiast' Gardner called him after their encounter, a meeting less dominated by car sales and much more by racing stories and discussions about the advantages of 35mm film over plates.

Gardner also had a soft spot for Kimber's cars. He had seen the effectiveness of MG's little Midgets at first hand a few months earlier at Brooklands when they romped home with the team prize in the Double Twelve whilst he was having a less-than-perfect race with the stern-faced Miss Burnett in their unreliable Aston Martin. Based on the Morris Minor chassis but around 300lb lighter, these tiny sports cars were the result of a chance visit in the late summer of 1928 by an MG engineer called Reg Jackson to the Morris factory. 'Jacko' as he was commonly known (and no relation to Robin Jackson the Brooklands engineer) saw the Minor chassis, immediately recognised its potential and reported back to MG. Kimber wasn't entirely convinced but visited the Morris factory after which he instructed Jacko to make a prototype. His effort – a boat-tailed design in wood and canvas – was then sent off to Carbodies of Coventry, who formed it into a working mule. This proved the car's worth: its low weight gave a top speed of over 60 miles-per-hour, much more than standard for the day and remarkable given the tiny 850cc engine. After around four weeks of development, Kimber committed to its unveiling at the London Motor Show at Olympia, held that October. It was received very well by both public and press, and the order book quickly filled with over 200 names.

Full production of the model, designated the MG Midget and known as the 'M-Type', started the following spring. One of the first owners to receive their car was Lord Freddie March, heir to the Goodwood Estate, who had just reconciled with his grandfather after a family feud. A few years previously, the Duke of Richmond had been outraged when the young man had stated his intention to marry a vicar's daughter,[91] and promptly stopped his allowance. Undaunted, March trained as a mechanic and enrolled as an apprentice at Bentley under an assumed name,[92] earning a salary that now enabled him to wed, with or without the family's blessing. The Duke relented and permission was given, and shortly before his grandfather's death he was accepted back fully into the family, with all the financial freedom that offered him. The Midget was to be his entry into motorsport, and he wasted no time booking his first event. So it was that in July 1929 he lined up in his MG[93] on the starting grid in the Junior Car Club High Speed Trial next to two other

---

91   Elizabeth Hudson.
92   He used the name Fred Settrington. *Driving Ambition*, Goodwood Road & Racing, 2018.
93   Registration WL7171.

brand-new Midgets[94] on his left and an Austin Seven on his right, the driver a slim man with angular features who would later in life transform the British motor industry with his revolutionary *Mini*: Alec Issigonis. Unbeknownst to the other competitors, Kimber had decided that the Midgets must perform as well as possible at the model's competitive debut and instructed the works mechanics to look after the cars. This they did, and the cars and drivers all managed to win gold medals, the highest award available.[95]

The little MG was Goldie's ideal car: small, powerful, and punching well above its weight in competition, but Kimber tempted him further by telling him to wait a few months. MG had just been approached by record-breaker George Eyston who wanted to break the 100 miles-per-hour barrier in a light car and saw a modified Midget with a small-bored 750cc Wolseley engine as the answer. Kimber immediately agreed, aware that arch-rival Herbert Austin had been trying to take the record for some time and seeing it as an opportunity to prove the Midget's dominance over the Austin Seven, its main competitor. The planned enhancements to Eyston's car, designated EX120 by the factory but later splashed across the headlines as 'the Magic Midget', would undoubtedly find their way to an improved road car.

Goldie listened, held his nerve, and waited. His racing successes of the previous season had not only raised Goldie's reputation, but also that of his red Amilcar YV91[96]. When, after the Brooklands Autumn Meeting in late September 1930 he mentioned in the Brooklands bar that the car may be for sale, fellow racer Harry Clayton[97] was quick to offer a very good price. Clayton's payment, added to the cash prizes

---

94   The owners were Brooklands regular Leslie Callingham and Harold Parker, both personal friends of Kimber.
95   Reg Jackson, Cecil Cousins and Frank Tayler.
96   There is some confusion between two Amilcars, this and another later also bought by Clayton. There is a photograph at Plate V in Magic MPH that clearly shows Gardner's car to hold the 'YV91' registration but other reports have listed this as 'YW91'. To compound matters, the registration 'YV91' is now on the other car, that was later re-registered 'NPA217' (just as Gardner's had been re-registered 'MPC207'. More information can be found in the excellent Motor Sport article of July 1978 and here: https://www.dylan-miles.com/vehicles/1927-amilcar-c6-ex-w-e-humphreys-extensive-brooklands-history/
97   Sorting out the Amilcars, *Motor Sport*, July 1978.

earned in the previous season, gave Gardner a bank account that for once wasn't struggling to cope with his expensive hobby, and so he went shopping. The following month at the London Motor Show he was seduced by the Talbot 75/90 and put down a deposit,[98] specifying that race preparers Fox & Nicholl bring the car up to his demanding specification. Although the model had enjoyed great success that year with the Fox & Nicholl team, the Talbot was for road use; he still felt that his racing future lay with the tiny MGs. When, in late January 1931 at the Montlhéry circuit near Paris, Eyston broke the light car record in EX120 averaging 101.87 miles-per-hour, Gardner had all the evidence he needed and immediately wired Kimber a deposit for one of his new C-Type 'Montlhéry' Midgets.[99]

The delivery of the car was an act of pure theatre. On the day of the first practice session for the JCC Double Twelve in early May 1931, the fourteen purchasers of the first tranche of Montlhéry Midgets had been asked to meet at Brooklands. Eagerly awaiting the arrival of their cars, they were astonished to see Lord Freddie March emerge from between the dark sheds, leading a procession of the tiny cars into the paddock, each painted in the colour specified by its new owner. Lord March, having made the most of his new-found financial freedom, had bought three of the cars which he intended to run as a team throughout the season[100] and sometime previously had suggested to Gardner that he do the same to give him some competition.

So, over a few drinks in the bar, a plan had been hatched. Gardner would link up with Robin Jackson and Ronnie Horton, two other drivers of the new Midget,[101] and the trio would compete as a team throughout the season in the Double Twelve, the Irish Grand Prix and

---

98   http://www.talbotportal.com/CarDDetails.aspx?KeyID=21660
99   *Magic MPH*, (ibid) p16.
100 MG Competition Cars and Drivers, Knudson, P27.
101 Barré Lyndon, *Combat*, (Windmill Press, 1933), p97. Lyndon states that all three cars were owned by Gardner, and he secured the services of Jackson and Horton as drivers. Allison & Browning in *The Works MGs* p39 state that Jackson and Horton had ordered the cars themselves. Understanding Gardner's financial situation, the latter is more likely to be correct.

the Ulster Tourist Trophy. So that the pit crew could easily identify their cars, the three friends chose different colours: Horton red, Jackson white and, setting a precedent that he was to return to in the future, Gardner decided that his car, 'RX8591' would be painted black.

As Gardner first glimpsed his new racing car, he was very impressed. The Midgets looked fantastic, their sleek bodies stripped down to the bare minimum for the challenges they faced. Side-mounted exhausts ran down their flank, splaying out in fan-shaped silencers that were pinned to their boat-like streamlined tail. To keep weight low, other additions were kept to a minimum: just a single headlamp was fitted and thin cycle-style mudguards to keep the spray at bay during bad weather. Inside, the compartment was tiny, just big enough to hold two men side-by-side and when the strapping Gardner climbed in, he quickly realised that the small, half-moon aero windscreen was far too low to afford any protection. This he noted to 'GP', George Propert the MG works manager, who was showing the new owners around their cars, and he promised to find Gardner a bigger screen.[102] Then, with the help of GP, Gardner fired the engine, happily blipping the throttle to warm up the car. 'Take her out', GP shouted over the din of the revving engines. 'Run her in on the track'. Gardner needed no more encouragement. Pulling his helmet onto his head and shifting the visor into place, he dropped the clutch and pushed the gear lever into first. He roared off, the car's gloss-red wheels[103] glinting in the sun as he gained speed up the start/finish straight towards the Members' Banking. For the very first time, Goldie was on a racetrack in an MG, the marque that was to define him.

All fourteen of the Midgets were entered into the 1931 Double Twelve in early May, joined in their class by ten Austin Sevens, but even before the race started teething problems abounded. During practice

---

102 Gardner's enlarged screen is obvious in photographs from later races, especially when lined up with C-Type Midgets with 'standard' screens.

103 Lyndon, *Combat* (ibid) p97.

on the day before the race, the engine in one of Lord March's cars expired and had to be replaced by red-faced MG engineers, Cecil Kimber himself driving it through the night to Portsmouth and back through torrential rain to run it in.[104] By the following morning the weather had improved a little, and as Goldie lined up for the 8am start, the rain had stopped long enough for Earl Howe, one of the grandees of the circuit and chairman of the BRDC, to come over and wish him luck and explain with croaking voice that he'd decided to withdraw on account of suspected tonsillitis.[105] Goldie, already soaked and with water pooling on the canvas tonneau that was the car's only weather equipment, thanked the Earl then pulled down his visor, keen to get going.

The first few hours of the first 12-hour stint of racing were grim but uneventful. Then, by 11am, the track began to dry out and the previously careful drivers started to stretch their legs. The Midgets, given a fair handicap by Ebby the timer due to their diminutive engines, started lapping consistently at around 65 miles-per-hour, and despite the supercharged Austins going a little faster, their careful preparation by the MG works team soon began to show. As the race progressed, many of the others fell by the wayside. One Austin broke a crankshaft, an Alfa Romeo damaged a valve, and a Maserati snapped its back axle, but the little MGs kept going. By the end of the first day, Gardner, with Pippin Murton-Neale, his old co-driver from the 1929 Irish Grand Prix, was sitting in a very respectable third place and Lord March was in a dominant lead.

The second day of the competition had a less auspicious start. Having been left in the paddock overnight, the Le Mans-style rules demanded that the cars had to be fired on their own electric starter and were not allowed to be pushed or cranked by hand. Robin Jackson's MG failed to respond, and even in the hands of Brooklands' master

---

104　Allison & Browning, *The Works MGs*, 2nd Ed, (Veloce Press, 2010), p40.
105　Boddy, *Brooklands* (ibid) p452.

engineer himself, Jackson took three hours to get the car started.[106] Meanwhile, Gardner had set off and was early into his stint when the car started to misfire. He pulled into the pits, and the MG mechanics immediately swarmed around it, checking ignition, fuel, and timing. Nothing obviously untoward could be found, so the lead engineer Cecil Cousins took the decision to remove the cylinder head to investigate. As the bolts were unscrewed and the head heaved off, the air was filled by a stream of profanities from Cousins that turned heads from across the paddock. He had found the cause: one piston had totally disintegrated. Scolded like naughty schoolchildren, Gardner and Murton-Neale professed their innocence and swore blind that they had not over-revved the engine. With a huff, Cousins turned and walked away. Their race was over.

But most of the other MGs kept going, and Cousins had more than enough to keep him busy. At 8pm that evening when the remaining fly-battered, oily, and scorched cars limped over the line and when Ebby had worked out the handicaps, Montlhéry Midgets had taken the first five places in the race,[107] with Lord March holding on to his substantial lead to take the winner's laurels. To Kimber's delight, the fastest rival Austin Seven had finished in a lowly seventh place and the MG press team made the most of their Midget's total dominance. It was prescient timing for both the Midget and the Seven; with the repercussions from the Wall Street Crash and burgeoning Great Depression starting to be felt in the paddock, Bentley on its last legs and even the grand old Rolls-Royce struggling to survive,[108] the emergence of a cheap car that could be sold to the masses but which also had the cachet of being a race winner was an immensely powerful combination.

Fortunately for Kimber, the Midgets' performance in the next major race was equally as impressive: the third edition of the Irish Grand

---

106 Boddy, *Brooklands* (ibid) p453.
107 Race programme, Brooklands archive.
108 For more, see Peter Grimsdale, *Racing in the Dark*, (Simon & Schuster, 2021).

Prix, held once again at Phoenix Park in Dublin, but which this year coincided with a torrential rainstorm. Through the floods,[109] the MGs battled and with ten laps to run, three were in podium positions: Norman Black, driving one of Lord March's cars, Ronnie Horton second and Gardner in third. Then, peering through the spray as he passed the pits, Gardner saw his pit manager[110] leaping around and wildly gesticulating for him to push harder. Black's leading car had started to misfire in the soaking rain, and Gardner realised he had a chance of a win. The bit between his teeth, he raced as hard as he could but to no avail; as the track dried, so Black's misfire had solved itself and he crossed the line the winner, Gardner retaining third. They may not have won the race, but two podium finishes earned Gardner the team prize for which he was delighted to receive a magnificent silver cup and was a 'deservedly popular' winner according to the *Motor Sport* write up.[111] Buoyed by his success, Gardner performed well in his next couple of Brooklands races, and very nearly took another win on 3rd August but was beaten on the line by a charging Amilcar. But later that month, Gardner and his team once again set sail for Ireland to take part in the last of their three team races and the one that Gardner looked forward to more than any other: the infamous Ulster Tourist Trophy.

Racing on closed roads had been banned in England in 1925[112] but the law was different in Ulster where the mix of twisting, undulating country roads set with a spectacular backdrop of hills and loughs made it the perfect location for such an event. The Ulster Tourist Trophy was the jewel in the crown, a road circuit at western end of the Ards Peninsula about ten miles from the centre of Belfast. In the three years the

---

109 *Magic MPH* (ibid), p17.

110 Jack Woodhouse.

111 *Motor Sport*, July 1931. The Irish Grand Prix was split into two 300-mile handicap races held on consecutive days. The first was for 1,500cc and under cars which competed for the Saorstát Cup. The second was for cars with larger engines, who competed for the Éireann Cup. The Grand Prix winner was the car that completed the race on either day in the fastest time. This made the dominant performance of the MGs, including an outright win for Norman Black (driving for Lord March), even more impressive. Robin Jackson's car was the third member of Gardner's team. He had to stop for four minutes to change plugs.

112 This was the result of an injury to a spectator at the Kop Hillclimb.

race had been run at this course it had attracted some of the best drivers in the world and had gained a reputation for being utterly unforgiving: a moment's lapse in concentration on the tight, snaking roads filled with blind corners and changes in camber could easily result in the driver ploughing into one of the ditches or massed blackthorn hedges that lined the route, 'ending up in the sheugh (shuck)' in local slang.[113] Starting just east of the village of Dundonald, each of the race's 30 laps took in level crossings, twisting rural roads through the undulating countryside, tight town-centre hairpins and narrow bridges; this six-hour race was as far from the sanitised, 100-yard-wide Brooklands track as you could imagine.

Eager but slightly wary of the challenging race ahead, Goldie and the rest of his team set up a headquarters in the town of Bangor, a few miles north of the Ards circuit. The cars were prepared differently than at Brooklands, this time in 'touring' form with twin headlamps and with a riding mechanic on board,[114] the pair being the only people allowed to work on the car during pit stops or if it should break down. Goldie had managed to get his way with GP, who had arranged for a tall cowl to be fitted on the driver's side of his car, complete with a large, square windshield which gave him a little more protection than the tiny half-moon screen had done and made his car instantly recognisable to his pit crew. The MG factory mechanics had also fitted another major improvement to the cars: a Powerplus supercharger which provided a very significant boost in both acceleration and top speed.[115]

At first, everything went well. During practice, the MGs all proved to be ideally suited to the circuit and the supercharger was performing exactly as Reg 'Jacko' Jackson, head of the MG competition department, had expected, giving the small cars a top speed of around 100 miles-per-hour. Due to their small engine size, the MGs all had good

---

113 My wife is from Northern Ireland. I first wrote, 'took a trip to the sheugh' and she laughed at me.
    'Nobody would say that,' she said. 'You'd end up in the sheugh.'
114 *Magic MPH* (ibid), plate VIII.
115 This was a development based on the one fitted to Eyston's record car. *The Works MGs* (ibid) p41.

handicaps that equated to around four laps on the biggest cars and were well positioned in the 44-car field.

Just like in Dublin, it was a racing start, and again Gardner was given permission to sit by his car and clamber in from there. Quickly, he pressed the starter and shoved the accelerator pedal to the floor, the rear wheels spinning before they gripped the tarmac, and he shot off amongst the other competitors. The first mile or so was relatively easy, the road wide and straight as the cars headed east towards Newtownards, all jockeying for position. But then came Quarry Corner, a big left-hander that funnelled the cars into the narrow Belfast Road that headed out into the country. As he made it around the bend, Goldie tightened his grip on the wheel as the road became much more treacherous, high tree-lined banks shrouding the roadway and a series of s-bends winding upwards towards the hamlet of Killarn, where roadside cottages flashed past. Here the road flattened, with big sweeping bends encouraging speed whilst the hard-packed blackthorn hedges on the verge urged caution before the road dropped away again through fields before reaching more esses at Bradshaw's Brae. Then it was a fast run into the town of Newtownards where the crowds, giant advertising hoardings and unforgiving granite walls awaited. Gardner dropped a couple of gears at the very sharp right in the centre of the town, then picked up speed again until he once again left the houses behind and headed back into the countryside, the shores of Strangford Lough down to the left and the Scrabo Tower looming like an ominous sentry on the right. Gardner dropped a gear and braked for the railway crossing, then picked up speed again as the houses of Comber started to flash past. Here again was another tight right-hander with stone walls ready to catch the unwary, and he concentrated again until he was once again out of the town and racing back through the undulating countryside. If the Belfast Road had felt small, this was even tighter, with no margin for error afforded by the hedges, trees, cottages, and spectators who lined the route. Then finally, he reached Dundonald again, swung around the tight right-hand hairpin and floored the accelerator again as he sped back towards the pits.

It was an unforgiving course, both on the driver and the cars. Most of the vehicles picked up some damage: some slid into ditches and had to be pulled free by spectators and others glanced off the grey stone walls that hemmed in the roads in the three towns. Even cars that avoided physical damage were placed under a huge amount of stress for hour after hour as they lapped the course, and abandoned vehicles were another hazard that the drivers had to avoid.

Although new to the race, Gardner took all of this in his stride and after a few laps had settled into a comfortable rhythm. He enjoyed the course, thriving on the twisting roads where he would make up time on his bigger-engined competition but accepting that they would speed away from him on the straights. About three hours into the race and feeling very good, he left Comber and decided that he would pit this lap for tyres and fuel. All he had to do was make it around the Dundonald hairpin and he'd be back with his mechanics in no time.

He didn't make it. Approaching the Carstrand railway bridge a huge shape loomed into his mirror, a Mercedes-Benz Super Sport, the largest car in the race.[116] It closed in tight to him as they sped towards the metal span of the bridge and Gardner pulled over to the right to let it pass.[117] 'I wondered why he was so long doing so,' he later wrote. 'I then saw out of the corner of my eye an enormous wheel much too close for my liking – the next thing I knew [it] had hit my rear off-side wheel.'[118]

The Mercedes had about 20 miles-per-hour on the MG and the impact threw the German car up and over the side of the Midget, smashing the bodywork as it went. Briefly disentangled, the car shot forwards again, only for the rear wheel to crash into the MG's front, the

116 Driven by B.O. Davis.
117 *The Works MGs*, (ibid), p45.
118 *Magic MPH* (ibid), p19.

two becoming forged together in a mass of bent metal. 'I was dragged along, and then, like a terrier with a rat, finally dropped,' Goldie wrote.

The little MG ploughed to a stop in a ditch, the mangled wings digging into the dirt and hurling the men forwards in the cockpit. Unbelievably, neither was hurt and as they sat, composing themselves in the twisted wreck, Gardner considered himself very lucky. Although they later managed to fit new wheels to the car and limp back to the pits, Goldie's race was over, and Gardner knew that it would need a full rebuild back at the MG factory in Abingdon. Of his other 'team' cars, Horton also failed to finish, Robin Jackson being the only one to reach the chequered flag. More successful was Norman Black, winning his second major race of the year in the MG to the sheer delight of its owner, Lord March. In an international field that included the racing superstar Tazio Nuvolari and 'Bentley Boy' Tim Birkin, both running in glorious 8C 2300 Alfa Romeos, the success was all the more sweet.

Gardner returned home dispirited but not deterred. Until the crash, which he did not consider to be his fault, he had been running a strong race around one of the most difficult circuits he had attempted alongside a field of other world-class drivers. He knew that, with his little MG fixed, he would stand a great chance of a top result. When just a matter of days later, his car returned from MG it was clear they had done a fantastic job.[119] He tested it at Brooklands and the car handled superbly, delivering performance totally out of proportion to its size. He ran it in the Brighton and Hove Motor Club meeting in early September earning himself a first-class prize, then returned to Brooklands on 3rd October to contest the BRDC 500 Miles. Although it wasn't the best of races, Gardner at least finished with his car running well, unlike Freddie March whose big-end bearing failed.[120]

119 *Magic MPH* (ibid) p19.
120 Jeffrey Clover, the sole MG entrant without a supercharger whose handicap had allowed him to set off a full 25 minutes before the next competitor, retired after 1½ hours when his rear axle broke, the car having averaged an extraordinary 83 miles-per-hour up until that point.

But better news was to come. At the final meeting of the Brooklands season on 17th October 1931, Gardner dominated the Cumberland Junior Long Handicap race to win easily, and when he pulled up in the paddock, Robin Jackson rushed over to tell him some even better news: Ebby had clocked Gardner's average lap speed at 100.61 miles-per-hour,[121] the first time any 750cc car had managed to break to 'the ton' on the outer circuit. As he climbed out of his car and walked out of the paddock, the handshakes came readily. This was a significant record, and he was a popular recipient of the honour. Beaming, he wiped the oil from his face, and went off to share a drink with his friends at the bar. It felt good being a record breaker.

---

121 *Brooklands* (ibid) p264.

8

BATTERED ABOUT

———————➤————

Things were looking up for Goldie Gardner. Barring the incident with the Mercedes-Benz, the 1931 season had been a great success, with a healthy amount of prize money. That, in addition to his income from work, meant that money wasn't as tight as it had been a few years previously. 'Work' wasn't very onerous either. He enjoyed his time at the Milne & Russell office, immersed in the business of cars. The other directors enjoyed his presence, too, and allowed him the time he needed to travel to race meetings. Having a notable racing driver on their books had benefits for the company, especially when Gardner placed his racing cars complete with laurel winner's garlands in the showroom that encouraged an influx of potential customers and hordes of fascinated children who pressed their noses against the window.

But for Gardner, the best thing was that he felt totally accepted by the extraordinary group of people with whom he raced. He had made some good friends: he was particularly close to the newly knighted

Sir Malcolm and Dorothy Campbell, and Lord Freddie March of the Goodwood Estate, but he'd also built strong friendships with some of the engineers and mechanics who worked with him, in particular the imperturbable Reg Jackson, or 'Jacko' from the MG works who ran their competition department. It was a relationship that in the future was to work hugely in his favour.

For the time being, there was more racing on the cards. His C-Type Midget was in fine competitive shape as was his Rover 20 Speed Special, a car he used for races requiring a larger engine. Throughout the spring and summer of 1932, he used both vehicles regularly at Brooklands, securing a host of strong results.[122] Then in June came the JCC 1,000-Mile event, a two-day spectacular in which Goldie enlisted the expert skills of Hugh Hamilton as his second driver.

'Hammy' as he was known to everyone in the paddock was a native of Omagh in Ulster, the son of a local solicitor who had died in 1927, after which his mother, Agnes, moved back to England. She settled in Great Bookham, Surrey, just ten miles from Brooklands where he quickly became a regular and instantly became very well known in the paddock. Not only was he a very big character and often slightly riotous after a drink, but he was also an extremely quick driver. Dick Seaman, arguably the most successful British Grand Prix driver of the era who later drove with him, said that he couldn't keep pace with Hammy. Now though, he worked as a salesman for University Motors, the London-based MG distributors, but yearned to race. Gardner had an eye for young talent, and when he approached Hammy to race with him, he quickly agreed.

The car though had other ideas. On day one of the event, the engine seized[123] and required a 3¼-hour pitstop to swap it for another one as the frustrated Hammy stood and watched, then on day two the fuel

---

122 A second-class award in the JCC Open in April, a third-place finish at the JCC High Speed Trial in the same month, and another third at the Whit Monday meeting in May.
123 Spun main bearing.

tank split and had to be replaced.[124] The pair completed the race some way down the standings, but another driver – Eastbourne butcher and novice racer Henry Leeson – wasn't so fortunate. Having lost control, he swerved off the course, hit the parapet of the entry tunnel and fell twenty feet onto the road below where he was killed instantly, gaining the dubious distinction of becoming MG's first fatal racing casualty.[125]

Undeterred, two weeks later Gardner returned to Brooklands and promptly won his next race,[126] but the big challenge of the year lay ahead: the return to the Ulster Tourist Trophy. This year, Austin had beaten a hasty retreat, giving MG a great opportunity to dominate their class, although the regulations had also been changed so their handicap was not as generous as before.[127] Gardner was convinced he could do well and so, like the previous year, he had linked up with two other owners to form a team: Randolph Jeffress, heir to the British American Tobacco empire whose car was to be driven by racer Cyril Paul, and Hammy, who had really impressed him during the JCC 1,000-Mile race and had become a firm friend. Their cars received a final shakedown at the MG works in Abingdon, and in mid-August they were ready for collection. Goldie, as ever immaculately dressed in double-breasted jacket, beret and with a pipe clamped between his teeth, arrived to collect his car, his '32' race number already emblazoned on a roundel on the side of the car. Next to it was number 31, Jeffress's car, that was collected by Cyril Paul. The men, joined by another MG owner,[128] pored over the cars looking to see what improvements Jacko and his team had made before setting off for Liverpool docks, Paul driving number 31 on trade plates, Goldie following in his rather more comfortable Talbot 75/90.[129] Crossing to Belfast, they then made the short

---

124 *Magic MPH (ibid)* p20.

125 *Brooklands,* (ibid), p 481.

126 The Stanley Cup on behalf of the JCC at the BARC Inter-Club Meeting, driving his Rover.

127 Supercharged 750cc cars received four minutes less of a head start than in 1931 but the cars were allowed to race in a more stripped-down trim. *Combat,* (ibid), p278.

128 Eddie Hall.

129 NMM Archive.

journey by road to the Number Nine Garage behind the Bangor Hotel, where the team made their headquarters. The garage was rumoured to be unlucky after its use the previous year by a competitor who rolled his car during the race, but ignoring any bad omens, the team got to work and once Hammy arrived the next day, they were ready to race.[130]

In first practice, Gardner had a narrow escape when his radiator cap blew off, sending a stream of boiling water inches past his head accompanied by a jet of steam that briefly blinded him, but otherwise all seemed to go well for the team.[131] Hammy was extremely fast, setting a succession of new 750cc lap records despite being forced by the scrutineers to change his supercharger. This didn't slow him and despite intermittent rain showers, on second practice on Thursday 18th August he set a new lap record speed of 74.5 miles-per-hour, a time that gave even the drivers of the biggest cars in the race something to think about.[132] The other two cars were also running well, and when Hammy pulled into the pits at the end of his session, the team looked to be in good form. As he climbed out of the MG, the mechanics set to work, lifted the bonnet, and carried out their routine checks. He was about to walk away when one called him back, showing him the state of the spark plugs: black, and burnt. Neither man was sure they'd hold up for the race, so Hammy decided to do one final, flying lap with a new set to see if they fared any better. The plugs quickly changed, Hammy pulled on his goggles and his white leather windcap and jumped back behind the wheel, his riding mechanic, the flamboyant Marquis de Belleroche, preferring to go bare-headed next to him.[133] Hammy had been fast before, but on this lap, he pushed even harder. Left through the sweeping Quarry Corner the pair roared, darting through the tree-shrouded esses on the way to Bradshaw's Brae then down into Newtownards. Turning right out of the town, they hit 100 miles-per-hour on the straight

130 *Combat*, (ibid), p280.
131 *Dundee Courier*, 18 Aug 32.
132 *Combat*, (ibid), p281.
133 *MMM Register Yearbook* (MGCC, 2016).

to Comber, slowed for the bend, then Hammy pushed the accelerator to the floor again as they shot back towards Dundonald. Just outside of the hamlet of Ballystockart they caught another competitor[134] going considerably slower than the MG and pulled over to pass but didn't make the overtake in time for the next corner. Hammy fought with the wheel, the tyres squealing as they skittered over the tarmac and thought they had made it as they cleared the apex, only for the wheels to lose grip on the still-damp road and for the car to violently spin 180 degrees. The shocked driver of the other car just managed to avoid them, then watched as the MG ploughed through a hedge into a cottage garden, very nearly hitting the owner who had to jump clear, before striking a bank which catapulted the two racers out, the car landing upside down. He screeched to a halt before rushing back to help his fellow drivers and found Hammy with blood streaming down his face holding his chest, and Belleroche prone on the ground complaining that his back hurt.[135]

Back in the pits, Gardner had an awful sinking feeling when Hammy didn't appear on time and the word soon reached him of his team-mate's incident. The practice session now finished, he jumped in his car, sped round to Ballystockart, and found Hammy sitting on a couch in the front room of the cottage. Shoeless, with dried blood on his face and still holding his broken ribs, Hammy then described, in colourful language, what had happened. Before long, an ambulance arrived and took him off to Newtownards hospital.

Gardner was shocked. He was very close to Hammy, and he had an extraordinary amount of faith in him as a driver. Not only was he quick, but he knew these roads like the back of his hand, and it once again reminded him how unforgiving the Ards course could be. That said, his immediate problem was to replace both car and driver and

---

134 A Riley Nine Brooklands driven by Victor Gillow.

135 The road is now the A22 and remains as tight as it was in 1932. Although on a map it looks relatively straight, the right-hand bend after Ballystockart is surprisingly long and the road drops away on the turn. Stanley Barnes, who had also used the 'unlucky' Number Nine garage, had crashed in a similar place the previous year.

Circa 1894. A look of determination was evident on the young Goldie's face from a very early age.

1908, Uppingham School. Gardner (middle, left) doesn't even manage eye contact with the cameraman as the school running team are captured for posterity. He excelled at sports, also making the school 1st XV rugby team and his house fives side.

Circa 1912, Ceylon. A young Gardner in his Ceylon Mounted Rifles uniform.

OFFICERS & STAFF OF B. BATTERY 72ᴺᴰ BRIGADE R.F.A.
BULFORD, JULY 8ᵀᴴ 1915.

8th July 1915, Bulford Garrison. Captain Gardner with his officers, warrant officers and non-commissioned officers of B Battery, 72nd Brigade Royal Field Artillery. At Bulford, they finally trained with real artillery pieces and live ammunition.

Summer, 1917. Posing with two other officers from 72nd Brigade Royal Field Artillery, Major Gardner's sunken cheeks and loose uniform tell their own story.

September 1928, Le Touquet. Gardner leaves the line in a cloud of smoke, the tyres on his Salmson spinning on the dusty road.

9th May 1930, Brooklands. Gardner and Miss Burnett pose unhappily in their Aston Martin before the start of the Double 12.

9th May 1930, Brooklands. The frantic first yards of the Double 12. Gardner and Burnett are near the back of the pack and did not finish; eventual winners Frank Clement and Woolf Barnato are to the right in 'Old Number 2' Bentley Speed Six.

18th July 1930, Irish Grand Prix, Dublin. Gardner arrives back in the pits in his Amilcar with Martin Jameson as passenger. During the race, they burnt a hole in the silencer, causing flames to leap out when he changed down a gear.

19 August 1932, Ards Circuit. Youngsters flock to gain Gardner's autograph.

20th August 1932, Ulster TT. Gardner and Paterson (Car 32) pull away at the start of their ill-fated attempt to win glory in the Ulster TT.

20th August 1932, Ulster TT.
Above: Gardner's crumpled MG sits by the side of the road as the medical
team treat Oscar Paterson while they wait for a stretcher team.
Below: Gardner is carried away from his car, writhing in agony.

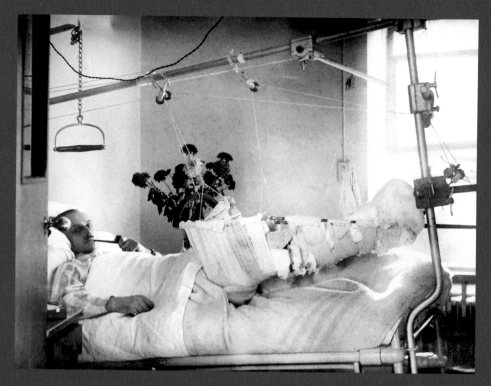

August 1932. A dejected Gardner reclines in his room at Newtownards Hospital, his right leg shattered once again. He spent four months in hospital.

August 1933. Still walking awkwardly after his crash the previous year, Gardner returned to the Ulster TT as Hammy's manager, here seen with BRDC badge, alongside Hammy's mother. Despite leading for most of the race and setting 750cc course records, he was pushed into second place by the masterful driving of Nuvolari.

15th September 1934, Brighton Speed Trials. Teddy Rayson, who later had a relationship with Gardner's first wife Mariel, shares a cigarette with racer Kay Petre. Photo taken by Gardner.

Spring 1935. Sir Malcolm Campbell (centre, rear) and his team on the sands at Daytona Beach. Gardner is back row, second from left. The group included Campbell's master engineer Leo Villa, Alf Poyser, sent by Rolls-Royce, and Roger Fuller from the Daily Mail.

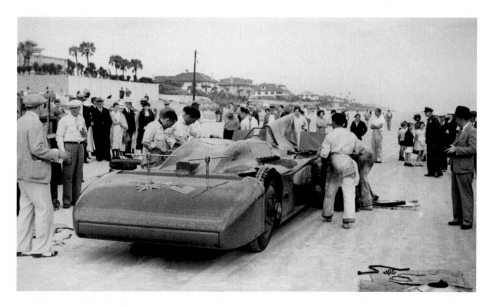

Daytona Beach, March 1935. Gardner's photograph of the team preparing Bluebird for Malcolm Campbell's land speed record attempt.

Seabreeze Swim Club, Daytona Beach, 1935. Mariel King-Boalt smiles between Gardner and Roger Fuller of the Daily Mail, with Alf Poyser of Rolls-Royce and two other local friends.

8th March 1936, Daytona Beach. Gardner, the sole non-American entrant in the first AAA-regulated stock car race, lines his borrowed Lincoln Zephyr up for an overtake at the Northern Approach as the crowds look on.

Photo: Courtesy AACA Library & Research Centre, Hershey, PA.

fill the gap in his team. There was one other MG C-Type, the works mule that had been the first fitted with a supercharger and nicknamed 'Hoodoo' by the mechanics because it was rumoured that everyone who drove it ended up crashing. Once some of the racing parts had been stripped off Hammy's wreck the car would be ready to compete, but what of a driver? Goldie asked Stan Barnes, the driver who had been almost killed the previous year when his car flipped, and this year was understudying for his brother. Keen to break his bad luck at the course, Stan agreed, and the race officials agreed to change both car and driver in the entry sheet. The following day the scrutineers passed the car fit to race and so on the morning of Saturday 20th August,[136] the weather cloudy but dry, *Hoodoo*, with Stan at the wheel, lined up alongside Gardner and Paul with the rest of the 32 entrants along the pit wall ready for the start.

Gardner, dressed in black coveralls and with his ubiquitous walking stick in his left hand, shook hands with Oscar Paterson, the local man he'd enlisted to ride with him as passenger. As his mechanic[137] checked that the Hartford dampers were set correctly and gave the wheel spinners one final whack with a hide hammer, he was surrounded by a gaggle of local teenagers, all keen to collect the driver's autograph. Then, just after half-past ten, a claxon sounded: it was time to race. One of the mechanics, a superstitious bunch, had tied a garland of baby toys and a horseshoe to the bonnet strap for good luck which Gardner now removed, before both he and Paterson donned their helmets and goggles, climbed in the car, and readied for the start.

The cars were lined up in their handicap groups in the pits, from where they would start. The roadsides were packed with spectators, some crammed into a scaffold-built grandstand, others hanging over the advertising hoardings that lined the route. Ebby, the timekeeper, stood by the start, Union Flag in one hand, stopwatch in the other.

---

136 In his book *Combat* (p284) Lyndon states that the start was on 29th August, but this is a misprint.
137 'Nobby' Marney. Barré Lyndon, *Circuit Dust*, (John Miles, 1934), p223.

Then, a ripple of applause spread through the crowd as Hammy, whose injuries had been diagnosed as some broken ribs and a dislocated shoulder, was pushed to the track side in a bath chair.[138]

Gardner smiled across at Hammy, but he was nervous; with the requirement to use the electrical starter and with all the noise on the grid, you could never be sure if the engine was actually running. He'd seen other cars, their drivers assuming they were running properly, left stranded on the grid as the rest of the field pulled away. But he didn't have long to worry; quickly, Ebby moved to the side of the track, stared at his watch, and raised his flag. Then, at exactly 11am, it fell.

Enveloped by a wall of noise, the first batch of drivers snaked their way off the line in a haze of tyre smoke, all except two cars[139] who had fallen foul of Gardner's feared scenario, their drivers frantically waving their hands to let the others know of their problems. Over the next few minutes, Goldie watched as small groups of cars were set off by Ebby according to their handicap. Finally, after an excruciating wait, Ebby raised his flag in front of Goldie's car and curtly dropped it. Paterson pulled the starter switch and Goldie, feeling the car rock into life, dropped the clutch and floored the accelerator. To his immense relief, the tiny MG leapt forwards, the supercharger screaming in a high-pitched wail as if to tell the other cars that they were on their way.

The three cars in Goldie's team had all made good starts. Stan Barnes in *Hoodoo* was first, but Goldie was only a car length behind and hugged the right-hand side of the road, ready for Quarry Corner ahead, and out of the corner of his eye, he caught a glimpse of Cyril Paul in number 31 to his rear left. Up to the Quarry they raced, and Goldie braked before dropping a gear and pulling the car around the corner. Close together now, the gaggle of little MGs roared past the crowd along the fast, winding road through the fields, then into the

---

138 The previous day, the *Belfast Telegraph* had reported that Hammy 'Is much better and has had a very comfortable night.' Friday, 19th Aug 1932, p 10.

139 Crossleys.

tree-shrouded cutting known as the Glen. As they reached the left-hand Mill Corner, Barnes still held the lead of the group, but in the melee, Goldie had dropped a place.[140] He wasn't worried – it was a long race, and anything could happen around this notorious course. Around the bend they drove to the cheers of the crowd, then out over the top of Brae Hill and down, through seven bends into Newtownards. At Conway Square they lined up for a tight right-hander then shot through the outskirts of the town and back into the country, keeping flat out until they reached Comber. Here Goldie concentrated as the road became narrower and the run-off evaporated; if he lost it here on the cobblestones they would side-swipe the sandbags that had been piled up on the notorious Butcher's Shop Corner. The car ahead slowed, and Goldie took his opportunity to regain the place. With clear air in front of them and desperate to catch sight of the cars ahead, Gardner and Paul dashed out of the town, under the Carstrand Bridge and past Ballystockart where Hammy had lost it two days previously. Then, it was back into Dundonald, around the hairpin, past the start and back down to the crowded natural amphitheatre of Quarry Corner.

Behind them, Goldie's teammate Stan Barnes had been jockeying for position with another MG in Freddie March's team.[141] As they passed the pits, they were wheel-to-wheel, but as they raced up Brae Hill, Barnes lost the place. Desperate to keep up with the other car, he pushed his car into the next corner at full speed but as he reached the apex, he knew he had overstepped the mark. His tyres squealing, Barnes fought his big steering wheel in vain, only to have the car slide sideways to a halt across the road. A driver following closely behind swerved but was unable to miss the MG, smashing into it broadside with a terrific crash and sending it lurching into a water trough. Shaken but otherwise OK, it was the end of Stan Barnes's race.[142]

---

140 He was overtaken by Eddie Hall in MG number 34.
141 Driven by Norman Black.
142 Talbot driven by Brian Lewis. He was able to continue the race.

Up ahead, Goldie was unaware of the drama. Now through New-townards again, he raced on, trying to catch the cars ahead, but it took him the rest of the lap before he caught sight of his target. Past the pits and around Quarry Corner he sped, supercharger screaming, as he pushed the little MG as hard as he could. Almost at the top of the Glen, where Barnes had crashed a lap earlier, he caught the first car, Paterson made the signal to overtake and Gardner pulled over to the right to push past.

But something happened. Whether it was the driver's instinctive reaction to the sight of Barnes's MG still stuck at the top of the hill ahead[143] or just an unfortunate dip in the road that unsettled the wheels, suddenly the slower car skipped slightly to the right.[144] Gardner instinctively steered away to avoid a collision, but his two right-hand wheels slid onto the grass verge where they immediately lost traction and the car swerved violently. He wrestled with the wheel, scissoring it back and forth but, just as he thought he had caught the slide, there was an almighty bang. Gardner felt himself being tossed into the air, then an impact, then nothing…

Those watching saw what had happened. The MG's front right wheel hit a deep gully, sending the car spinning up into a full somersault with parts strewn across the track and Paterson being dumped out into the soil bank that edged the road. Gardner wasn't so lucky. Still in his seat, the car somersaulted again before he too fell out, taking the full impact of the crash head-first, the chassis landing on his right leg before bouncing to a halt on its wheels a few feet away. Spectators rushed to help, finding Paterson conscious but in a state of shock, but Gardner covered in blood, his helmet split in two and his right leg a mass of

---

143 Gardner wrote that Barnes's crash happened after his, but this is unlikely to be correct. In *Combat* (p289) Lyndon writes that Gardner's incident happened a lap after Barnes's, and a hand-written race programme held by the MMM Register shows Barnes marked with one completed lap, Gardner two. Gardner was therefore on his third complete lap when he crashed.

144 This is the way Gardner tells the story in *Magic MPH* but in an official press release for his 1951 Bonneville record attempt, it states that the accident was caused when Gardner 'glanced at his mechanic's hand signal for a split second'. Gardner states a number of times that he remembers nothing of the accident, so either is possible.

bone and vivid flesh. Shocked, they called for medical help while other flat-capped spectators pushed the crumpled MG off the road.

Within minutes, three white-clad nurses had arrived, one quickly applying a tourniquet to stop the blood that was shooting from Gardner's leg and strapping a bandage around his face. Then, as another MG flashed past, a stretcher party arrived to take him to an awaiting ambulance. As the stretcher bounced along, Gardner gradually came to, aware both of the terrible and familiar pain in his right leg, and also conscious that he had been very fortunate to emerge from the wreckage alive.

That evening, a doctor visited him at his bed beside Hammy's in Newtownards hospital, introduced himself as Dr Sandy Calder and explained just how lucky Gardner had been. His right thigh, already damaged from his wartime injury, had taken the full force of the car's weight, splintering the bone which had been thrust out through the skin. Behind his knee, the main artery had split and had to be sewn back together, a procedure that was very rarely successful, but which was Gardner's only chance of avoiding amputation. Other injuries – both clavicles broken, considerable damage to both wrists and a fractured neck vertebra that wouldn't be spotted for some time – would eventually heal.[145] Despite his condition, when a group other drivers visited the pair the following day to tell him how the race had finished,[146] he was on good form, even when he discovered that the third member of their ill-fated team, Cyril Paul, running strongly with the leaders, had been forced to retire with ignition trouble. At least Oscar Paterson, his riding mate, had been virtually unharmed by the crash.

Hammy was kept in the small hospital for three weeks, but Gardner's stay was much longer. His leg in traction, he started to heal but then the wound became septic, and Calder was advised by his seniors to amputate. He refused, each day coming by to tweak Gardner's toe

145 *Morris Owner* magazine, July 1939, p468-469.
146 This group included race winner Cyril 'Whitters' Whitcroft, Earl Howe and many others.

in what the driver thought was 'playful nonsense' but was his method of seeing if the leg's circulation was still intact. Gardner didn't realise, but if he hadn't reacted to the doctor's pinches, he would have lost his leg for good.

In all, he spent four months in the cottage hospital and in a strange way he enjoyed it; there was little to do but chat to the nurses and other patients, read his newspaper and smoke his pipe. He regularly received letters from back home, mainly from friends telling him about the latest rumours fresh from the Brooklands paddock, but on occasion formal-looking correspondence from Abingdon keeping him abreast of the repairs on his car.[147] But after a while, his leg now healing well, he started to yearn for a return to the bustle of life and just before Christmas 1932, he hobbled out of the door for the final time.

1933 was a strange year for Gardner. Still recovering for the first few months, he spent his time at work, watching racing or visiting friends. By July, he felt well enough to enter a race, the new Mannin Beg, or 'Little Man' competition on the Isle of Man. He travelled over but his heart was not in it and his brother Edgar took his place in his C-Type Montlhéry Midget but crashed on the first corner of his qualifying lap and retired before the end of the race. Hammy, driving one the latest racing K-Type MGs,[148] dominated the race until he too was forced out with a rear axle problem. Two days later, Gardner watched as the larger-engined cars ran the Mannin Moar or 'Great Man' race and one of them caught his eye, a glorious eight-cylinder 2300 Alfa Romeo driven by his Brooklands friend Kaye Don. With a long chassis clad in a wonderful body by Zagato, the car had been built for the Alfa Romeo works team to compete in the 1931 Le Mans 24-hour race before being purchased by Don.[149]

---

147 Ironically, the MG was fixed before he was. The current owner of the car, which is in fine health and still raced, still has a letter addressed to the hospital asking Gardner's permission to release the car after the repairs.

148 A 1087cc MG K-Type Magnette.

149 Don had made an agreement with F.W. Styles from Alfa to buy the car for £1,000 after the race.

The following month, Goldie returned to the Ulster TT, this time acting as pit manager for Hammy who finished a close second after an
almighty scrap with the eventual winner, the great Italian Tazio Nuvolari, also driving an MG.[150] Then, in September, Goldie returned
to Brooklands and took part in the MCC High Speed Trial, but his
old winning form had still not returned. With an assuredness common
amongst racing drivers, he decided that a more powerful car would
provide the answer and made a deal with Kaye Don for his Alfa Romeo,[151] stretching its legs for the first time in the Brighton Speed Trials
later that month. He also wrote to Cecil Kimber, enquiring about the
new MG, the K3 Magnette, and received a reply that he didn't expect,
Kimber offering him the loan of one for the following season.[152] The
car, a works entry in the Mille Miglia that had achieved a respectable
second-place class finish driven by Giovanni 'Johnny' Lurani, arrived
in time for his first race of 1934 at the Brooklands race meeting in
May. Streamlined, with a boat tail enclosing its fuel tank and lacking
wings, lights, and windscreen this was a serious machine and throughout the summer Goldie raced it regularly in all the Brooklands events.
Between races, he kept himself busy with hillclimbs and speed trials at
Lewes,[153] Shelsley Walsh and Craigantlet in Belfast in his Alfa Romeo
(partnered there by Alec Calder, his surgeon from Newtownards) but he
found the long-chassis car 'rather cumbersome on bends'[154] compared
with the nimble cars he was used to. Consequently, when he heard that
Alfa Romeo was selling a short-chassis 2300 he jumped at the chance,
travelling to Italy to pick up the car as soon as he could, driving it back
through Europe despite the lack of a windscreen or any weather equip-

---

150 A full report of this race is in *Magic MPH,* (ibid) p25-27.
151 This was chassis 2111011, registration GT6074. More information is in Simon Moore's *The Legendary
   2.3 Alfa Romeo* (Parkside, 2000) and *The 8C Story Continues* (Parkside, 2022). It is possible that the Mannin
   Moar race result made Don decide not to take on the Alfa, and to pass it to Gardner.
152 Some sources state that Gardner owned MG K3 chassis K3015 but it was loaned to him by the factory.
   For more see Leonard Goff, *Magnette-ised* (Biddles, 2007).
153 Details in Jeremy Wood, *Speed on the Downs* (JWFA Books, 2005).
154 *Motor Sport,* July 1934, 'Shelsley at its best'.

ment, hunching down behind the tiny aeroscreen.[155] Back home he had various engine parts of his old Alfa transferred on to his new one, then sold his old four-seater to another Brooklands driver.[156]

At the end of August, in the borrowed works MG K3, Goldie had his best result so far of the year: a third place in the Esher Senior Short Handicap at Brooklands. He was very pleased with himself that evening as he set off on the long journey to Ulster where he had once again promised Hammy that he would run his team for the Tourist Trophy race. The following day he arrived in the paddock in Dundonald expecting the usual friendly welcome from the other drivers but was instead faced with sombre expressions. The news had just reached them: Hammy, driving a Maserati 8CM in the Swiss Grand Prix, had skidded off the track just before the end of the race. His car had disintegrated as it crashed through the trees and Hammy was killed instantly.[157]

It was a huge shock; Hammy had been more than just a teammate, he had been his best friend. Their time convalescing together in hospital had cemented that friendship, and the realisation of his death just seemed so otherworldly. Sure, Hammy had crashed before – just after the 1933 Ulster TT race he had survived a serious crash in an MG J4 Midget during a race in Czechoslovakia – but he had always come back smiling. For a friend who was such a superb driver to die so suddenly was a great blow to Gardner. There was nothing else for it; Goldie packed up and sadly went home.

The next few weeks were a testing time. Hammy's death really affected Gardner, probably more so than his own crash at the Ards circuit. It just seemed as if every time he visited that place, something ter-

---

155 The second of Gardner's two Alfa Romeo 2300 cars, chassis 2111016, registration BGO246, was the final 2300 to leave the factory in 1931 and first registered to the before being sold on. (Shelsley Walsh archive). Chassis number 2111016 was the final 2300 to leave the factory in 1931 and first registered to the *Scuderia Ferrari as SF31* (Shelsley Walsh Archive) It was registered for the road in Great Britain on 27th July 1934 as 'BGO246' (*The Legendary 2.3 Alfa Romeo;* ibid.) Gardner's wife Una later recollected that he told her he had driven to Italy to collect a car that had once been personally owned and raced by Enzo Ferrari himself (interview with Ros Gardner).

156 James Wright.

157 The post-mortem showed that Hammy's heart had stopped before the crash, but this was not revealed until much later.

rible happened, but he did what racing drivers always do and remained focused on the next meeting. What a race that was: the BRDC 500 Miles at Brooklands, the jewel in the crown of British motorsport, in which he was partnered with one of the most famous racing drivers of the time, Dr Dudley Benjafield, one of the 'Bentley Boys' who had won Le Mans in 1927[158] and who was the founder of the BRDC.

The race started well for the pair. 'Benjie' took the first session and was keeping up a good pace until just before half distance when the heavens opened. A few laps later, he pulled into the pits and after a quick dash of fuel, Gardner clambered in. 'The conditions about this time were appalling,' Benjafield said. 'The straights were covered with large puddles of water and if a car or two happened to be a short distance ahead, one could see nothing more than a large cloud of spray which appeared to extend right across the track.'[159] As Gardner pulled out onto the circuit, he couldn't quite believe how bad the conditions were: rain was cascading down the banking and when he reached the Railway Straight it looked like a river, with standing water pooled across the surface. As water soaked through his clothes and ran down his back he rubbed at his goggles, desperate to try to improve his vision, but to no avail. Every car was enveloped in a shroud of spray, a grey mass of water in which he *knew* there was another driver fighting the same battle. Many didn't make it. Lining up for a pass on the Railway Straight, Gardner was shocked to see a car pirouette out from the spray, slew across the track in front of him and crash out through the corrugated iron fence. Shortly afterwards, the race-leading car[160] suffered a similar fate and skidded off the Members' Banking which prompted the extremely experienced John Cobb, the other front runner, to retire saying that the conditions made it impossible to race. Other cars fell by

---

158 With Sammy Davis in a 3-Litre Bentley.
159 Dudley Benjafield, *BBC Radio* interview, 22 September 1934, 9.50pm (NMM).
160 Driven by Wal Handley who was partnered with George Eyston.

the wayside, either through mechanical problems or through the terrible weather, but Gardner doggedly kept going.

Then, suddenly the skies cleared, and the rain stopped. Visibility improved, and as the damp Gardner passed his pit, he saw Benjafield gesticulating wildly. 'I saw Benjie dancing about on the pit counter, hanging on to an upright with one arm and waving furiously with the other,' he wrote. 'I realised then that something was in the wind, so pushed the little car round as fast as I could.'[161] Gardner didn't know it, but the race was nearly over. Driving hard now, he saw another MG[162] hove into view and gradually gained on him, finally managing to overtake with just minutes left of the competition. Exhausted and bedraggled, he was utterly relieved when the chequered flag was finally waved and when he pulled into the pits was greeted with the sight of a delighted Benjie running over to clap him on the back. Just seven cars had finished the race, and by overtaking Wisdom, Gardner had not only taken a third place overall but also won their class and the prestigious Barnato Trophy (including £50 prize money). Benjafield thrust a glass of champagne into Gardner's hand and was quickly joined by Cecil Kimber who had come over to congratulate the pair. After they were presented with their third-place pennant, a pair of bronze medallions and the Barnato Trophy by Woolf Barnato himself, Gardner, Benjie and Kim posed for a photograph.

During the previous year, Gardner had almost come to terms with the fact that his racing life was nearly at an end. He hadn't found the success he'd previously been used to and found himself just taking part rather than competing because he loved it. But that third place at the BRDC 500 with Benjie made all the difference. It had been a brutal race, through which he had battled and earned the pair a very well-de-

161 *Magic MPH* (ibid) p28.
162 Tommy Wisdom's K3.

served podium and the heartiest congratulations of the other drivers.[163] For Gardner, that meant a lot. Also, putting the borrowed K3 on the podium in such an important race repaid Kimber's generosity and cemented the relationship they had built up. It was a turning point; at his next Brooklands race, the last of the season, Gardner dominated and took an outright win. His heart was back in the game and a few weeks later he decided to buy a K3 of his own, a streamlined single seater belonging to his old teammate Ronnie Horton, that he immediately sent off to be tuned by Robin Jackson. This was a very serious racing car, and he had big plans for it, but for the time being, it would have to wait. Goldie Gardner had another, more pressing engagement, this time overseas.

---

163 Gardner was included in a humorous montage in that month's *Tatler* (10 Oct 1934) entitled *A group of real knuts and bolts of the high-speed world.'*

9

DAYTONA

The weather was dry and, at 8 degrees centigrade, relatively warm for the time of year as Gardner climbed the gangplank of the *RMS Aquitania*[164] on 23rd January 1935 and looked up at its four red funnels gently breathing thin twists of steam into the Southampton sky. The old ship, with over 20 years' service on the North Atlantic route, was showing its age but still an opulent form of transport with nearly one member of the Cunard White Star Line crew for every two passengers. Not since his return from Burma before the war had he been on such a vessel, but some things never changed: his first task was to fill out the forms that would be used to process his entry into the United States. Within a few minutes the ledger had been completed stating that it was his first trip to America, that he was an engineer by trade, and that for the duration of his visit he would be staying at the Hotel Issens in Daytona Beach,[165] part of Sir Malcolm Campbell's world land speed record team.

---

164 In *Magic MPH*, Gardner says it is the Lusitania, but the Southampton embarkation records clearly show the group departing on the RMS Aquitania. He later hand-corrected this in his own copy.

165 It's a sign of the times that the mechanics stayed at another hotel, the *Williams*.

Gardner had been delighted when Campbell asked him to accompany him. He was very fond of both Malcolm and his wife Dorothy, and this venture would give him the opportunity to see a world record attempt up close. This wasn't just a couple of days on the sands at Pendine as he'd experienced with Parry-Thomas, but a properly planned and financed expedition with a clear target: to set a new world record of over 300 miles-per-hour on the sands at Daytona Beach. As he was shown to the first-class cabin that would be his home for the week-long crossing to New York, he allowed himself a broad grin.

That evening, after the ship had pushed away from its berth and the passengers waved their farewells, he met up with the rest of the team for cocktails before dinner. Alongside the Campbells and their 12-year-old daughter Jean was Robin Grosvenor, a friend of Malcolm's and another man with an extraordinary war record, as the Military Cross and Bar that adorned his tailcoat attested. Originally a cavalry officer, Grosvenor had transferred to the newly created Royal Flying Corps and subsequently shot down 16 enemy aircraft, one of the highest tallies of the war. Next to Grosvenor was Roger Fuller of the *Daily Mail*, who greeted Gardner with a firm shake of the hand. Below decks in steerage, the large engineering team led by Campbell's trusted chief mechanic Leo Villa[166] settled into their slightly less salubrious rooms, as did Clifford Lyon of the *Daily Express*, whose editor wasn't as generous as that of the *Daily Mail*.

A high-pressure system sat over the Atlantic for the duration of the crossing, giving good weather and relatively calm seas for that time of year. Even Villa, who had a history of being badly affected by motion sickness,[167] survived without any ill effects and by the time they docked in New York on 29th January, the team was raring to go. The work

---

166   The others included Ted Allen, Harry Leech, (an engineer whose day job was at the Air Ministry), Walter Hicks and David McDonald from Dunlop, and George Lovesey and Alf Poyser, who Rolls-Royce had sent to support the maintenance of the engine.

167   Leo Villa's own book *The Record Breakers* gives a very detailed report of this and Campbell's other record attempts (Hamlyn, 1969).

started immediately with the mechanics unloading the car and spares and processing their passage through customs, while Campbell, Gardner and the rest of the first class group departed immediately by train. Two days later, they arrived at St Augustine, a pretty seaside town on the Florida coast some seventy miles from Daytona, where they were welcomed by the local mayor[168] who brought bad news: not only was a gale blowing but the sands were in poor condition. Daytona Beach is twenty-three miles long, but experience had shown Campbell that only ten miles of it was suitable for the record runs, and it was the state of this stretch that was of critical importance. A strong north-easterly wind was needed to build the heavy surf that pounded the sand flat enough to be suitable, and this hadn't yet appeared. The spring tides due in a couple of weeks would probably create the right conditions, but for the time being, they would have to wait.

Two days later, Villa and the rest of the team arrived with *Bluebird*[169] but it was a frustrating time. Every morning Campbell, Gardner and Grosvenor took to the sands to see if there had been an improvement overnight, but it was always the same story: a rutted surface of sand ridges and eroded dunes meant that the best that could be achieved were a few slow-speed runs. The local authorities did what they could, sending men to manually flatten the humps and lay a line of tar to guide the record breaker down the best course, but by the time the wind changed enough for the first full-speed attempt on February 14th, it still wasn't anywhere near the surface Campbell had been expecting.

The first run was not a success. Campbell was desperate to stretch the car's legs, and immediately ignored advice to keep the revs low.[170] The team watched as Campbell thundered off in the enormous car, his goggles glinting in the winter sunshine, but after just one quick run, he drifted to a halt to the consternation of the thousands of onlook-

---

168 Mayor Armstrong.
169 Malcolm Campbell, *My Thirty Years of Speed* (Hutchinson & Co, 1935).
170 From mechanic Alf Poyser.

ers who lined the dunes.[171] When Villa arrived at the car, the smell of burning was obvious and he quickly diagnosed a seized universal joint, but that wasn't all that was wrong. The condition of the beach, so Campbell complained, was causing the car to slide around in an alarming manner and the huge twin rear wheels to spin in the soft sand.[172] As the team wheeled *Bluebird* back to their garage, Gardner mused that he was learning a great deal, not least of which was that, despite meticulous planning, record attempts could be frustrated by many unseen challenges.

While the mechanics worked and they waited for the conditions to improve, the rest of the group made the most of their time. They had hired an aircraft to track *Bluebird*'s progress, which they used for day trips, heading as far afield as Tampa on the other side of the Florida peninsula, visiting alligator farms and watching dirt-track racing in the nearby town of DeLand. But it was the social scene of Daytona Beach itself that made the biggest impression on Gardner.

Daytona was then, as now, a place of two halves. The main settlement sat back from the shore and resembled any other Floridian town, but the beachfront houses were something else: huge, wood-clad winter homes of the rich and powerful whose bored owners were fascinated by the arrival of these motoring gladiators from across the water. Invitations poured in, which the British group were more than happy to accept. In late February, Campbell received a card from E.L. King, president of the J.R. Watkins company of Minnesota,[173] then (and now) one of the country's biggest manufacturers of health remedies, baking products and other household items. He quickly accepted an invitation to visit on behalf of the group.

---

171 *The Record Breakers*, (ibid) p156.

172 A power increase from 1,400hp to 2,500hp without any additional weight compared to their previous run at Daytona two years previously was another cause of this trouble and an issue that required an aerodynamic solution. The frustrated Campbell duly telephoned Reid Railton for advice.

173 https://forgottenminnesota.com/forgotten-minnesota/2011/09/a-grand-estate-for-the-owners-of-the-watkins-medical-products-company

The King house exuded American wealth and status. The walls
of the drawing room were adorned by game trophies and a roaring
fire warmed two golden retrievers[174] who sat up and yawned when the
British arrived. Framed shelves of exotic seashells lined the walls next
to beautiful Remington paintings of the Old West[175] which Gardner
was inspecting when the King family entered the room. E.L. King was
pleasant, just as Gardner expected, but it was the two women of the
household who caught him off guard. Grace Watkins King, his wife,
was the daughter of the company's founder and a two-time women's
World Trap Shooting Champion. The game trophies were hers, she
quickly told him, and it was instantly clear to Gardner that she was
a force to be reckoned with. Behind her came their daughter Mariel
holding the hand of Patricia, the two-year-old girl who she had adopt-
ed as a baby. Mariel was tall with a broad smile, dark curled hair in the
style of the times and wide, shining eyes. Gardner was immediately
enthralled and listened attentively as Mariel explained that she had
collected the shells during various worldwide expeditions. When, at the
end of the evening she invited him to accompany her to a dance at the
Seabreeze Swim Club[176] a few days later, he instantly accepted.

Mariel's confidence, her keen intelligence and her sense of adventure
made a strong contrast with the rule-bound and class-conscious women
he'd known in England. The now-pleasant sub-tropical weather and
general party atmosphere of a country having recently emerged from
prohibition helped to create a heady atmosphere, and Gardner quickly
found himself relaxing the stiff demeanour he'd worn as a uniform for
many years. He found that he enjoyed the company of this new set, a
strange mix of the ultra-rich, Hollywood stars and racing drivers. One

---

174 Mariel was a renowned breeder of Golden Retrievers and a keen conchologist who even had a species of
   cone shell named after her. https://repository.si.edu/bitstream/handle/10088/5316/SCtZ-0203-Hi_res.
   pdf?sequence=1&isAllowed=y
175 https://casetext.com/case/mertes-v-estate-of-king
176 NMM Archive.

night, he looked over at Mariel and realised that this woman made him feel alive like nobody else had done. He was falling in love.

But there was still work to be done. In a fortnight the sand had improved enough for another high-speed attempt, and on 2nd March the local police department cleared the beach of pedestrians and placed marker flags. The word had spread rapidly through the local area, and thousands of people turned out to see the British daredevil and leviathan of a car charge down the beach.

At first, all went well. The car launched perfectly, and accelerated southwards along the sand to the delight of the crowd. A speed of 200 miles-per-hour was easily achieved… 220… 240… then, suddenly the big air brakes deployed, and the car slithered to a halt. The crew quickly mounted up and drove towards the car to find out what had happened, finding Campbell clambering out of the car, a grim look on his face. Suddenly, the cockpit had filled with fumes and scorching heat. Sure that the engine had caught fire, Campbell had stopped as quickly as he could, but once static Villa realised that the cause was less dramatic: part of the bonnet had been bent by the airflow, directing the exhaust fumes directly into the car. After some percussive maintenance and some temporary strapping, Campbell agreed to give the car another run, but the same problem occurred on the return leg and the day's activities were ended there. Other problems remained. 'I had been strapped into the cockpit,' Campbell wrote, 'Otherwise the bumps would have thrown me out, while the sand was even worse than it had been during the first test… sand had smothered the cockpit, clogging my nostrils and ears.'[177] That night, Villa and his men fitted extended exhaust pipes to the car and replaced the badly burned bonnet. The car was ready.

Early the next morning, to the delight of passing children, Campbell drove the huge, 27-foot-long car down the main street from the garage to the beach. This time, the Police had cleared a larger expanse

---

177 *My 30 Years of Speed* (ibid) p262.

of sand to give him a better run at the record, but that meant driving underneath the pier. When given the all clear, Campbell pushed his accelerator to the floor, the wheels spun and then he was off, quickly picking up speed towards the tiny-looking 40-foot gap between the steel and concrete legs of the pier that was his only route to success. Faster he charged, reaching 130 miles-per-hour as the enormous car shot under the stanchions, almost deafening the onlookers who had packed onto the walkway above. Beyond the pier was a bend in the beach, and the onlookers watched as Campbell fought with the steering wheel to correct the inevitable slide. The bumps on the beach were still as bad as on the previous day and just before the start of the measured mile, despite his harness, Campbell was nearly thrown out of the car. At a speed of more than 270 miles-per-hour, his head was instantly pummelled by the wall of air that ripped his goggles downwards, clamping them over his nose and mouth. Suffocating, with sand being forced into his eyes, Campbell ignored the instinct to lift, and kept his foot flat to the floor. Almost blind, he completed the measured mile at 270.43 miles-per-hour but a check of his tyres at the far end reiterated just how close to disaster he had been: huge chunks of tread were missing. Sensibly, Campbell drove the car back to the garage and joined Gardner for a drink. Two days later, with a more robust seat harness fitted, Campbell tried to make another attempt but just before the run began, a strong wind picked up. This time it was Lady Campbell who was the voice of reason, forbidding her husband from running that day.

Then, on Thursday 7th March, conditions finally improved[178] and *Bluebird* set off beautifully again, although it nearly clipped the pier as it passed underneath. Patches of water still dotted the beach and the sand was not in perfect condition, but Campbell kept the car on course and thundered through the measured mile. Gardner positioned himself about 20 yards from the car's track and was nearly blown over as it thundered past, then watched as it completed its run, rolled to a halt,

---

178   The Record Breakers, Villa, p70.

had new tyres fitted, and set off on the return leg. Just before the start of the measured mile, the car hit what Campbell later described as 'an ugly bump', the five-ton car flying some thirty feet through the air before landing with an almighty impact. Sure a crash was imminent, Gardner watched Campbell fight with the big steering wheel as the car swerved violently towards the dunes, tyre treads stripping into the air through a cloud of sand. The tail slid outwards, but at the last moment Campbell managed to correct the slide and straighten the car, then forced the accelerator to the floor once again. Snaking from one side to the other throughout the mile, the car passed the final marker then slid to a halt by the pier.

He had done it… just. A new average of 276.816 miles-per-hour made Campbell the fastest man on the planet, but for him, it wasn't enough. He had set himself the target of 300 miles-per-hour, and in the days that followed tortured himself by working out that he had missed the target through the mile by just four fifths of a second. Two more weeks they waited, hoping in vain that the weather would improve, but after Campbell's rather sombre fiftieth birthday celebrations they started to pack up. It was clear a more reliable surface was needed at these speeds.

On 20th March, the people of Daytona said their farewells to the British in typical style. Gardner went from party to party becoming more and more merry as the night went on. He met all the friends he'd made during the two-month stay[179] but there was only one person he longed to see: Mariel. With his heart thumping in his chest, he asked her to meet him again. Of course, she replied, with her usual beaming smile, she'd love that. She would be back in London in a matter of weeks, staying at the Savoy with Patricia, and she couldn't wait to see him. Then, as they parted, the warm evening air still filled with the sounds of dancing and laughter, she leant over and kissed him.

---

179 They included Pop Myers and Ted Allen from the AAA, 'Wild Bill' Cummings and Doc MacKenzie of Indianapolis 500 fame, Gar Wood the famous designer of speed record boats and more.

10

FASTER AND FASTER

On 5th April 1935, Gardner looked down at the waving crowds thronging the Southampton docks as the *RMS Berengaria* berthed. Tanned, lean and, as ever, immaculately dressed, he felt conflicted: sad because this most excellent adventure to Daytona Beach had ended, but elated that he had experienced another world, a world filled with laughter and love. He had also learned a huge amount about speed record attempts, not just in a practical sense but also about the public adulation that resulted. Everywhere they had been, Campbell's group had been feted, by the rich and powerful, by the press and by the general public. On their return journey they'd even stopped off in Washington DC where the Vice President, John Nance Garner, had presented them with a plaque. Now, as they waited for disembarkation, Gardner could see the gaggle of press photographers jostling for position. He had known for some time that this was what he wanted, and Daytona had given him the impetus to actually get on with his own record breaking. He wanted his name in the record books, representing King and Country as the best in the world. The adulation of the press and public he could take or leave, but their *respect* was another matter. He cared about that.

Heading back to Reigate and the normality of work at Milne & Russell was hard at first, especially as his thoughts kept turning to Mariel, but he soon fell back into his old routine and within a couple of weeks was back at Brooklands. Here he was reunited with the other obsession that had dominated his attention over the last few months: the sleek MG K3[180] that he had bought from Ronnie Horton at the end of the previous year and which he had entrusted the famous racing mechanic Robin Jackson to prepare while he was away in America. The car was already very quick, Horton having taken class wins at the Shelsley Walsh hillclimb, set six international class records in 1934 and lapped Brooklands at 123.88 miles-per-hour, earning him the coveted '120 MILES-PER-HOUR' badge, the first time it had been given to the driver of a 1,100cc car. The car, combining MG's six-cylinder supercharged engine with a custom, offset streamlined body was the perfect basis for what Gardner had planned but he wanted more speed. Money, for once, wasn't a major issue as he'd received a fair price for his beautiful Alfa Romeo 2300 Zagato Spider.

After testing the MG during the Easter Meeting, during which Campbell also did some demonstration laps in his now world-record holding *Bluebird*, Gardner felt his car handled well. It was undoubtedly quick and after a few post-race adjustments back at Robin Jackson's workshop it was on top form by the time of the Whitsun Meeting on 10th June. It looked great, too: he had sent the car off to be painted in his old Royal Artillery colours, a dark blue line superimposed with a vivid zigzag of crimson snaking along its flanks and a Union Flag on each side of the tail. A 'very quick specimen' as Bill Boddy described it,[181] the car drew a great deal of attention, especially from Ebby who slapped him with a harsh 31-second handicap. It was too much to make up, but it encouraged Gardner to push the car to its limits and as he pulled up after the finish, Jackson's beaming smile told him that he had joined

---

180 Chassis number K3007.
181 *Brooklands*, (ibid), p650.

the exclusive club of those who had lapped the outer circuit at more than 120 miles-per-hour. The following day he was presented with a car badge, mounted on a plinth onto which was engraved, '10.6.35 Presented by the proprietors to Major ATG Gardner MC for having officially lapped the track at 120 miles-per-hour with his MG Magnette (1087cc).'[182] It was one of just 84 of the famous badges ever presented by the Brooklands Auto Racing Club.[183]

A few days later, the badge was firmly affixed to the grille of his car as he made his way towards London, his destination the Savoy. He felt his heart give an uncharacteristic flutter as he turned off the Strand and pulled up outside the famous old hotel, and he hesitated before switching off the engine and climbing out. Tentatively, he made his way up the steps, through the front doors and headed left into the American Bar… at least the location was appropriate, he thought to himself. There she was, sat at the bar, cocktail in hand. She turned, and that huge smile of hers shone from her face. Instantly, his nervousness dissipated, and once again he felt that surge of happiness and freedom that he'd experienced in Daytona. He went to shake her hand, but she pulled him close and kissed him.

The rest of the month was a blur as they rekindled their romance. For the first time in many years Gardner seemed to forget his racing and only paid it any attention at all when Cecil Kimber contacted him with the news that Lord Nuffield, the head of Morris Motors, had stated that MG was no longer to build racing cars. 'The Directors have decided that… racing for the purpose of development has, in our case, served its useful purpose. Another reason… [is] that we are handicapped out of British racing.' It was half of the truth. Although Ebby's harsh handicaps were one element, what Kimber didn't say was that

---

182 Engraving on badge (www.sworder.co.uk/auction/lot/lot-480).

183 Some online resources record that Goldie Gardner took part in the 1934 and 1935 Le Mans 24 Hours, partnered by Arthur Beloe. This is incorrect; the driver was Rodney Gardner (no relation) who entered and raced a Singer 9 and an Aston Martin Ulster. He is mentioned in the October 1935 *Motor Sport* report of the Brighton Speed Trials.

a deal had been struck with Austin to call a truce on their ever-more expensive competition against each other.[184] At any other time such an announcement would have affected him most deeply, but with Mariel there, his K3 in top form and plans being hatched for racing and record attempts elsewhere, it did not dampen Gardner's mood. Even when, on Independence Day, 4th July 1935, Mariel returned with Patricia to America on board the *SS Bremen*, his happiness did not abate. He knew Mariel would be back and within a month she was, this time alone and staying in rented accommodation in the village of West Wickham, just five miles from his office.

Throughout the late summer and autumn of 1935, Mariel experienced the British 'motor set' season for the first time. Gardner invited her to accompany him to watch the Ulster TT, back at the Ards circuit that held so many memories for him.[185] She eagerly agreed, and the pair travelled across by ferry to watch the race. There, surrounded by the rolling green hills of Ulster and with this beautiful woman next to him, he hardly took note of the racing. Summoning courage, he proposed. Mariel accepted.[186]

Soon, the happy pair returned to England and, deciding to keep the engagement secret until Gardner could speak to Mariel's father, focused instead on his racing. The BRDC 500 was the highlight, and with his new car, Gardner thought he had a great chance of bettering his previous third-place finish. He enlisted Bill Everitt as his second driver, a very competent racer who had partnered George Eyston to 4th place in the same race the previous year. At first all went well, with Everitt keeping a steady pace that by 3pm had pulled him up to 3rd place on handicap despite throwing a tyre thanks to a very rough track. Mariel then watched as Gardner jumped in at the half-way point and roared off. He needed to exceed an average speed of 114.49 miles-per-hour

184 John Thornley, *Maintaining the Breed* (Motor Racing Publications, 1950) pp 95-96.
185 7th September 1935.
186 *Dundee Evening Telegraph*, 10 Feb 1936, p4. 'Racing Motorist to Wed'.

and Everitt had done his part admirably, maintaining a steady 117-118 miles-per-hour, but it wasn't to be. Almost immediately Gardner's engine started to misfire and, aware a spark plug had fouled, he pulled into the pits to change the offending item. It didn't work. Over the next few laps, Gardner returned to his mechanics and swapped out other plugs, finally resorting to changing all six. That, finally, did the trick and he sped off, lapping at nearly 120 miles-per-hour in an attempt to catch the leaders. Despite his efforts, it wasn't enough, and Gardner was flagged back into the pits having not made the time cut-off. He was very disappointed; he had expected to do better and wanted to show Mariel what he was made of. But Mariel saw other things: the way the other drivers clapped Gardner on the back and bought him drinks at the bar. He was a popular man and obviously well respected within this tight-knit group.

Soon, it was time for Mariel to return to America. In her absence, Gardner kept himself busy at Brooklands, attending the last race of the season on 19th October, after which he entrusted his MG back to the care of Robin Jackson, asking him to improve the streamlining and refresh the engine. His car safely away for the winter Gardner booked his own transatlantic voyage, leaving Southampton on 15th January 1936 aboard the *RMS Majestic*[187].

It was a sombre affair compared with his previous crossings. In the chilly January dawn, *Majestic* was on her last voyage before being scrapped, her place taken in the Cunard-White Star Lines fleet by the new *Queen Mary*, and the crew were more reserved than usual. A conversation with a young stage actor called Rex Harrison who was about to make his West End debut lightened the mood a little, but just as they docked in New York, the Captain made the sad announcement that every British passenger had been expecting for some time: after a long illness, His Royal Highness King George V had passed away the previ-

---

187 In *Magic MPH* Gardner recalls incorrectly that he travelled across 'In the late autumn' 1935 but embarkation logs show he crossed to New York in January 1936.

ous evening. By the time he walked down the gangplank, Gardner had a black crepe mourning band affixed to his right arm and, outwardly at least, had a serious look on his face. Inside, he just couldn't wait to see Mariel again and to relive some of the excitement he had felt in Daytona Beach when he had last visited. This time, he wasn't there to accompany Malcolm Campbell – the salt flats in Utah had now taken over as *the* place to attempt land speed records – but to race himself. The Daytona Beach authorities, keen to retain the income of all the motoring fans that had crowded into their town every spring to watch the speed record cars, had commissioned the creation of a 3.2-mile racecourse that looped along the beach, through two 'approaches' cut through the dunes, then back along the town's main street and put up the huge prize fund of $5,000 to entice stock car racers from all over the country.[188] Gardner, no doubt aided by Mariel's connections, had been the sole overseas invitee.

Once he had arrived in Daytona there was still more than a month before the start of the race, time to spend with his love, Mariel. Heady with an excitement he'd not felt before, he received the permission he sought from her father, then helped Mariel in her preparations for the wedding. Paperwork was organised, a pastor in Volusia County in Daytona found to conduct the ceremony on March 10th and decorations booked for *Oceanfront*, Mariel's family home. Now, as his future wife went shopping for a dress, Gardner had a little time to prepare for the 250-mile race which was scheduled two days earlier on Sunday, March 8th.

The event would go down in history as the first American stock car race officially sanctioned by the American Automobile Association (AAA), some 11 years before the formation of the National Association for Stock Car Auto Racing, or *NASCAR*. Until then, a few local races had been held on farms, mainly raced by moonshiners who thrived in

---

188 The course was created by racer Sig Haugdahl and local attorney Millard Conklin. Haugdahl, was a Norwegian by birth but now a resident – like Mariel – of Minnesota.

the flat-out, dirt-track conditions. This though was different, attracting all sorts of professional drivers.[189] In all, 27 cars entered, 20 of them Fords, but Gardner was in a borrowed Lincoln Zephyr saloon and was astounded at the pre-race scrutineering. The race was classed as 'Strictly Stock', allowing for no changes from the production line, and the scrutineers were brutal. 'The car was literally torn to pieces,' Gardner wrote. 'The cylinder head [was] removed, sump dropped, rear axle drawn back and opened up and also the top of the gearbox removed. Everything was then checked against the manufacturers' certified specification.'[190] Once content that everything was as expected, the scrutineers and their mechanics reassembled the car and officially sealed the engine. Gardner was then told his entry had been accepted and immediately instructed that his race number '7' should be painted on the sides and rear of the car.

The following day he arrived, ready to race. Immediately, he was taken aback by the crowd: every square foot of the dunes was packed with onlookers, all straining to see the drivers and especially this crazy Brit with a walking stick. 'Goldie' (as they all loved to call him) lived up to their expectations, wearing his white shirt emblazoned with the BRDC crest and donning a borrowed American football helmet to comply with the rule that stated head protection was compulsory.

After a few qualifying laps to gauge the average speed of the cars, the drivers lined up for the 1pm start.[191] In the style typical of the razzmatazz that was to follow in stock car racing of the years to follow, four swimsuit-clad young women in high heels[192] waved off the racers according to their qualifying handicaps, who then roared along the sands towards the Northern Approach corner. Gardner started well and pushed the car up to 90 miles-per-hour by the time he reached the

---

189 The starting grid included 1934 Indianapolis 500 winner 'Wild Bill' Cummings, 1935 Eastern States AAA Champion George 'Doc' Mackenzie, the young Sam Collier, who was later to become the sole American importer of MG cars and NASCAR founder Bill France Snr.

190 *Magic MPH*, (ibid) p36.

191 The race was recorded on film and is available at https://youtu.be/bxWYPqcHlt4

192 Getty images 156389105.

first corner. During qualifying, he had realised that the best way to take the approaches was to drive in at top speed, fling the back of the car out and keep the accelerator pressed to the floor. At first, it worked; taking a wider turn[193] than most other drivers, he slid around the corner in a cloud of dust and maintained a steady speed until his tyres gripped the surface of Highway A1A and he shot off towards Ponce Inlet and the Southern Approach. But after twenty laps the sand at the two corners had turned into a morass of high ridges and deep furrows, causing the cars to crazily bounce through the dust and Gardner was very nearly thrown out through the window of his Lincoln. As the laps went on, the ground became worse still and eventually the cars started to get stuck. Approaching a corner at speed, Gardner saw a gaggle of cars stranded on the course, their drivers all frantically trying to dig, push or drag them out of the sand. With inches to spare, he maintained his speed and dived between them, hoping to keep enough traction to make it around the corner and up the small incline to the highway, but it wasn't enough. To his dismay, he felt his wheels slip and then finally spin, his Lincoln grumbling to an undignified stop. He then sat, awaiting a tow car, all the while being barracked by the joyful onlookers.[194]

And so, the race progressed. Cars drove, cars got stuck, cars were pulled out. Sometimes, Gardner joined a circle of other racers biding their time on the beach until a gap in the breakdowns appeared long enough for them to have a go at the corner. Finally, after 150 miles, both he and the car had had enough, and he decided to retire. Not long afterwards, the race organisers came to the same conclusion, the race was ended and the winner announced.[195]

The race was a partial success. The chaos of the later stages wasn't exactly what the formal officials of the AAA had envisioned and Day-

---

193 Getty images 83558166.
194 *The Sports Car*, June 1936, p188.
195 The winner was announced as Milt Marion, driving a Ford, one of just ten cars left on the track. Bill France, later to become the founder of NASCAR, came in fifth although he claimed to have lapped Marion twice. Neal Thompson, *Driving with the Devil*, (Crown, 2007).

tona Beach lost over $20,000 on the event, having failed to prevent spectators from watching without buying tickets, but the onlookers loved it. Despite the conditions, so did the drivers and the $5,000 winners' purse, split between the top five finishers, made this a very lucrative pastime for those at the front. The event's greatest success was to bring stock car racing to the attention of the masses, something that after World War 2 led to the creation of one of America's biggest sporting spectacles.

Two days later, still buzzing from the race, Gardner stood in the grounds of *Oceanfront* with American racer 'Doc' Mackenzie and *United Press* sports-writer Henry McLemore at his side as his groomsmen. Suddenly, the music began and he turned; clad in a stunning dress of cellophane lace of a colour described as 'ashes of orchid' and holding a huge white gardenia bouquet, Gardner beamed a smile as his bride approached.[196] Minutes later, after a short ceremony, it was done; Gardner was a married man. A week later, the couple accompanied by Mariel's daughter Patricia, embarked the *RMS Berengaria* in New York, bound for Southampton and their new life.

---

196 *The Winona Republican Herald*, 6 April 1936, p6. Mariel was attended by McLemore's wife and Marie Metille.

11

THE FIRST RECORDS

The newlyweds arrived in a blustery England at the end of March and quickly set about finding a house. An advantage of marrying one of America's richest young women was that the King fortune encouraged things to progress faster than normal and before long, they were moving into their new home, the grand Oakhurst Court in Surrey, not far from Godstone[197].

By the time of the Brooklands Whitsun Meeting at the end of May, Gardner was keen to get back on track in his single-seater MG. Trial runs had shown a marked improvement in speed, and it seemed that Robin Jackson's fettling over the winter had been very successful, but the event itself was to be one of Gardner's more frustrating races. During morning practice, another competitor lost control of his car and crashed on the Railway Straight, the impact killing him instantly. Too late to clear the wreckage before the event, the crumpled remains of the vehicle were covered in a tarpaulin, an ominous

---

197 Immigration records show that during this time Mariel and Patricia briefly visited America, returning on the *Corinthia* on 16th May 1936. Oakhurst Court is now a care home.

reminder to everyone of the risks involved.[198] Undaunted, Gardner was still looking forward to his race, the prestigious Gold Star Trophy, in which just ten cars were entered, but the prize money had tempted the big names and the line-up was a veritable *Who's Who* of top drivers. Nevertheless, it was Gardner who the bookies had their eye on but it was not to be; by the third lap, he developed engine trouble and coasted back into the pits where a concerned Robin Jackson ran over, keen to find out what had gone wrong.[199] It wasn't the way Gardner had planned to reintroduce his new wife to his home track, and dispirited, he climbed out, got changed and drove Mariel home. The next Brooklands meeting, held over the first weekend in August, was much more successful. With his car performing beautifully in the first race, Gardner started scything through the field and was about to overtake two other drivers when the leading car's engine exploded with a huge bang, showering him with shards of hot metal and enveloping the trio in a thick cloud of oil smoke.[200] Unable to see the wreckage, Gardner and the other driver, experienced racer Charles Follett, pushed on through the haze, trusting one another to keep the line. 'Motor racing,' Follett remarked, 'is a perfectly safe recreation in the company of experts.'[201]

Gardner completed the overtake, took a comfortable win and later that day repeated the feat in the five-lap Locke King Trophy race after lapping at what was described as the 'astonishing speed' of 122.07 miles-per-hour.[202] He knew that both he and his car were in top form and saw an opportunity to set a record of his own. He immediately spoke to Ebby and Percy Bradley, Clerk of the Course, and they agreed

---

198 Kenneth Carr, driving an Alfa Romeo 8C 2300 Monza. The race, the Gold Star Trophy, *Brooklands*, (ibid), p673.
199 Cobb, Earl Howe and Woolf Barnato were in the starting line-up but 'Much was expected' of Gardner's car according to *Motor Sport*, (July 1936) p347.
200 Follett was driving an Alvis Speed 20 and remembered the car that exploded as being a Bugatti, but in *Motor Sport*, September 1936 (p422) it was recorded as the 'Grenfell-Rapier-Special' of K.O. Biarritz
201 *Motor Sport*, November 1946, p262.
202 *Brooklands*, (ibid), p678. The race was won at an average of 114.27 miles-per-hour.

to support an attempt on the 1,100cc outer lap record on 27th August. Maybe that would impress Mariel.

When the day arrived, conditions could not have been better. The car was running well, and Gardner was feeling very confident. He spoke to Bradley and asked him to start timing him and only wave him in once the record was his and it was clear that he could not improve on his time. Four flying laps later, Bradley made the sign and Gardner returned to the pits, to be met with the beaming smiles of Mariel, Robin Jackson, Bradley and Ebby. He had done it: his speed of 124.4 miles-per-hour set a record that still stood when the circuit closed in 1939.[203]

Encouraged, Gardner returned the next day, keen to try to gain another British record, this time for the fastest average speed over an hour. After six laps everything looked good, his speed well above what was required to gain the record but the old track, now a patchwork of rough concrete after nearly 30 years of racing, was taking its toll on his tyres.[204] As he exited the Members' Banking, a huge patch of tread detached itself from his front offside tyre and whizzed past his head. He had no option other than to coast into the pits, swap all four wheels and go out again, this time driving slower to protect his tyres. It worked, but only for a while; having just reached the 50-mile point, Robin Jackson waved him in, and he was amazed to see that his rear tyres were worn down to the canvas.

Although he had failed to achieve the hour record, the day was far from being a failure. Gardner had taken two other British records, his first national awards, and proved that both he and the car had greater potential.[205] Not only that, but it had sparked an excitement in Gardner

---

203 Gardner was presented with another Brooklands badge, this time engraved, *27.8.36 Presented by the proprietors of the Brooklands Auto Racing Club to Major ATG Gardner MC after having gained the 1100cc Outer Circuit Lap Record at 124.40 miles-per-hour.* https://www.sworder.co.uk/auction/lot/lot-0----a-brooklands-auto-racing-club-enamelled-12440-mph-badge/?lot=256426

204 He was averaging 123.5 miles-per-hour.

205 The records were the British 50km standing start (SS) record at 118.96 miles-per-hour and the 50-mile SS at 119.664 miles-per-hour. In *Maintaining the Breed* Thornley states that the records were 'Subsequently disallowed because of a misunderstanding with the timekeepers' but in *Magic MPH* Gardner states that these records still stood in 1952.

that he'd not felt for a long time, and he was keen to do more. If he could find a more forgiving surface, he mused, he was sure he could break international records.

More importantly, the achievement drew the attention of both the British press and Gardner's old friend Cecil Kimber. Twelve months after Lord Nuffield had cancelled the MG works racing programme, Kimber was keen to get an MG presence back on the track and into the papers, and saw Gardner's record attempts as a perfect opportunity to do both. Kimber offered him factory support for his next outing, including the services of Reg 'Jacko' Jackson and suggested he talk to Jack Woodhouse, MG's German distributor, to discuss whether the use of the new *Reichsautobahn* near Frankfürt could be arranged. Gardner agreed, and immediately wrote to Woodhouse, suggesting a record attempt be launched the following year.

The support of 'Jacko', as Gardner always called him[206] was hugely important. A flame-haired, good-looking thirty-year-old, he was responsible for all MG racing and had a reputation as a meticulous engineer with infinite patience. Hired by MG in October 1928, he had worked with George Eyston in 1931 to attempt to break the 100 miles-per-hour barrier in a 750cc car and it was MG legend that, in a single week before the attempt, Jackson put in 146 hours of work.[207] His phenomenal hard work helped deliver Eyston the record from under the nose of a rival bid by Malcolm Campbell and gained Jackson an inscribed silver cigarette holder from Eyston which he used to resupply his almost insatiable appetite for tobacco.[208] Having worked with him during the Ulster TT races, Gardner liked Jacko a lot, and was very happy with this arrangement.

206 In later life he preferred 'Reg' or 'Reggie' but to Goldie he was always 'Jacko'. Wilson McComb, *The Story of the MG Sports Car* (Littlehampton, 1972).
207 *Sports Car,* January 1975, p20.
208 Property of Tracey Rose, Jackson's granddaughter, who can remember his permanently tobacco-stained fingers.

In the meantime, Mariel's society connections had created another phenomenal opportunity for Gardner in America. At Westbury on Long Island, New York, a purpose-built, four-mile racing track had been created and a spectacular race planned for the opening on 12th October 1936. The Vanderbilt Cup race was intended to showcase American motorsport at its best, with the top drivers from around the world invited to take part and the inclusion of Goldie Gardner, the Brit who had taken part in the first stock car race, was seen as a win all round. Gardner leapt at the opportunity but knew that his chance of any sort of success would be slim at best, especially with the dominant Alfa Romeo racing team taking part. 'Nuvolari will win,' he proclaimed. 'There isn't a faster racing car in the world than that new Alfa of his. All out, it's good for 200 miles an hour. And he's just as good as his car.'[209]

With his MG away being prepared for its 1937 record-breaking season,[210] Gardner needed another mount for the race. He enlisted the help of Edward 'Teddy' Rayson, the 32-year-old smooth-faced son of a leading London barrister who owned a very capable Maserati 4CM.[211] The dashing Rayson, who Gardner had met at the Brighton Speed Trials,[212] readily agreed and followed on with his car a few days later aboard the *Queen Mary*. The car now on its way, Gardner was able to relax, and on arriving in America he and Mariel set off for a short break at her family home in Winona, Minnesota.

Rockledge was an impressive home by any measure. Tucked into the bluff overlooking the Mississippi river just south of the town of Winona, it had been designed for E.L. King Snr in 1912 by Chicago architect George Maher, an associate of Frank Lloyd Wright. The 10,000 square-foot mansion had been recently updated to the contemporary

---

209 Interview with his best man, Henry McLemore in *The Bend Bulletin*, (Oregon) Sep 8, 1936 p2.

210 The car may also have not fitted the very strict race regulation size of a track between 4'2" and 5"5 and being at least 31" wide at the seat.

211 This had previously belonged to Giuseppe Farina, the *Scuderia Ferrari* grand prix driver.

212 (NMM Archive photograph, 15 Sep 1934.

Art Deco style, with zebra-print sofas, brightly coloured vases, mirrored bathrooms and chrome fireplaces.[213] The couple spent two weeks there before heading back to New York and the opulent Vanderbilt Hotel on Park Avenue, where the suave Rayson was waiting with the Maserati. Gardner met him with a handshake then introduced his wife, the dashing young Englishman just three years Mariel's senior making an instant impression on her. They chatted, then the two men got down to business. Gardner had decided not to race the car, so Rayson was left to take on the new circuit.

And what a circuit it was. Four miles in length, with a hard-packed sand and gravel surface winding around 16 unbanked corners and a colossal 3,775-foot-long main straight, the purpose-built Roosevelt Raceway was unlike anything either of the men had driven on before. The outfield included huge, multi-layered stands, concrete and steel crash barriers and a chain-link fence to keep the 70,000 spectators at a safe distance from the cars, a novelty at the time. More impressive still was the prize money which the *London Daily News* proudly announced was a total of £20,000, (worth over £1.5M in 2023) and that 'Famous Britons to Compete'.[214]

It wasn't just famous Britons who were drawn by the cash reward: the dominant Scuderia Ferrari entered their three current Alfa Romeo Grand Prix cars, each a V12 four-litre supercharged 12C-36 model. The team's attendance had been sweetened by the race organisers paying passage, accommodation and chauffeurs for all 32 team members and their wives, four racing cars and a full inventory of spares.[215] On paper, the sleek Alfa Romeos should have been challenged by the hugely powerful dirt track racing cars of the American drivers, but once qualifying began it was clear that the Italian cars' suspension, steering

---

213 https://forgottenminnesota.com/forgotten-minnesota/2011/09/a-grand-estate-for-the-owners-of-the-watkins-medical-products-company
214 *London Daily News*, Thursday 24 September 1936, p11.
215 Brock Yates, *Vanderbilt Cup Race*, (Iconografix, 1997), p17. Driving the cars were Nino Farina, Antonio Brivio and ace driver Tazio Nuvolari, fresh from his Grand Prix win at Modena and who Gardner had tipped for success here.

and brakes totally outperformed the local specials, despite their sheer grunt. Rayson too was struggling: the little 1.5-litre engine of the Maserati was no match for the bigger cars and the loose track surface very difficult to navigate, especially around the winding course. He qualified a lowly 36th.

On the day of the race, the sun shone brightly as the crowds flocked into the circuit. Mariel, to her disgust, was forced into the stands by a course rule that forbade women in the pits and was joined by Gardner once he had made a tour of the cars and spoken to the drivers. They watched as a one-lap warm-up exhibition race of vintage cars took place,[216] then as the 45 qualifiers lined up on the grid for the main event. The cars were a very odd mix: state-of-the-art Alfa Romeos sat purring next to immense Indy 500 cars and brutally powerful dirt-track racing cars.[217] Nuvolari, who had experienced transmission trouble during qualifying, was on the third row and Rayson back in row 12.

The crescendo of revs rose to the starting flag then the cars stormed off the line in a cloud of dust. By the first corner, it was obvious that there was only one dominant force on the track: Nuvolari, who had already taken the lead and, other than a brief pit stop for spark plugs, kept it until the end of the 300-mile race. The 'Madman from Modena' as the local press dubbed him beamed as he was presented with the huge cup by George Vanderbilt while Rayson finished a lap behind, in a fair 18th place.[218]

That Gardner didn't race in the Vanderbilt Cup wasn't necessarily a problem for him. That he had been invited to enter and been mentioned as one of the *Daily News*'s 'famous Britons' was enough: it kept him in the company of the great drivers of the day, and that was essential for what he wanted to do next: travel to Germany and win his first

---

216 Won by Indy veteran Ralph Mulford in a Stutz Bearcat.
217 The front row was Brivio in his Alfa on the left, Billy Winn in a dirt-track racer and Wilbur Shaw in his two-man Indianapolis car. Shaw understeered into a fence and Winn's rear axle disintegrated, putting both out of the race.
218 Period newsreel: https://youtu.be/_RPa8KCCVkM

international speed records.[219] To do that, he needed sponsors other than MG, and that would take all of his powers of persuasion. With a lot on his mind, he travelled back to England.[220]

Back at Oakhurst Court though, life wasn't as straightforward as he had envisaged. His single-minded focus on his record-breaking plans was difficult for a strong, independent woman like Mariel to bear and the cracks in their relationship started to show. There was another element, too: it seemed that the dashing young Rayson had made a larger impact on Mariel than Gardner realised. Just days after she travelled back to the USA with Patricia for Christmas at the family home on Daytona Beach, Rayson also embarked, bound for Florida. Whether he knew the truth of what was going on or not, Gardner tried to reconcile with his young wife, but without success. She told him she would return to Britain on 23rd April to finalise her affairs, and when she embarked at New York she pointedly used her father's central-London bank as a holding address on the immigration paperwork.

It was too much for Gardner to bear. In the early hours of Thursday 22nd April 1937, the day before she was due to dock at Southampton, he roared down the Albert Bridge Road, Battersea, in his Mercedes-Benz SS, his fast and powerful cabriolet. His emotions for once got the better of him, and he returned to the one thing that made him feel alive: speed. His foot remained flat on the floor, pushing the vast, six-point-eight-litre engine to its maximum, and the tyres screamed as he pulled the wheel violently around every corner as if to shake the anger from his mind. Finally, he pushed it too far: the car clipped a kerb, smashed head-on into a street refuge, and rolled through two 'keep left' signs and a lamp post before coming to a steaming halt, slewed across the road, with parts scattered all around. Both front wheels had been ripped off by the initial impact, which left the front wings a crum-

---

219 Class G (750cc to 1,100cc) international records.
220 His details are included in the immigration paperwork for the SS Aquitania, departing New York 20 October 1936, but are lined-out in pencil. There is no mention of Mariel or Patricia. It is possible he travelled back with them by air later, as all three were in England by December 1936 (www.ancestry.com)

pled mass of twisted metal and the chassis bent almost beyond repair. Gardner's limp body lay trapped in the wreckage, the broken steering wheel pinned to his chest and blood streaming from cuts all over his face, arms, and body. Passers-by rushed to help and were soon joined by twenty firemen who arrived in five fire engines. He told them he had skidded on a wet road and didn't mention the turmoil going through his mind.[221] Taken to Battersea Hospital, he was found to have no broken bones but was kept in for observation. While there, he regained some of his stoical disposition and wrote to the editor of *The Evening News* to complain that he had been described as 'one-legged' in their coverage of the crash. A full retraction was printed that Saturday.

Mariel's trip back proved to be the final act in their relationship. On her return to Daytona, she filed for divorce and within twelve months she was openly travelling with Rayson, the pair of them entering the E.L. King residence as their final destination.[222] Meanwhile, Gardner had been released from hospital after a week and although battered and bruised, tried to pull himself together. The loss of his marriage after such a short time and falling so deeply in love with Mariel was deeply distressing and for a while he wondered how he would continue, but two small rays of sunshine glinted in the darkness.

The first was a letter from Jack Woodhouse, the MG agent in Germany, informing him that the German authorities had agreed a date in June for his record attempt and would provide time-keeping apparatus, police to secure the road and accommodation at the Frankfürter Hof Hotel. Although there was much more to do, his first major speed record attempt had been given the green light.

The second was a strange one. Gardner was quite surprised by all the press attention given to his Battersea accident and the way in which he was reported: as he had been in America, he was always referred

---

221 *The Standard*, April 22 1937.

222 Goldie's knowledge of Mariel's relationship with Rayson was assumed although largely unspoken, given the norms of the time (Interview Ros Gardner).

to as 'Goldie Gardner' and usually either 'racing motorist' or 'famous racer'. Although he had always been Goldie to his friends, this was different. ATG Gardner the Brooklands racer was put to bed and Goldie Gardner the speed record driver stepped up. It was the incentive he needed; his stiff upper lip came firmly back into place, he instructed the engineers at Milne & Russell to rebuild his Mercedes-Benz, and he threw himself into his preparations for the Frankfürt run.

The first priority was the record car which was left in the hands of Robin Jackson who removed the 'Brooklands' fan-tail exhaust and carefully rebuilt the engine to include a purpose-built bronze head and new supercharger.[223] Next, the problem of transporting the car was solved thanks to Eric Fernihough ('Ferni'), a contender for the motorcycle speed record who offered the use of his truck, which he told Goldie he was happy to drive.

The date the Germans had suggested was in mid-June at the Frankfürt - Darmstadt autobahn when other German drivers would be attempting speed records. Desperate to show that German engineering was world-beating and keen to create a sport that would regenerate a sense of national pride, Hitler and his propaganda chief Joseph Goebbels had state-funded the Auto Union and Mercedes-Benz racing teams to the point at which they were almost unbeatable by the mid-1930s. Their drivers became German heroes: Rudolf Caracciola winning the European Drivers' Championship – the forerunner of the F1 world championship – an unprecedented four times for the Mercedes Silver Arrows, his main rival being Auto Union ace Bernd Rosemeyer whose marriage to the glamorous aviatrix Elly Beinhorn made them the 1930s equivalent of the Beckhams. Having dominated racing, the Nazi spin machine decided that speed records were next, a display not just of German automotive strength but also a chance to highlight their impressive new autobahn network to the world. The inclusion in this

---

223 No 10 Supercharger. Jackson also fitted a special camshaft and added parts from the larger No. 11
      Powerplus to increase the supercharger's pressure. *Maintaining the Breed, (ibid)* p101.

of a disabled, 6'3", 47-year-old British war veteran in a repurposed racing car delivered in a borrowed truck was extraordinary but possibly seen as the chance to humiliate the old British foe, especially as he wasn't attempting the more prominent record classes. Anglo-German relationships were still civil – just – but Hitler's support of the nationalist cause in the Spanish Civil War and his growing talk of *lebensraum*[224] had created a growing tension between the two countries. Nevertheless, when Goldie, Ferni, Jacko (lent by Kimber) and Robin Jackson (travelling in his Bentley with Freddie Clifford along for the ride) arrived at the 'sinister'[225] border post at the German frontier, they were waved through with a smile. After an overnight stop in Cologne, they arrived in Frankfürt where Goldie and Clifford wasted no time in reporting to Prince Richard von Hesse, *Group Führer* of the Nationalsozialistisches Kraftfahrkorps (N.S.K.K.), the paramilitary German group responsible for 'fitness in motoring skills' and the organisation responsible for running the event. After an embarrassment of heel-clicking and Nazi saluting, von Hesse made it clear that the British team really were *very* welcome and told them that the track was theirs from dawn on 15th June. Goldie couldn't (or wouldn't) speak German, so an official interpreter was supplied who remained with them throughout, no doubt reporting back to his superiors.

At dawn on 15th June, the MG was unloaded from Ferni's truck and was immediately surrounded by inquisitive Germans, most of them in uniform, who were ignored by the team. Jacko and Robin Jackson, wearing a garishly striped blazer, checked over the car whilst Goldie donned his brown leather racing helmet and puffed on a cigarette. Just one track of the dual carriageway was shut, but it was enough; the smooth surface, long straights and gently sweeping bends were just what Goldie had longed for to see what the car could do. With a push, the funny-looking car was away, the revs building as it flashed past the

---

224 Living Space, the expansion of Germany to include what Hitler saw as ethnic Germans.
225 *Magic MPH*, (ibid), p45.

watching Germans and through the measured section. By the end of the day, Goldie had set new Class G world records in both the flying kilometre and flying mile[226] but was fortunate with the weather; the following day Bernd Rosemeyer took to the same track, but crosswinds twice pushed his car onto the grass verge, only his masterful driving preventing catastrophe.[227]

Goldie was pleased with what they had achieved, but the team knew that both car and driver could do more. At top speed, the engine had developed a misfire, preventing him from hitting the 150 miles-per-hour target he'd set himself. Although the Germans couldn't give them any more time on the road now, von Hesse promised to allow them back in October, but that was too long for the impatient Goldie. Before leaving England, he had provisionally arranged to use the banked track at Montlhéry on the outskirts of Paris, and the team quickly packed up and set off to France. This time, the border crossing was more painful; whether the Englishman was seen as an upstart for breaking two world records in their back garden or whether it was just a particularly officious guard on the post that day, the result was a long delay during which the British men were pushed around and their car stripped of all belongings. Eventually allowed to proceed, the team headed west, Jacko and Ferni directly to Montlhéry and Goldie, Jackson and Clifford taking a detour to watch the 24 Hours of Le Mans.

It wasn't a happy experience. On the eighth lap of the race at the tricky Maison Blanche corner a French amateur driver[228] rolled his car and was thrown out to his death. British driver Pat Fairfield was following close behind and was unable to avoid the car now slewed across the track, smashed into it and was then shunted by another car. Fairfield was pulled from the wreckage and taken to a private hospital, but his situation was grave. Goldie, Jackson and Clifford were old friends

---

226 Flying Km at 142.2 miles-per-hour (old record 138.84 miles-per-hour).
       and Mile 148.5 miles-per-hour (old 131.96).
227 https://www.topgear.com/car-news/big-reads/bernd-rosemeyer-trail-auto-unions-269 miles-per-hour-hero
228 René Kippeurt in a Bugatti.

and quickly left the circuit to sit with him until his wife could fly over from England. The following day, Goldie and his team departed for Montlhéry and soon after, having never recovered full consciousness, Fairfield died.

At the Montlhéry track, other challenges beset the group. Jacko had to leave for home soon after their arrival, and despite their best efforts, the car's misfire continued to get worse, Robin Jackson even changing two of the pistons in an unsuccessful attempt to solve the problem.[229] Nevertheless, the run on the huge, banked oval track was a success, setting four new international Class G records for flying five- and ten- kilometre and mile targets.[230] An attempt to break the hour record ended when the induction manifold split, but as Goldie had passed the 50km point, he established a new record at that distance at 123.21 miles-per-hour. The achievement also gained Gardner the coveted Montlhéry gold button-hole badge for lapping at over 200kph and the rare 'Record Man' pin. With Ferni on the way back to England carrying the car, the rest of the team celebrated in Paris before heading home.

Back in England, work to improve the car started. A Zoller supercharger replaced the Powerplus unit and Jackson designed a new inlet manifold to replace the troublesome item that had ended their Montlhéry attempt. Stub exhausts were fitted and the radiator fairing adapted to clean the overall appearance and improve streamlining.[231] By the time they were due to depart again for Germany, the team were sure that the car would run well.

This time, having been given a *Laissez-Passer* (free passage) document by the German Embassy in London, they had no issues crossing the border but on their arrival in Frankfürt were amazed by the scale of the event which was much larger than back in June. Keen to

229 *The Works MGs*, (ibid), p120.
230 5km at 130.5 miles-per-hour, 5 mile 130.0 miles-per-hour, 10km 129.8 miles-per-hour and 10 mile 129.4 miles-per-hour.
231 Gas entered this new induction manifold at the centre, rather than the end. *Maintaining the Breed* (ibid) p102.

showcase Nazi automotive power, the N.S.K.K. had closed the autobahn for a week, designating it *Rekordwoche* (Record Week) and inviting Mercedes-Benz, Auto Union and BMW teams to make attempts
on various records. Goldie was in glittering company, with every star
driver there: Rosemeyer and Carracciola, Englishman Dick Seaman
who had been appointed as one of the Mercedes-Benz Grand Prix
drivers, motorcycle record-holder Ernst Henne and all-round Italian
speed man Piero Taruffi.

But it was Gardner's turn first. On Monday 25th October, in crisp
but dry weather, he removed his overcoat and leather driving gloves,
donned his helmet and was pushed to the start by Jacko and Ferni. By
11am, he had finished, setting new flying mile and kilometre records,
but still found that over 6,100rpm the engine misfired and slowed. On
Wednesday he ran again but could not improve on his times so Jackson
again decided to again replace two pistons. This helped, and when he
drove again on Friday he raised his Class G records once more despite
the misfire still lingering at higher speeds, but the 150 miles-per-hour
barrier still eluded him.[232]

Between his own runs, he watched the others and learnt. On 26th he
saw Rosemeyer battling his Auto Union around the autobahn bend at
phenomenal speed, becoming the first person to break the 400kph (248
miles-per-hour) barrier on a public road and later having to be dragged
unconscious from the car, having peaked at over 250 miles-per-hour. By
the end of the week, Rosemeyer had set three world records and was a
national hero. Goldie recognised Rosemeyer's fortitude, but was more
interested in the shape of his car: the Type C was a smooth, low silver
bullet with fully enclosed wheels that made the most of its V16 power in direct contrast to the upright, open-wheel Magnette. Later, with
Jacko, he spoke to chief Auto Union designer Robert Eberan von Eberhorst, who congratulated Goldie on his achievement and commented

---

232 Flying KM to 148.8 miles-per-hour, flying mile to 148.7 miles-per-hour, 5km to 143.6 miles-per-hour
     and 5 miles to 144.6 miles-per-hour.

with Germanic[233] directness that the next logical step in the MG's development should be an all-enclosed, streamlined body.[234] Goldie knew he was right.

But in the meantime, Goldie basked in the praise he received. Back in Britain, despite having added limited value to the record attempt, MG jumped on his success and printed full-page adverts that announced his success with the headline 'International records BEATEN!' In Germany, the response was just as positive, with the *Berliner Illustrierte Zeitung* devoting a page header to two photographs of him in the MG on 28th October, announcing that he was England's *Meisterfahrer* (Master Driver). 'It was certainly a most memorable event,' Goldie wrote with his usual lack of drama, but his thoughts were already on the following year and how he was going to create a car that would not just stretch the records but smash them. For that, he needed money. He needed the full support of Lord Nuffield's Morris empire.

---

233 Although at this time he may have been considered 'German', Eberan von Eberhorst was born in Austria.

234 *Maintaining the Breed*, (ibid), p102.

12

THE STREAMLINED JOB

Back in England, Goldie spoke to both Jacko and Robin Jackson to see what they thought about creating an even faster machine. Both agreed that the body had already achieved its full potential but the engine had more to give, although the engine misfire was still a sore point. Robin Jackson had been entrusted with its build and Jacko, feeling that this could reflect badly on the MG Car Company, suggested that the valve seats had cracked. The egotistical Robin Jackson did not take this criticism well and refused to let Jacko look at the engine, an already frosty relationship between the two degenerating further.

Meanwhile, Goldie set off for Abingdon to try to persuade Kimber to build a record car for him. Kim loved the idea and told him he would like nothing more than to get back into the racing world, but he had been strictly forbidden from doing so. None of the current Morris models were suitable to use as a base and the thought of building a record car around an obsolete chassis would not have been acceptable to the company. At this point, Jacko came up with an idea: George Eyston's old EX135 record-breaking car was currently up for sale at Bellevue Garages, which he suggested would make a perfect chassis as it was an 'official' MG experimental car. Syd Enever, the head of MG's experimental department, was asked his opinion and replied that with a streamlined body, it should be capable of 170 miles-per-hour. A now-excited Kim told Goldie that he would have to approach Lord Nuffield directly. Goldie wrote to him without delay, setting out his plan.[235]

Nuffield replied on 20th December 1937. 'I think your proposition is a very good one,' he wrote. 'I shall be only too pleased to authorize (sic) the M.G. Company to do as you suggest… I think it will be best for you to settle details direct with him [Kimber].' Goldie kept the letter, writing on it, 'THE OK TO GO AHEAD WITH THE SPECIAL STREAM-LINED 1100CC JOB.'[236]

He didn't need to be told twice and immediately made an arrangement to purchase EX135 and transport both cars to Abingdon, starting work in the new year. Robin Jackson was to continue with the development of the engine but Jacko, supported by Enever, was to run the project, seeking whatever external help he needed. The plan was to use the engine out of Goldie's Magnette, mated to a framed body covered in a smooth aluminium body. The original engine out of EX135 would be put into the other car which would then be sold.

Enever was another huge addition to Goldie's team. A self-taught engineer who built go-karts and boats as a young boy and almost killed himself when a home-made cannon exploded in his face, Syd joined Morris Garages aged 14 in 1920. In his first few years there, his 'near wizardry'[237] for rapid diagnosis and rectification of engine problems became the stuff of legend and he was appointed head of the experimental department in 1929. His propensity for hard work matched even that of Jacko, and as a pair they became an extraordinary force to be reckoned with and firm friends. Away from work, both men had

235 More details are given in *The Works MGs*, (ibid) p120-121.
236 Letter, NMM Archive.
237 David Ash, *Sports Car* magazine, January 1975, p19.

few other interests except they both had an 'eye for the ladies',[238] a pastime that nestled comfortably with their frequent all-expenses-paid overseas jaunts.

Jacko, Enever and Robin Jackson concentrated on the engine, trying to solve the high-speed issues. It wasn't a happy time; Jackson's testbed couldn't replicate the problem and he bridled when the sometimes-blunt Enever suggested that it lacked the air pressure required to run the engine at very high speeds. The engine was brought to Abingdon, and on the MG factory testbed the cause of the misfire was quickly identified: the exhaust valves were overheating and the cylinder head began to lift at over 6,000rpm, allowing a fine spray of water to escape into the cylinders and short-circuit one of the spark plugs, seemingly a different one each time. It was no wonder that the frequent swapping of pistons had achieved no effect. The troublesome inlet manifold also caused friction between the two Jacksons, with Reg stating that it wasn't much better than the factory one. Robin, unsurprisingly, didn't like this one bit.[239]

Reid Railton, maker of speed-record cars and boats who had just completed John Cobb's world land speed record car, was enlisted to build the body. First, the car was stripped down to its basic components and a plan drafted to put the driver just 7 inches from the ground. At over 6-feet tall, Goldie was too big to sit upright without affecting the frontal area, so a 45-degree back rest was fitted, leaving the driver in a very similar position to that of today's Formula 1 drivers, with a vertical height (seat to shoulders) of only 22". The propshaft was mounted in a 6-degree offset position to the left of the driver which kept the overall height (and centre of gravity) low and the fuel tank positioned to the driver's left, balancing weight distribution. Special road wheels with restricted steering movement reduced the track and gave just ¾"

238 Peter Thornley, *Mr MG* (Magna Press 2003), p35. Jackson was remembered as a 'bit of a philanderer' by his family. (Interview Tracey Rose, Feb 23).
239 There is a more detailed explanation of how the engine issues were solved in *The Works MGs*, (ibid) p121.

clearance when on full lock, and bespoke Dunlop tyres inflated to 60psi were fitted and carefully balanced. The structure now complete, the streamlined body could be designed.

On 28th January 1938, on the same day that Bernd Rosemeyer died,[240] Rudolf Caracciola took back from him the speed record for a car on a public road with an astonishing run of 432.7kph (268 miles-per-hour) over the flying kilometre in his Mercedes-Benz W125 *Rekordwagen*, a speed that was not bettered in an officially timed run until 2017.[241] Using the Mercedes as inspiration, Railton penned a smooth outline complete with enclosed wheels and pointed tail but quickly discovered that the design was covered by a patent owned by W. Keller and Company of Stuttgart, the work of master aerodynamicist Paul Jaray.[242] This worked out to the British team's favour though as Keller were happy to license the original design, allowing the new EX135 to be an almost carbon copy of the W125 that had benefitted from many hours of aerodynamic development. In addition, the underside of the body was completely flat, creating a ground effect, decades before Colin Chapman designed this into his Formula 1 cars. The body of the car was designed to be easily removable from the chassis and quick-release panels fitted to cover the wheels. An aircraft-style Perspex bubble canopy was provided to shield Goldie's face, left open to allow air to circulate.[243] The two Jacksons, aided greatly by the objective practical advice of Syd Enever, had managed to solve the engine woes with a combination of sodium-filled valves and a modified coolant channel that redirected water away from the head. Fuel supply too was im-

---

240 Just two weeks previously on 12th January 1938, Gardner had travelled to Frankfurt once again to watch Rosemeyer pilot the Auto Union *Stromlinienwagen* along the autobahn. Afterwards, they posed for a photograph, Gardner linking arms with the awkward-looking German (Getty Images).

241 The record was finally beaten by Koenigsegg factory driver Niklas Lilja in an Agera RS in November 2017 at a closed-road event in Nevada, averaging 277.9 miles-per-hour. https://www.topgear.com/car-news/supercars/koenigsegg-has-smashed-worlds-fastest-car-record

242 *The Autocar*, June 29th 1938 p193. Jaray was an Austrian Jew and as such his key involvement in the design of the record-breaking German cars was officially suppressed. Thornley stated that 'The nose of the body was designed to have a fairly steep fall-off towards the front, a feature it was subsequently found to be covered by the German 'Jaray' patents' *Maintaining the Breed*, (ibid), p103.

243 A very detailed description of the build is given in *Maintaining the Breed*, (ibid) p104-109.

proved; Les Kesterton of S.U. Carburettors was drafted in to support the team, and the Shell company developed the fuel mixture to include nitromethane, which MG called 'Dynamin A' to prevent details of their secret ingredient from escaping.[244] As a result, Reid's calculations, when combined with Robin Jackson's expectations for the motor, suggested the new car should indeed be capable of 170 miles-per-hour, as Enever had surmised.

Goldie's personal life was also progressing at speed. The previous year, he met a 20-year-old young lady called Hester Jackson (no relation to either of his teammates), they had an intense affair and on 23rd December 1937 they announced their engagement in *The Times*. This came as a shock to her father, a Mexico City-based financier, who did not take kindly to his young daughter taking up with a recently divorced racing driver who was almost as old as he was. Another person surprised to read the announcement in *The Times* had been Mariel, who was still using the surname Gardner. Despite having been granted a divorce in America, she was not happy about her ex-husband moving on from her quite so quickly (despite herself own relationship with Teddy Rayson[245]) and took legal advice. She was told that her divorce was not legally binding in Britain and started legal proceedings in London, alleging adultery.

Refusing to be distracted by this, he pushed ahead with the development of EX135. By the early summer of 1938, the car was coming together nicely and the full weight of the Morris Motors press team swung into action. Photographs of the wooden buck were published in *The Motor* and a picture of Goldie being measured by Reid Railton was printed in the *Daily Mirror*. A two-page article in *The Autocar* included a cut-away drawing and published technical details of the engine and drivetrain. By August, it was ready, and Goldie accepted an invite from

---

244 An interesting article about MG racing fuels is included in the April 2022 edition of *Safety Fast* magazine.
245 The affair seems to have started in January 1938 and lasted until December of that year. During this time, they travelled together across the Atlantic at various times, and on 25th March 1938, Rayson flew into Miami, stating he was going to the King residence in Daytona Beach. (www.ancestry.com).

the BARC to demonstrate the car at the August Bank Holiday Meeting at Brooklands, seeing it as an opportunity to run the car at speed. The car was very well received by the inquisitive spectators, who marvelled at its sweeping body, clad in British Racing Green paint and emblazoned with the MG octagon behind the driver's compartment and another on the nose, a Union Flag on each side and a white lightning bolt along the length of each flank. Held back by a fence, the crowd surged to watch as Goldie donned his goggles and leather windcap and climbed in the car. He set off down the start/finish straight but immediately the combination of rock-hard tyres, unforgiving suspension and the pock-marked surface of the Brooklands track wasn't a happy one. 'I was shaken up and down like a sardine in a tin… being kept in the car only by the flat underneath portion of the steering wheel hitting my tummy, and the top of my head cracking up against the top of the Perspex blister,' he wrote.[246] Nevertheless, the run gave him a great deal of confidence as the car had behaved beautifully despite the jarring. On the billiard table-flat surface of the autobahn, he mused, it should run perfectly.

He didn't have long to wait to find out. The next set of speed tests in Frankfürt was scheduled for November but Jack Woodhouse had been in touch, telling Goldie about rumours that the Germans were building a very special autobahn section between Dessau and Bitterfeld to the north of Leipzig that would be perfect for record runs. At the Donington Grand Prix on 22nd October, Goldie tracked down General Hühnleim, the *Korpsführer* of the N.S.K.K. who had just been promoted to the second-highest political rank in the Nazi Party, and Leo von Beyer-Ehrenberg, another top N.S.K.K. official. Hühnleim said that the Dessau stretch was unlikely to be available in time but agreed to meet Kim the following week in Berlin by which time he would know for sure. True to his word, they met as planned but the news wasn't ideal: Kim telephoned Goldie on 31st October to tell him that Des-

---

246 *Magic MPH*, (ibid) p56.

sau wasn't ready but he had been given authority to use the road at Frankfürt again.

This would do. By now, Goldie knew the Frankfürt road extremely well and it gave him a chance to compare the two cars, his old one and the new EX135. On 1st November, the team set off from England, meeting at their destination two days later. Compared with his privateer attempts of the past two years, this group felt much more professional: a sign-painted Morris commercial lorry had been provided, and both Jacko and Syd Enever were there officially as was 'Kes' Kesterton from SU Carburettors. Kim couldn't stay away, and met them directly from Berlin, keen to see how this new EX135 would run. Nor could Goldie's fiancée Hester, who he allowed the rare privilege of accompanying him, and who donned a stylish Germanic hat complete with pheasant feather over her curled blonde hair. In a photograph taken at the time, she looks smug. Goldie looks uncomfortable.[247]

But the weather wasn't on their side. Sheets of water flooded the track over the weekend, and the group were forced to wait. Jack Woodhouse did his best to entertain them, hosting a party on Monday evening that ended with Freddie Clifford immersing himself completely in a pond, but otherwise they just waited for the skies to clear. Finally, on the morning of Wednesday 9th October, the rain stopped.[248] Quickly, the team deployed in the cold of the dawn: Robin Jackson to point 'Kilometre Nr. 12' where he would turn the car around, leaving the others at the start, 'Kilometre Nr. 2', near the airport. The car was quickly fuelled, fired up and shot off down the road, only to splutter to a halt within a few yards.[249] Rolled back to the start, the team scratched their heads. The engine had run perfectly on the testbed and the only difference anyone could think of was that the carburettor intakes were

---

247 Unpublished photograph. Gardner was later very unwilling to allow his wife, Una to accompany any of his record attempts (family reminiscence).

248 Gardner incorrectly recorded this as 4th November in *Magic MPH*.

249 In *Magic MPH*, Gardner remembers that he drove this test run; in *The Works MGs* p122, Jackson was said to be the driver. However, in *Maintaining the Breed*, Thornley states that Jackson was already at Km 12 at this point.

now under pressure from air being forced into the front of the car. Kes was brought in to investigate and started pulling apart the carburettors, only to exclaim in surprise as a piece of wood, ½" long and the diameter of a pencil, floated out with the fuel. Quickly removed, the parts were reassembled, hard spark plugs and racing wheels fitted and the engine restarted. Goldie was ready to see what the car could do.

He set off and by the second kilometre post had hit what he thought was top gear, but the instruments made him doubt himself. Without a speedometer he had to rely on the rev counter and had been told not to exceed 7,300rpm on the first run, but by the time he arrived at the timing strip, the engine was pushing 7,500rpm without anything like the full use of the throttle and he felt the car had a lot more to give. Worried that he had missed a gear and was actually in third, and terrified that he could blow the engine on the first run, he held the revs back until he finally saw Jackson waving his arms at the finish.[250] Instinctively, he stamped on the brake pedal and the cold rear drums locked out on the damp road, the car fishtailing to a halt and providing a moment of alarm for the onlookers. Having turned, he pulled up next to Jackson and yelled, 'What gear am I in?' Jackson's heart sank, but just then a German signaller ran over with a message that had been sent by telephone from the timing officials. The speed was 288.692kph, or 179 miles-per-hour. Jackson smiled, relieved: the car had been in top. On the return run, Goldie could let the car stretch its legs; he now realised their calculations of 170 miles-per-hour had been very cautious. He told him to go flat out; even if the engine gave up half-way through, it would probably coast fast enough to take the record.

After Jackson had checked the plugs and refilled the fuel tank, Goldie rolled off again, building up speed. This time, he did as Jackson had instructed, pushing the accelerator flat to the floor until he saw 8,300rpm on the rev gauge, then eased as he passed through the end of

---

250 Laurence Pomeroy later reported in *The Motor* (Nov 22 1938) that the car had run out of fuel at the mile marker on the first run and coasted for three miles until the turnaround point).

the timed section and slowed until he saw his colleagues. As he climbed from the cockpit, the official timer had reported: an average of 194.52 miles-per-hour, giving him both flying kilometre and mile records in excess of 186 miles-per-hour[251], and with his top speed reaching over 196 miles-per-hour. The team were jubilant, and while Goldie was given hearty congratulations, they checked the car over, ready to run again to improve on his 5km and 5-mile records.

But it was not to be. Aluminium shavings were found in the engine[252] (later found to be caused by the supercharger vanes scraping its end cover) and any future runs were called off as a precaution. Only then was it realised that Robin Jackson had been marooned at the finish line, and was recovered by Laurence Pomeroy, writing for *The Motor*, who lent the freezing Jackson his coat. The German authorities were astounded at the speeds reached and said that they would not have allowed it to go ahead with traffic driving down the opposite carriageway had they known. Herr Mikle, chief assistant to Dr. Ferdinand Porsche, immediately travelled down from Stuttgart to see the car and offered some advice on further improving its streamlining.[253]

That night, once the German scrutineers had inspected the car, the results were made official. Celebrations ensued: at first a pleasant but rather tame dinner party at the Frankfürter Hof Hotel hosted by Kim, later degenerating into *bierkeller* drinking that ended with Goldie and Freddie Clifford being challenged to a pistol-shooting competition at four in the morning at a German cavalry officers' mess.

But as they walked back to their hotel just before dawn, there was a tense atmosphere in the city that the two British men were aware of even in their inebriated state. This night, for all its jollity, was one that would become infamous; as they climbed into their beds just after 6am, they heard the sound of glass shattering from the hotel across the street,

---

251 Flying Km at 186.6 miles-per-hour, flying mile at 186.5 miles-per-hour.

252 Gardner reports these as having been found in one of the exhaust stubs; Thornley says they were coating the spark plugs.

253 *The Motor*, 22 November 1938, p737.

immediately followed by what Gardner described as 'the most awful pandemonium'. This was *Kristallnacht*, the pogrom of the Jews. By the end of the following day, nearly 300 synagogues and over 7,000 Jewish businesses had been destroyed, with 30,000 Jewish men rounded up. The 'Nazi bestiality was clearly visible throughout our return run out of Germany,' Gardner wrote, 'and we were very glad to find ourselves back again in Belgium.'[254]

Back at home, Goldie considered what the team had achieved. In a year, he had gone from driving a car that couldn't quite reach 150 miles-per-hour to one that very nearly broke the 200 mile-per-hour barrier. Everyone was enthused: Goldie himself, keen to return to the wonderful German roads to prove himself and the team who were convinced they could generate more speed with a few tweaks. There was no question of stopping now and Jacko and Syd immediately set about disassembling the car. The new sodium valves and piston crowns were found to be in excellent condition as were the tyres, which manufacturers Dunlop stated had nevertheless reached their speed limit and would have to be redesigned for future use. Once the supercharger issue had been identified and solved, the team took Herr Mikle's suggestions and removed the large 'MG' badge from the nose, redesigned the projecting air intake and angled the stub exhausts angled backwards at 45 degrees.[255] Enever was now convinced it could easily exceed 200 miles-per-hour.

Meanwhile, the world slowly awoke to the presence of this new British phenomenon. On Friday 18th November, a banquet was held at the Savoy Hotel in London to celebrate Goldie's achievement and that of George Eyston, John Cobb and Dick Seaman, *The Daily Mail*[256] call-

---

254 *Magic MPH*, (ibid), p63.
255 The engine was found to have run well over its peak delivery of just under 7,000rpm during the Frankfürt run, hitting around 185bhp. As a result, the gear ratios were changed from 3.6 to 3.09:1. The supercharger gearing was also changed, leading to a 17% increase in blower speed. The result, run on the testbed in January 1939, was a peak of 202bhp at 7,500rpm. *Maintaining the Breed* (ibid), p116, *The Motor*, 22 Nov 1938, p737.
256 *The Daily Mail*, 19 Nov 1938.

ing the four men, 'strong, silent speed kings' and announcing that they were all heroes. The following month, with EX135 already on a tour of MG showrooms around the country, Viscount Nuffield held a luncheon at the *Trocadero* restaurant, again inviting the stars of the motoring world. Kimber spoke first, taking time to criticise the British press for their previous 'general disregard of the M.G. achievement' but otherwise everyone remained in the best of spirits. At the end, Nuffield presented Goldie with a mounted silver model of EX135, cufflinks were presented to the other team members and Kimber told Goldie that he would be given a new Tickford-bodied drophead MG WA when they were released, the most luxurious car that the company had on their books.[257] It was a significant gift, but Kimber understood the importance of what Goldie had achieved for MG. 'From a sales point of view this record cannot be stressed too much, the point being that the brains behind the design of the record car are also responsible for the cars you are selling,' he wrote in a letter to all sales departments. Kim knew that not only would plaudits follow, but also increased sales of road cars.[258]

The press loved the fact that a British racing car driven by a war hero had broken records in the Germans' own back yard, but it was the awards from within the motoring world that meant most to Goldie. The British Racing Drivers' Club (BRDC) awarded him their prestigious Gold Star award, marking the pre-eminent British driver of the year[259] and Prince Richard von Hesse sent a beautiful leather-bound book from himself and the N.S.K.K., emblazoned on the cover with the Nazi eagle and swastika, recording the event with photographs taken by his men.[260] Then, on Thursday 26th January 1939, the Segrave Trophy Awarding Committee met at the Royal Automobile Club in Pall Mall, London, and decided that the 1938 recipient should be Major A.T. Goldie Gardner.

---

257 The dinner was on 15th December 1938.
258 Sales Letter No 6 dated June 1939. Malcolm Green, *The MG Story* (Herridge, 2020), p200.
259 To put this in context, the 2021/22 BRDC Gold Star winner was Sir Lewis Hamilton.
260 NMM Archive.

This was a huge accolade. The Segrave Trophy was (and remains) arguably the most prestigious award for achievement for the 'British subject who gives the most outstanding demonstration of the possibilities of transport by land, air or water,'[261] its roll of honour a who's who of racing and record-breaking greats. 'When the average man is nearing his fifties, he usually seeks a quiet life,' the official Segrave Trophy award proclamation stated, 'So it is curious to find that one of the greatest motor drivers of our generation, Major A.T.G. Gardner, captured the world's record for light cars at the age of 48. '"Goldie" to his innumerable friends – though the quietest of men – has never sought a peaceful existence... This splendid performance has greatly raised the reputation of British cars throughout the world. Everyone in motoring circles has a great opinion of "Goldie" – except "Goldie" himself.'

Despite the plaudits, and with newspapers as far afield as Tasmania[262] now having woken up to his achievements, Goldie couldn't wait to get away from the limelight and back on the road. He now had something to prove: he wanted to be the first person to travel 200 miles-per-hour in a light car.

---

261 The 1939 Segrave Trophy award document.
262 *Hobart Mercury*, 'Capabilities of New MG Machine'. 19 November 1938.

13

THE DOUBLE TON

By the end of March 1939, EX135 had finished its tour of showrooms and was back at the MG factory in Abingdon. Meanwhile, the storm clouds of war had been growing ever darker over the continent. The Germans marched into Czechoslovakia, prompting Great Britain and France to guarantee the borders of the Polish state in an attempt to deter any more German expansion. Goldie, reading the headlines, was deeply concerned; he had experienced the descent into war once before, and this felt just as ominous. He decided to call the team together to discuss whether they thought another record run that summer in Germany was still a good idea.

A few days later, the men met in Abingdon. Goldie gave each a chance to have their say, listening as they each voiced their opinions. Arrangements were in place for another run, this time at the new motorway near Dessau starting on 31st May, but if the team felt it was too risky, he would postpone the venture. By unanimous agreement, it was decided to press on. Their experience over the last few years was that the Germans had done everything in their power to facilitate the team and, more importantly, this new autobahn promised to be the best possible location to try to break the 200 miles-per-hour barrier. Unbeknownst to the British men, the dead-straight road between Dessau and Bitterfeld, just north of Leipzig, had been built as an auxiliary aircraft runway. 25 metres wide, with no grass central reservation, pillarless bridges and a marble-flat surface, it was perfect for the task of breaking speed records. The risk, the men decided, was worth it.

The next couple of months went quickly. The car was prepared while Goldie worked on the logistics of the trip and built press interest in his next attempt. Finally, the car, spares and team departed from Dover, and on arrival in Germany on Monday 29th May, it seemed as if their fears had been unfounded. The O.N.S., the German motorsport authority, seemed to have gone out of their way to help the British, and had set aside a garage and yard at the Dessau police station for their use, complete with a fully equipped timing lorry, a refreshment van, a fire engine, a meteorological unit and even a loudspeaker van to play music while they worked on the car.[263] Impressed, the British group retired to their hotel, the *Goldener Beutel*[264] to decide a plan of action. The team – this time significantly expanded from the previous year but with the notable absence of Robin Jackson[265] – were keen to see the road, and a reconnaissance of the autobahn was made that evening where there was much poring over a *Hallwag* road map[266] and discussion about where Goldie should accelerate and brake. The following day, having fitted the race wheels to the car, they returned for a final look and were amazed to see the lengths to which the Germans were going to prepare the road, with the centre line being repainted and a sweeper brushing the concrete dust away.

By 8am, the team was at the start, the car was ready and Goldie raring to go. The Germans looked on with interest. Compared with the

---

263 *Maintaining the Breed*, (ibid) p116.
264 Golden Bottle.
265 The team consisted of Goldie, Jacko and Syd, with George Tuck (MG), Chris Shorrock (superchargers), Les Kesterton and A. Bicknell (SU Carburettors), Johnny Lurani and a representative from Dunlop's German office.
266 The original is now part of the NMM Archive. It has a large, pencil cross over Dessau.

young, chiselled Silver Arrows drivers they were used to dealing with, Gardner seemed a throwback to an earlier generation: dressed in baggy trousers secured at the ankles by puttees, his shirt was covered by a short-sleeve knitted tank top with his BRDC badge hand-sewn on over the left breast and a winged MG insignia pinned above it. He had put some weight on in recent months and his stomach bulged slightly over the leather belt strapped around his middle. The look was completed with white windcap, spotted silk scarf, goggles perched on his brow and ubiquitous cigarette hanging from his lips. He didn't look like a record breaker but looks could be deceptive; the Germans were aware what he had achieved previously at Frankfürt and knew better than to discount this old racer.

As the team bustled around the car and the swastika-clad O.N.S. officials concluded their preparations, Goldie remained placid. 'I know most racing men, but I have seldom seen one so singularly unmoved as Major Gardner,' later wrote *Autocar*'s John Dugdale who had been asked by Goldie to accompany them. 'Even at the uncomfortably early hour of 6am at which we were constrained to have breakfast on that memorable morning, he was the same as ever, speaking a little and only to the point in his deep, gruff voice. There were few of those pre-racing signs of tense nerves that reveal themselves in some men.'[267] That morning didn't just mark the first record attempt, but also Gardner's birthday. With that too, he made no fuss.

Finally, the O.N.S. men indicated that they were ready. Goldie climbed into the car and sat patiently as Jacko and Syd screwed the lid back into place. With a shove, the car roared into life and he took a leisurely run to fully warm the engine, but at the far end he overshot the turning point by some way. On his return, he switched off the engine and called Reg Jackson over. 'I say Jacko, it's going to take some pulling up,' he exclaimed. 'Why, I was only doing 4,000 [rpm] and she ran the devil of a way.' 'Well, Major, you know that you're shifting some even

---

267 *Autocar*, 9th June 1939, p1001.

at 4,000,' Jacko replied. It may have felt slow, but the car was still travelling at 140 miles-per-hour and with only two brake drums on the rear,
stopping wasn't the car's strong point.

After a short wait for the timing officials to get into place, and with
the spark plugs and wheels changed, EX135 was finally given the green
light. After a quick push, the car rolled off again and Goldie pressed
the accelerator to the floor. This was it: the chance to break that elu-
sive double ton.

Quickly, the car gained pace. Up and up went the rev counter,
climbing towards the 7,300rpm target that Syd had set for him. Inside
the cockpit, all the usual sights and sounds were there: the blast of the
air passing the canopy, the deep howl of the engine and the feeling of
heat pulsating off the bulkhead by his feet, but it all felt good, it all felt
poised. As he hit his target revs and kept the needle still until he had
passed the 5-kilometre mark, he started to wonder if he was really going that fast and absentmindedly noted the presence of an ambulance
pulling into place by the side of the track, but then felt a chill as it
dawned on him what it meant. 'I suddenly realised that I was the only
bloke using the road,' he later reminisced. There was only one person
who would be using that ambulance if something went wrong.

Outside the car though, it was a very different story. John Dugdale,
standing on a bridge about a kilometre after the end of the timed section, watched with a sense of awe as the tiny green car flashed past at
an extraordinary rate. Goldie was going very, very fast indeed.

The run over, Goldie backed off the throttle and applied the inade-
quate brakes, slowly losing speed until he saw Jacko by the side of the
road ahead. His mechanic ran over with a broad smile on his face: the
Germans had just telephoned through the results: the mile, kilometre
and 5-kilometre speeds were all over 200 miles-per-hour, with the mile
an astonishing 207.37 miles-per-hour.[268] As Jacko checked the car over,
Goldie realised that all he had to do was keep the speed up on the re-

---

268 Kilo was 206.36, 5km 201.74 miles-per-hour.

turn leg. He turned the car, and with a shove from his mechanic, he was heading back towards the start.

Using the middle of the huge, eighty-foot-wide road, he darted under the bridge where Dugdale was still standing, the rev counter pushing on to its maximum. All going well, he started to relax but then, just as the road entered a more exposed stretch devoid of any roadside banks or trees, he felt the wind catch the slab-sided flanks for the car and shove him off centre. His heart thumped in his chest and he instinctively corrected, fighting the crosswind to get back on the centre of the track. Fingers white-knuckle tight on the black steering wheel, he tried to keep the revs constant but it was a struggle just to stay in line as the gusts danced around him. It was with a significant sense of relief that he finally saw the finish line hove into view and slowed to a halt. He wasn't sure if he had done enough, but as he climbed stiffly from the car, the O.N.S. officials approached him, wide smiles on their faces.

He'd done it. The mean speeds were 203.54 miles-per-hour for the kilometre, 203.16 for the mile and 197.54 for the 5km.[269] He was officially the first person to break the 200 miles-per-hour barrier in a light car, just twelve years after Sir Henry Segrave had been the first person ever to drive at that speed, using a car of 45-litre displacement[270] compared with Gardner's tiny 1.1-litre power unit. It was an extraordinary achievement, but more was yet to come; when they returned to their police station headquarters that evening, the engineers set to work. The British had another trick up their sleeves.

Without saying much other than to Goldie and Kim, back in Abingdon Jacko and Enever had hatched a plan. They had decided to bring a cylinder-boring tool with them which they could use to enlarge the piston chambers. That, combined with new pistons, would increase the

---

269 Return legs were kilo 200.78, mile 199.22 and 5km 193.54 miles-per-hour. At the time of writing, two of these records (1 mile and 1km flying start) still stand.

270 The '1000hp' Sunbeam was powered by two Matabele aero engines each of 22.4 Litre capacity mounted fore and aft of the driver. The actual horsepower was closer to 900 but rounded up for publicity purposes (NMMT).

displacement of the engine just enough to qualify it for another category of records: Class F (1,100cc to 1,500cc). So, having attained the
Class G records, Gardner spoke to Herr Dienemann, the O.N.S. representative, to request an attempt on the Class F records in two days'
time. Unperturbed, Dienemann agreed, but asked how it was to be
done, then listened with amazement as Goldie told him.

Given the go-ahead, Jacko and Enever, helped by Chris Shorrock
and Kes Kesterton, started stripping out the engine. All was going well
until late that night, when Jacko awoke with a start, a concern nig-
gling him that he had to speak to Enever about right then. It had just
dawned on him that he had never used the Van Norman electric boring
machine they had brought with them but assumed Enever had. What
if he hadn't? He woke Enever and, true enough, Syd hadn't used the
machine either, but told him that as it was a new machine, it came with
an instruction manual. Semi-satisfied with his answer, Jacko went back
to bed. The next morning, the pair found the manual and started to put
the machine together but quickly discovered that the 110-volt electrical
supply in the police station wasn't enough to power it up. Enlisting the
help of the German Army signal corps, they ran a wire several hundred
yards along poles to the nearest 3-phase electrical supply and plugged
it in. The machine immediately sprung to life and started spinning itself around the room. As it was hard-wired and the switch was on the
machine, the two had to chase it around until they managed to grab it
and switch it off. The pair looked aghast at each other, convinced they
had ruined this precious tool, but they had nothing to lose: they tried it
on the first cylinder, and the result was a beautifully honed bore. Much
happier, they removed it and attached the second cylinder, switching
on the machine again. This time though, something was very wrong.
A deafening howl immediately filled the workshop and Jacko rushed to
flick the switch to the off position. Syd looked inside and his heart fell;
the chamber was terribly scored. Puzzled, they removed the blade and
realised they had put it in the wrong way around. Quickly corrected,

the machine ran again well and even the scored chamber polished up perfectly. Before long, the block was ready for the new pistons.[271]

The two engineers' challenges had not finished though. As they re-built the engine, Jacko noticed that one of the camshaft housings was cracked and they had brought no replacement. Previously, Goldie had been offered the services of the local Junkers aircraft factory should he need them and decided to call in the favour, so the British group trooped down to the facility. They were well received but warned not to look around the factory; it was obvious to the team that intense military preparations were taking place there. A good repair was quickly made and before long the housing was back in place.[272] The German military preparations were not limited to the factory. The 'motorised police' at the team's base were constantly rehearsing with arms and equipment that Goldie commented made them 'more like an armoured regiment' than a police force. It was a prescient observation.

The following morning at 6am, the team were back at the auto-bahn. Gardner was keen for an early start to avoid the crosswind that had plagued him during his later runs earlier in the week, but as the team fired up the car, he felt the breeze pick up. He had no time to lose; the engine had not been run in and even the fuel mixtures[273] and car-burettor jets had not been changed from the earlier record attempt, but he wanted to get out there and set a time. On the outward journey he overran again, the relatively tiny brake shoes unable to effectively slow the charging car, and on the return leg the wind again caught the sides of EX135, shoving him sideways in another nerve-racking moment, but he knew it wasn't too far from the speed he'd managed a couple of days earlier with the smaller engine. Soon after he pulled up back at the start, the timekeeper's results came in: all three target records had

271 The cylinders were bored from 57mm diameter to 59.5mm, enlarging the engine from 1,087cc to 1,105.5cc.
272 There is a much fuller description of this process in *Maintaining the Breed*, (ibid) p117-118.
273 For more information on the fuels used, see Mike Allison's superb article in *Safety Fast!* April 2022.

been beaten with all averages over 200 miles-per-hour.[274] The team were jubilant but their celebrations were short-lived as they were quickly ushered away so that another record attempt could be made, this time by Goldie's old friend Johnny Lurani.[275] They watched as Lurani took six records[276] and became the first person to exceed 100 miles-per-hour in a 500cc car. The runs over, the Germans quickly set up tables on the autobahn and brought out food and drinks for the crews, with local dignitaries attending to congratulate the drivers including the Burgomeister of Dessau and a black-clad Sturmbannführer in the SS[277] who Goldie shook hands with, politely but stiffly. The well wishes were not confined to the Germans; on his arrival back at the *Goldener Beutel* a stack of brown telegrams awaited them: Nuffield and Kim were expected, but congratulations from the other speed men of the day – Campbell, Eyston, Howe, Sammy Davis and Charles Follett – really meant something to Goldie. He was in exalted company.

The following day, the British team took the Germans who had helped them for lunch in a local hotel by a picturesque lake, then made their way slowly back to England. There, a stack of congratulatory letters awaited Goldie, as did the motoring journalists of the day who all wanted to report his story. John Dugdale, *The Autocar*[278] journalist who had accompanied the team, wrote a long article and *Motor Sport* noted that, 'Major Gardner sounded the British trumpet very loudly when he sped along the Dessau autobahn… these records are a valuable piece of propaganda for this country, and we shall do well to realise it – even though the daily press did not appear to do so.'[279] The criticism wasn't quite fair – prior to the run, the *Evening Standard* had included a small report that a 'One-Legged Driver Seeks New Record' to Gardner's an-

---

274 Kilo 204.28 miles-per-hour, mile 203.85 miles-per-hour, 5km 200.60 miles-per-hour.
275 Gardner knew the Italian Count Giovanni Lurani Cernuschi (Johnny to his friends) well from their days driving at Brooklands. Lurani had also driven the same works MG K3 in the 1934 Mille Miglia (K3015) as Gardner drove the following year in the BRDC 500 race.
276 International class I (350-500cc).
277 Postcard by Bruno Stindl (NMM Archive).
278 *The Autocar*, June 9th 1939, p1000.
279 *Motor Sport*, July 1939, p218.

noyance – but on his return the press were slightly more forthcoming with the BBC interviewing him and syndicated articles appearing as far afield as Calcutta and Ceylon. Dinky, the toy car manufacturer, soon realised that the exploit was good for business and quickly commissioned a scale model of EX135 entitled '23P, Gardner's Record Car.'[280] More importantly for the continuation of the attempts, Nuffield and the other companies that had supplied parts saw this as excellent publicity. EX135 was once again toured around MG showrooms, starting with his own at Milne & Russell,[281] and his exploits touted in advertisements for everything from Lucas ignition to *Smiths* instruments. Finally, on 17th July 1939, Goldie received the prize he had been promised by Kimber when John Thornley delivered an opulent four-seater MG WA drophead, registration 'EOY672' clad in light blue paint (which Gardner thought would be safer during wartime blackouts) complete with specially ordered twin spare wheels and Lucas P80 headlamps.[282]

Goldie quickly found a reason to take a long drive in the car. In mid-August he was invited by his old friend Sir Malcolm Campbell to witness the first run of his new speed record boat, the K4, inevitably named *Bluebird*. He drove up to Coniston Water in the Lake District and watched as the tweed-suited, eighteen-year-old Donald Campbell christened the boat with the traditional bottle of champagne before his father took to the mirror-flat water and smashed the record with a run of 141 miles-per-hour. Then, two weeks later, Goldie was asked to demonstrate EX135 at the Imperial Trophy Race at Crystal Palace, after which Lord Howe presented him with a silver plate marking the Dessau run as the crowds surged around him, keen to see this new British hero and his futuristic car. For Goldie though, there was only one

---

280 23P was the designation, not the price. There were two versions made: the pre-war example produced in 1939 and early 1940 was stamped on the bottom as 'MG MAGNETTE' and post-war models as 'MG RECORD CAR'. An approximate version of Gardner's earlier Magnette is also available, designated 23A.

281 *Croydon Times*, 10 June 1939 'Record Breaking Car on View', then Pointings in Leeds from 21-25 July (*Yorkshire Post*, 21 July 1939).

282 Auction catalogue entry, Brooklands, June 2000.

August 1936. Goldie takes the offset single-seat
MG Magnette high on the Brooklands banking,
on his way to victory in the First August
Short Handicap race.

April 1937. The battered remains of Goldie's
Mercedes-Benz SS 680 show how fortunate
he was to survive the crash in Battersea on the
day before his estranged first wife returned to
England to settle their separation.

Photo: Courtesy Mike Jones Family Archive

October 1937. Robin Jackson (striped blazer)
and Reg 'Jacko' Jackson prepare the Magnette
for a record attempt. Goldie's speeds, averaging
very close to 150mph in what was not much
more than an MG 'special' astonished his
German hosts.

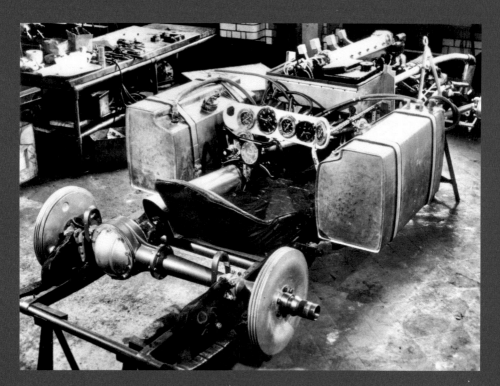

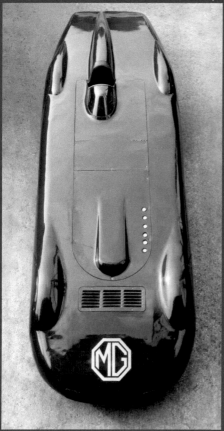

1938. Goldie's new record car was extraordinary: using the chassis of George Eyston's 1934 record-breaking MG K3 and powered by the engine from his previous Magnette, it was fitted with a new super-lightweight frame onto which was bonded a streamlined body designed by Reid Railton from a Jaray patent. The result was potent. (The internal shot is later, as the early car had a rounded oblong steering wheel).

Photo above right: Courtesy Mike Jones Family Archive.
Photos top & left: Courtesy Magna Press.

The autobahn at Dessau in 1939 was perfect for its task: wide, straight and immaculately prepared by the Nazis for their *Rekordwoche*. They did not expect a disabled old British veteran to drive at over 200mph in an 1100cc car.

Photo: John Dugdale Photograph Collection, courtesy of Revs Institute.

Dessau, 1939. Reg 'Jacko' Jackson was more than just Goldie's mechanic. The head of MG's competition department, he and Syd Enever accompanied Goldie all over the world to support his endeavours, sometimes even taking leave to do so. Both men were exceptional engineers and central to MG's production of successful sports cars from the thirties through to the sixties.

Photo: John Dugdale Photograph Collection, courtesy of Revs Institute

1st June 1939. Surrounded by fascinated Germans, Jacko and Syd rebore the engine in situ, allowing Goldie to take the Class F records the following day.

Photo: Reg Jackson family archive, courtesy of Tracey Rose

One of the benefits of having Goldie as a Director was that Milne & Russell was
given the use of EX135 for promotional purposes. Here the record car tours the
streets of South Croydon on its return from Dessau, 1939.

Photo credit: Courtesy Mike Jones Family Archive.

August 1940. Within months of being posted to Scarborough, Goldie had met and proposed to
Una Eagle-Clarke. This engagement photograph, posed in front of his MG WA given to him from
the factory, was printed in various newspapers and prompted a story in *The Tatler*.

July 1946, French/Italian border. The war over, the team reassembled for another record attempt. Johnny Lurani, to Goldie's left, had found a stretch of road near Bergamo that he believed was suitable.

The autostrada between Brescia and Bergamo was the opposite of the smooth autobahn on which Goldie had driven at Dessau before the war. Narrow, rough-patched, with a bend half-way down and a humped-back bridge at one end, the road was almost impossible to navigate at speed. The attempt was a failure.

1946 Italy. Facilities in Italy were basic. The team camped by the side of the road and carried out repairs in the shade of the lorry. Here, changing the rear axle are (L-R) Enever, Alec Baines on ground, Jacko in the car, and Stan Baines with flat cap.

1946, Italy. Despite the failure to secure any new records, the team immediately bonded again. Jacko grins as Goldie finds a new friend.

The locals were enthralled by the record team. Having just emerged from a brutal war, and with Allied forces still present, the car and its crazy British driver drew crowds wherever it went. Everyone was happy to help when needed.

The Jabbeke strip was everything Goldie had been searching for: straight, wide, with no traffic and very close to home. His runs there led the way for a succession of high-speed tests and record attempts.

Jabbeke, 1946, the team pose with EX135. From left, Goldie,
Alec Baines, Belgian onlooker, Reuben Rutter-Harbott,
Chris Shorrock, Syd Enever, 'Dunlop Mac,' Jacko.

A small crowd watches as Goldie flashes past the Jabbeke finish line.

thought: to get on with the next record attempt. Watching Johnny Lurani had reinforced what he already knew; he needed to run again, this time with a smaller engine to take the Italian's record. He approached Lord Nuffield who quickly agreed to fund the development of a one-off, six-cylinder 750cc engine. The scene was set.

But then, a few days after the cheering crowds of Crystal Palace, everything changed. On 1st September 1939, Goldie listened in great sadness as the radio reported that German forces had advanced into Poland. He knew what was coming: two days later, in concordance with their treaty obligations, Great Britain and France declared war on the aggressor state. Once again, Goldie's driving ambitions were to be thwarted by war, and once again he was to find himself at the very heart of it.

14

A RETURN TO THE COLOURS

The darkening clouds of war changed everything. On 24th August, a few days before Gardner appeared before cheering crowds at the Crystal Palace racetrack, royal assent was given for the Emergency Powers (Defence) Act, 1939. This gave the British government the right to 'take possession or control... of any property or undertaking... for the efficient prosecution of any war [in which] His Majesty may be engaged, and for maintaining supplies and services essential to the life of the community.' British companies could be compelled to refocus on war production, with motor manufacturers at the forefront of the urgent requirement to create the tanks, aircraft and other equipment that would be required to counter Hitler's cutting-edge military juggernaut.

The MG Car Company didn't wait to be told what to do. Once war was declared, the Abingdon factory was immediately emptied, ready for the task at hand. 'It was soon clearly obvious that if we were going to handle major war work, the first thing would be perfectly clear factory floor space,' wrote George Propert ('GP'), the man who had delivered Goldie's C-Type Midget at Brooklands and who later became General Manager of MG. 'So, our expensive paint plant and all other motorcar producing equipment was removed and put into cold storage. This all sounds relatively easy, but… we had to get a premises practically half as big as our own factory… we should have to clear many hundreds of tons of extremely valuable motor car parts… Fortunately, we were able to acquire a very dilapidated dis-used local factory which, at some considerable expense, we were able to put into suitable condition as a stores.'[283]

It wasn't just the uncompleted road cars that were forced into storage into the basement of what had been a *Clarks* shoe factory, there was also no place in the MG works for the sleek, green shape of EX135, its partially built 750cc engine and assorted spare parts. Racing and record breaking, although great for British prestige before the war, were reduced to frivolities once the conflict proper began. The chassis, body and parts, still the property of Goldie Gardner, along with the engines, were carefully boxed by the MG staff and moved to their store for the duration of the war.[284] Goldie didn't mind. Having lived through the Great War, he knew what would be required of both the country and its subjects if they were to vanquish the old foe. Immediately, his thoughts turned away from racing and back to the prospect of fighting Germans once again. Within days, he had visited the Royal Artillery branch of the War Office and, with the help of what he described as a 'tame M.O. (Medical Officer),'[285] somehow persuaded them that he was fit for employment as an officer on active service. This time though, there were to be no trenches and no artillery guns; sensibly, Goldie suggested his skillset best suited a role as an M.T. (Mechanical Transport) officer, responsible for vehicles and their crews. He was duly reinstated as a Second Lieutenant (a rank he last held in 1914) and given posting orders to a training unit in Scarborough, North Yorkshire. He quickly packed up the WA and set off.

---

283 George Propert, *MG War Time Activities*, (MGCC, 2018) p3.
284 West St. Helen's Street *Enjoying MG*, Feb 2013 p15.
285 *Magic MPH,* (ibid), p78.

Another factor may have aided in his application to rejoin the Army: for months, Goldie had been attached to a Territorial Army unit run by his old mentor, Sir Malcolm Campbell. Officially designated 56 (London) Provost Company, but unsurprisingly known to everyone by their nickname, the *Bluebirds*, the Croydon-based group were ostensibly created to provide a motorcycle-based quick reaction force in Sussex to aid in traffic control should a German invasion happen, but known to only a few trusted individuals, they had another, much more secret task. The *Bluebirds* were part of a covert force that became known later as the *Coats Mission* after its leader, Major James Coats of the Coldstream Guards. The detachment was formed for the personal protection of King George VI and Queen Elizabeth and their job, should a German invasion become imminent, was to whisk the Royal Family out of London to one of four pre-arranged stately homes dotted around the country. Hand-picked and armed to the teeth, the *Coats Mission* soldiers were seen as the nation's last line of defence. The *Bluebirds* were recruited almost overnight thanks to Campbell's fame and drew in a group of expert motorcyclists including Brooklands racers, stunt riders and AA patrolmen, all riding Norton International Model 30 racing motorcycles, but the fastest cars on the road were there too, driven by their owners: hand-picked racing drivers like Goldie (who arrived in his Talbot 105[286]) and his old Brooklands colleague A.F.P. Fane.[287] Unfortunately for Goldie, the task was a short one and he felt he should be back in uniform, hence his trip to the recruiting office.

Back in the real world, Scarborough was an inauspicious place for this old warrior to restart his military career. Previously a thriving seaside resort on the North Sea coast, it was now one of the areas identified as a possible landing zone should the Germans try to invade Britain. His job was to maintain a flow of qualified drivers to shift all the

---

286 This car, registration 'GO51' was one of the original Talbot team cars. (Photo, NMM Archive).
287 Coats Mission report from Royal Military Police Archive and transcript of interview by Major Hancock, (IWM).

heavy machinery of war about the land: Royal Artillery anti-aircraft guns, jeeps and logistics trucks. Scarborough itself was in the process of being fortified; as he drove into the town he was stopped at a barricade by soldiers who checked his papers before letting him pass with a stiff salute. He passed pillboxes being built at Springhill Lane and Scalby Mills, saw concrete anti-tank blocks being manoeuvred into place along the Royal Albert Drive and watched as rolls of barbed wire were unfurled along the slipways. Never did he think he would see such defences on British soil.

Mind you, it was far from being a harsh posting. Whilst most of the soldiers were billeted in the N.A.L.G.O.[288] holiday camp, the officers were housed in the rather more comfortable *Pavilion Hotel* which had the honour of being the first such hostelry in the area to be given an extended music and dancing licence until midnight on account of it having its own air-raid shelter that could accommodate all the guests. The Odeon Cinema and the Olympia Ballroom had also reopened after being briefly shut following the onset of hostilities, although if you fancied a dance, you had to bring your gas mask. At the end of January 1940 there was even a ball laid on for the troops at the *Grand Hotel* by the local Licensed Victuallers Association.[289] With his original rank restored, Major Gardner led a very comfortable life indeed.

Unfortunately, another matter dominated his thoughts during this period. At the end of October 1939, a barrister representing his ex-wife Mariel entered the High Court in London. On her behalf, he presented his case to Mr Justice Hodson: upset when she read of his engagement to Hester Jackson in 1937, she alleged that Goldie's conduct amounted to adultery as the divorce she had obtained in Florida wasn't valid under British law. The judge wasn't impressed, almost accusing her of connivance, stating 'The question to be considered was whether Mrs Gardner was in a position to complain if a man who she divorced com-

---

288 National Association of Local Government Officers.
289 Richard James Percy, *Scarborough's War Years*, (Sutton, 1992).

mitted adultery with a woman, the adultery being founded merely on the fact that the divorce was invalid.'[290] Nevertheless, he granted her a decree nisi with costs. It was a very sad end to the affair. Goldie wanted nothing to do with it and did not attend the hearing.

The weather didn't lift Gardner's mood, either. As a winter that was to be the worst in a generation set in, he looked for any distraction he could. One evening, he joined the other officers for an evening of music laid on to entertain them in the Officers' Mess but had low expectations – most of the acts were from the local holiday camp – but it helped to pass the time. But then, a pretty young girl, no more than 20-years-old, with dark, curly hair loosely gathered at the back, walked out onto the stage. Even before she had started singing, Goldie was captivated.

After the set was over, Goldie moved over to talk to her and quickly discovered that the young lady's name was Una. She had been living in London, training to be a professional singer when the war broke out, and wasn't very happy about the resultant recall back to the depths of the Yorkshire countryside to the family home in the hamlet of Saxton. At first, she wasn't very interested in this man who walked with a stick and was 24 years her senior, but as they chatted, she felt herself warm to him. He was kind, interesting, and she recognised a streak of determination and single-mindedness that they shared. She had been at school in Weybridge and had grown up to the sound of racing cars lapping the banking at Brooklands, then later at college in Dublin had watched as the racing cars had charged around the circuit in Phoenix Park every summer. She was fascinated that this man may have been one of the drivers she watched. His tall, upright bearing, smart service dress jacket covered with medal ribbons and kind smile made her forget the age difference.

The couple arranged to meet again and quickly love blossomed. Sometimes, they met as a group with other officers who had also made female friends, on other occasions they took trips up the coast together

290 *The Times* 24th October 1939.

in one of his cars, the WA or another MG, a T-Series Midget that he kept as a runabout. When she mentioned her frustration at being stuck in Saxton over the winter without any reliable means of transport, he insisted she borrow his Midget, which she duly did.

Before long, Una brought Goldie home to meet her parents. Francis Eagle-Clarke, a local solicitor and his wife Elspeth lived in the comfortable Willerby Lodge with their housekeeper, Edith Digby. Neither Francis nor Elspeth were very enamoured by their daughter's new beau, nearly a quarter of a century older than Una and a racing driver to boot. The recent reports of his divorce, other engagements and adultery in the court and social pages of the newspapers didn't help. Although Elspeth later grew to love him, initially she was dead against the pairing,[291] but she knew her daughter's character and when, in August 1940 she returned home to tell them they were engaged, she knew her protestations would fall on deaf ears.

Preparations were quickly made. Wartime restrictions meant that a lavish wedding was out of the question, but a simple ceremony suited them both given his divorced status. A few photographs were taken showing the couple posing with the blue MG WA, Una in flat shoes, simple dress and striped blazer, Goldie in his service dress and holding his ever-present pipe. A few papers published them and *The Tatler* covered the story with the headline, 'A Famous Racing Motorist Married.'[292]

Even as the Battle of Britain raged over the south of England and with the threat of invasion sharp in everyone's minds, Major Gardner was still granted a short period of leave to honeymoon with his wife. Given the situation their options were limited, so they decided on Surrey and London but their timing could not have been worse. Their wedding day coincided with a change of tactics by the Luftwaffe who initiated a concerted bombing campaign on London. At 4pm on 'Black

291 Interview with Ros Gardner, August 2022.
292 *The Tatler*, London, 11 Sep 1940.

Saturday' as 7th September 1940 became known, nearly 1,000 German aircraft swarmed over London dropping high-explosive bombs and incendiary devices. Standing on the balcony of their hotel in Surrey that evening, the newlyweds watched what Una later described as a 'funny sunset' before the pair realised they were observing a huge fire raging across the capital.[293] A few days later, having moved up to their hotel on Park Lane, they experienced the Blitz for themselves first hand, the bombs falling close enough to entomb their car in the building in which it was parked.[294]

It was an unexpectedly eventful honeymoon, but they soon returned to Yorkshire to start their married life together. At first, it was very comfortable; before long, Goldie was posted to a new unit in Wakefield, but it was still an easy drive back to the family home in Saxton. Then, in late 1941, he was posted again, taking on an appointment as Second-In-Command of an Anti-Aircraft Driver Training Regiment at Congleton in Cheshire before moving again in July 1942 to Rhyll where he became Deputy Chief Instructor Mechanical Traction (D.C.I.M.T.) at the Royal Artillery Mechanical Traction School. With this new job came promotion to Lieutenant Colonel.

For someone looking for an easy war, it would have been an ideal posting. The rank came with a lot of perks and the coast at Rhyll was every bit as lovely as the Scarborough beaches had been, but Goldie yearned for more. He still hadn't lost sight of his record-breaking aspirations; when a Mr. French wrote to him asking to purchase EX135, he said the car wasn't for sale, explaining that 'I still have another job to do with the MG before I consider selling it. Just before this war broke

---

293 As told to her daughter, Ros.
294 A catalogue entry from Brooks Auctioneers in June 2000 for MG WA EOY672 states that this was the car which was covered up, only to be unearthed in 1947 during clearance of the bomb site when it was sold to dealer on the Bayswater Road after which it was sold to a Mr Geoffrey Lambert. It either couldn't have been the WA, or it was recovered a lot sooner as there are photographs of the car in 1942 in *Magic MPH* and Goldie mentions that his friend Reuben Rutter-Harbott used it during the 1946 trip to Italy. It is also possible that it was a yarn spun by the dealer or that the tale was confused and it was actually his MG TA that was buried under rubble. This is possible, as the TA seems not to appear in photos after this time and Gardner is known to have a YA Tickford, possibly in its place.

out, we had finished a new 750cc engine with an eye on 200 miles-per-hour… and as soon as I see any chance of getting going I intend wheeling it out.' He did however offer Mr French first refusal if he did decide to sell, explaining that 'with the record body removed, [it] could very easily be converted into a road model!'[295]

Goldie knew that there was no chance of his attempting another record while the war raged and, in the meantime, he wanted to play a more active part in the proceedings. Soon, the perfect opportunity appeared: Gardner was approached by his postings branch who told him that a new headquarters was being formed. They needed someone with motor trade experience and the job would include overseas service. It was just what he was looking for and despite knowing little more about the role, he jumped at the chance.

The new job was in the Civil Affairs branch, created to provide active military headquarters with the support they required in managing the local infrastructure and population, to ensure that basic civil welfare and order were maintained. It was an attractive job and as Civil Affairs officers were classed as holding staff roles, they attracted an additional wage of five shillings a day. 34,000 people applied to join between 1943 and 1946 and were a mixed bag: of those rejected included a legless candidate, 'a potential murderer' (according to the War Office Selection Board psychiatrist), a 78-year-old general, a solicitor struck off the rolls and an officer certified as insane.[296] Some specialist civilians were hired and given ranks appropriate to their position, to Churchill's disgust. He said, 'It is most undesirable to scatter the much-prized military titles among people who are not going to do any fighting or exercise military command.'[297]

---

295 Letter reported in the *Autosport* forum by Roger French, the son of the correspondent.

296 *The development of British civil affairs and its employment in the British sector of allied military operations during the battle of Normandy, June to August 1944* (E Flint, PhD thesis, Cranfield, 2009).

297 Donnison interview with Colonel Bruce for Official History, 23 June 1954, reported in CAB 101/73, Edward (Flint PhD Thesis, Cranfield 2008).

But Goldie was the selection board's dream. Not only did he have specialist knowledge, through his record attempts and that of Malcolm Campbell he had experience of planning complex projects overseas. He was also a 'real' Lieutenant Colonel and had a Military Cross after his name; far from the 'bogus ranks' that Churchill had complained about. He was snapped up and sent straight to the Civil Affairs Staff Centre (C.A.S.C.) at Southlands House, Wimbledon. Then, in late April 1944, Lt Col Gardner was called with other members of the headquarters of what was now 21st Army Group under General Montgomery to South-wick Park, a stately home on the escarpment overlooking Portsmouth.

There, he found a hive of activity. Under a clump of huge trees, the vehicles and tents of Monty's forward tactical headquarters were setting up. Some men were doing arms drill, others running in squads. Jeeps, 2½ Ton trucks and steel-helmeted Americans were everywhere. Inside the house, guarded by military policemen, Goldie was briefed on the plan: Operation Overlord, the largest military invasion force ever assembled. A painted wooden map of the objective had been erected on the wall of the main briefing room: Normandy in northern France.[298]

Over the next few weeks, the headquarters carried out rehearsals. They practised moving, at first quite short distances, to Horndean then further afield, across the South Downs to Petworth and Crawley. Lt Col Gardner, in charge of the Civil Affairs Transport Section, was responsible for finding sufficient vehicles both civilian and military to deal with the needs of the civilian population and bring in food, water, fuel, and clothing.

Then, on 3rd June, under cover of a final movement exercise, the headquarters slipped away to a marshalling area where life belts, rations and seasickness tablets were issued. At 5pm, the operational maps were brought out and everyone on the staff briefed. There was no going back now. At 4am the following morning, as the morning light start-

---

298 Maj Paul Odgers, *A Tac Chronicle*, 30 Jul 1945. This is a superb report by an officer in 21 Army Group HQ (IWM).

ed to filter in from the east, they set off through Fareham to Gosport Hard. Here they loaded onto L.S.T.s, the large landing ships that could disgorge tanks, trucks and soldiers directly on to a beach. Manned by American troops, they were embarked by mid-afternoon and set sail before anchoring west of Cowes in the Solent.

'The weather had been worsening all day and there was considerable wind and choppy sea by nightfall, and it was with no little relief that [we] heard of a 24-hour postponement. Next day at eventide, the lines of assault craft moved steadily past the port beam. The expedition was at sea.'[299] Goldie was now one of 156,000 soldiers at sea in 5,400 landing ships. He didn't know at the time, but the worsening weather had caused much consternation in the planning headquarters back at Southwick Park, where General Eisenhower had finally given the go-ahead after a day's delay. It was a big call, but he made it: D-Day was set as 6th June 1944.

'There were ships in the channel as far as the eye could see and suddenly ahead appeared the coastline of France', Major Odgers, an officer in the headquarters remarked. 'But it was the mass of shipping rather than the quiet coast that staggered the eye as the convoy dropped anchor off JUNO beach.'

Tides, enemy action and the squally weather mean that it took them a long time to disembark. Even the forward 'Tac' headquarters weren't together on dry land until the morning of 8th June, and the HQ leap-frogged between locations for the first couple of weeks as the battle progressed. Finally, by mid-June, Goldie's group (part of the 'Rear' HQ) had settled in a huge, tented camp at Vaucelles, just west of the town of Bayeaux. Here, he set to work, building sixteen French motor transport companies manned by 600 Frenchmen from Rennes who were outfitted with uniforms, equipment and vehicles. They were loaned to various Army formations, delivering food and other supplies to distribution points.

---

299 *A Tac Chronicle*, (ibid).

It was a strange time. On the one hand, they were at the vanguard of the biggest offensive operation in Europe; by the end of August, two million Allied troops were in France. The Germans were still conducting a bitter fight, tenaciously holding key terrain, and with sporadic German tanks still causing a nuisance behind the Allied lines. The effects of war were never far away. Goldie, with the other members of the headquarters, watched as huge formations of Lancaster bombers flew over and the distant noise of war was ever present. But it was also very different to his last war in France: there was a Sunday football league, and the troops were able to discover some of the delights of the local countryside. 'All will remember the almost continuous rain, the few days of misty heat, the Camembert cheese, the Tiger and the Panther tanks' wrote Maj Odgers. Even His Majesty the King, Winston Churchill and Charles De Gaulle made visits, the latter causing a mild panic when he went for a walk and became lost.

Over the summer the headquarters moved, first just west of Bayeux, then through Falaise and on to Brussels by early September. A bitter winter set in, and although the Nazi machine continued to fight to its death, there were no longer any Tiger tanks to worry about and Goldie's life settled into a comfortable routine. Then, one Monday morning in early February, he walked into the Officers' Mess and absentmindedly flicked through the newspapers that had just been delivered. For once, the front pages were filled with something other than reports of the war: at King's Cross Station on the previous evening, a train had rolled backwards, derailing the rear coach which had hit a signal gantry and badly damaged the first-class compartment. A handful of people had been injured and two killed; without much thought, Goldie read the list of the casualties, then froze. Cecil Kimber, the founder of MG, had been one of those killed.

It hit Goldie harder than it should have done. He was at the heart of the bloodiest conflict in human history, a racing driver who had already lost many friends along the way, but Kim's death in such a seemingly benign accident felt utterly unfair. 'At that moment, I lost a very great friend, whom it would be impossible to replace,' he wrote. 'A brilliant and kindly enthusiast who had done so much to prove that a British car could hold its own against the products of any other country in the world.'[300] Sadly, he placed the newspaper down and went back to his room.

It took nearly three more months of bitter fighting before the word spread through the camp on 30th April 1945, carrying the news they had all been waiting for: Hitler was dead. Over the next few days, German emissaries met with their Allied counterparts and on 8th May, the surrender was made official. Victory in Europe had finally come. 'Now that it was all over, many of us merely felt very tired and suddenly rather anxious for the future,' wrote one of Goldie's colleagues, but he was impatient: he wanted to get back to Una, and to his record breaking. When given the order to demobilise in July, he wasted no time, heading straight for Ostend and then to Earl's Court in London where, for the second time in his life, he handed in his uniform and walked out a civilian.

---

300 *Magic MPH, ibid)*, p82.

15

BACK TO WORK

As quickly as the British motor industry had changed its role to war production in the autumn of 1939, once the war in Europe was won it instantly started looking to the future. Less than two months after VE Day, the country went to the polls and Clement Attlee's Labour Party won with a landslide. The country had been almost bankrupted by the war and the incoming establishment knew that exports were essential to create the money to buy the food the country so desperately needed. Attlee also knew that America's Lend Lease programme that had supplied Great Britain with raw materials, food and fuel would not last long. He was correct; less than three weeks after VJ Day, President Truman signed an executive order and Lend Lease was no more.

Exported British cars were one obvious source of valuable foreign export income, but the motor manufacturers of Coventry, Crewe and Derby were starting from a position of distinct disadvantage compared to their American rivals. Not only had the Luftwaffe bombs decimated British factories, but the necessities of a war of national survival meant that any development of civilian motor cars was outlawed for the duration. Not so in America where GM, Ford and Chrysler had continued to evolve new methods of pressing complex 'jellymould' panels, creating modern designs that appealed to a demanding public. To break into this huge market was going to take a miracle.

Back in Abingdon, part of that miracle took a very unlikely shape. Desperate to create something to sell, MG once again cleared the factory floor and replaced the machines that had been torn out in August 1939. They also brought back the old pre-war MG TB 'Midget' bodies and ladder chassis and set to work: with a few tweaks, these cars could be out in the showrooms in the late Autumn of 1945 and making money. The new car, unsurprisingly called the MG TC, looked almost identical to its pre-war sibling but the 'new' car resolved many of the earlier car's foibles. The two-seat interior was widened by four inches across the seat, with the doors longer and lower. The scuttle compartment now housed the new 12-volt battery and tools, next to the 1,250cc XPAG engine that now featured a much-needed timing chain tensioner and the ride quality was improved. By September 17th 1945, the first TC models were trundling off of the production line.

The TC unashamedly used pre-war technology and build methods, but with a revvy engine that gave a quick response, a good four-speed gearbox and minimal weight, it was (and remains today) a very fun car to drive. This combination of what we'd now call classic design and exhilarating, analogue performance hit the sweet spot for an unexpected audience: American GIs, now back in the USA after the war with demob checks burning in their back pockets, nostalgic for the little open-top sports cars they had driven around British country lanes before D-Day. And, happy to take their money and supply them with one of the new 'Midget' cars was the unlikely pairing of a one-legged ex-Etonian Coldstream Guards officer called Jocelyn Hambro and his lead salesman, a Norwegian ex- US Navy pilot called Kjell Qvale. Hambro, part of the banking dynasty of the same name, had established an export trading company in New Orleans immediately after the war and, as an MG owner, had decided to see how the American market reacted to the car. Qvale test drove one and was hooked.[301] Even in that first year of manufacture, exports exceeded home market sales.[302]

Back in the UK, John Thornley had just returned to MG in late 1945 after wartime service and saw the need to reinforce this initial export success. Despite Nuffield's ban on MG works racing in the mid-1930s, the brand had maintained its reputation for competition cars, so when Goldie Gardner contacted Thornley to inform him that he intended to try for another speed record the following spring, it was an opportunity too good to miss especially as Goldie would bankroll most of the attempt himself.

In fact, he had already made a start. Having recovered the record car from the storage site in Abingdon after its miraculous survival of a wartime fire that claimed the engine, supercharger and all spares but hardly singed the car, he set to work trying to find replacement parts. With EX135 tucked away in the Milne & Russell garages, he quickly re-established all his pre-war contacts, writing on work notepaper embossed with the company's address of 1 Brighton Road, South Croydon. They all wrote back, offering different deals: Dunlop agreed to provide tyres and wheels, S.U. would provide carburettors and Lucas various electrical items. Chris Shorrock, one of the designers of the *Centric* supercharger that had helped power EX135 to its pre-war records, promised to help Goldie create a new, improved 'blower' and told him he'd put two aside straight away.[303] Most importantly, Goldie wrote to his two old friends Jacko and Syd who had remained at MG.[304] The pair leapt at the chance; not only would it mean a return to their pre-war adventures but it would give them an escape from the bureaucratic morass that had descended on Abingdon in the economic gloom

---

301　For more about the post-war British motor industry, I thoroughly recommend Peter Grimsdale's excellent book *High Performance, When Britain Ruled the Roads* (Simon & Schuster, 2020).

302　1945 MG TC production was 34 home market, 47 export. Anders Ditlev Clausager, *Factory-Original MG T-Series*, (Herridge & Sons, 2019).

303　*Magic MPH,* (ibid), p83.

304　Syd's name had just been found on a Nazi list captured during the fall of Berlin, detailing all the most important British engineers who would have to be captured and nurtured at the end of the war. This story was told by Syd to Alec Poole and noted in his book *A Life by the Poole* (Self-published, 2021).

of the late 1940s. Raw materials were extraordinarily scarce, money was very tight; paperwork seemed to be required to do anything.[305] The chance to forget all of that and work on the record car again with Colonel Gardner seemed too good to be true.

Working in their spare time, Jacko and Syd started work on EX135 but despite a hefty cheque from Lord Nuffield (rumoured to be £1,000)[306] the team were not allowed to use the MG works to run up their engine for fear of the company being accused of frivolity in a time of national rebuilding. For Goldie, this presented a major problem as he considered that bench-testing the engine an absolute necessity prior to a run and was so disgruntled that he immediately arranged for the MG emblem to be removed from the car. It was Chris Shorrock, the supercharger builder, who came to his rescue. He and his brother Noel had been working on their new blower which they named the *Clyde*, using the Sterling Engineering Company Ltd of Dagenham, Essex to carry out the manufacturing process for them. Chris told Goldie they were of the right quality and 'knew their stuff', suggesting he should go to see their general manager, Mr. Redgrave. Goldie quickly agreed, and within a few days had the agreement of the firm to allow Jacko and Syd to use their equipment.

Quickly, the two engineers started putting EX135 back into racing condition. The car was disassembled, cleaned and checked over. Packages of parts arrived almost daily, some fitted immediately and others put aside for testing later. It is a mark of their extraordinary talent that, working almost exclusively in their spare time, the pair managed to get the car into a race-ready condition by early 1946. Now all they had to do was find a suitable location for the run.

In a continent that until five months previously had been embroiled in the biggest conflict the world had ever seen, nobody saw the breaking of speed records as a priority. Nobody that is, except a fifty-six-year-old

---

305 *The Works MGs* (ibid) page 128.
306 *The Works MGs* (ibid) page 128.

recently demobbed Lieutenant Colonel (now with 'bowler hat and bar' as he liked to joke) who had decided that this was what he wanted to do. And once Goldie had decided to do something, he was very persistent indeed. Hand-written letters in his distinctive scrawl were despatched to the automobile clubs in France, Belgium, Denmark, Holland and Sweden, but no suitable road could be found. He even enquired whether the roads he'd used in Germany in 1938 and '39 could be used, but one was submerged under a constant stream of American army trucks and the other was in the Russian zone. His letter to the Soviet authorities gained a very polite reply, telling him that his request had been forwarded to the proper department and he would receive a fuller response in time, but this letter never materialised. Unperturbed, Goldie started sending letters to his friends abroad to see if anyone could suggest a likely location. Soon, he received an encouraging reply from his old Brooklands pal Count Giovanni 'Johnny' Lurani, who had identified an autostrada (now the A4) between Brescia and Bergamo. A length of about 12km on the outskirts of Brescia was, Lurani told him, quite suitable for record breaking. Quickly Goldie arranged a date for late July.

It was a miracle that they made it and a testament to Goldie's tenacity. A sheaf of export licences had to be filled in, processed and signed off. Travel documents had to be procured and routes planned across countries still very much repairing the damage caused by the war. 'Apart from being a successful racing driver, he was also a war hero from the previous conflict, having the MC to prove it,' wrote Peter Browning. 'He was not afraid to use the morale-boosting or flag-waving cards to achieve what he wanted, or to bypass the official paperwork channels if he thought it possible to get what he wanted by talking to those he knew in the Government and the Opposition.'[307] Then there was the crew he assembled: Jacko and Syd (who both took annual leave to accompany him), Les Kesterton ('Kes') from S.U. Carburettors,

---

307 *The Works MGs*, (ibid), p129.

Chris Shorrock and his friend Reuben Rutter-Harbott who owned an engineering company and, most importantly, a lorry capable of carrying EX135. This disparate group of men, plus a few other keen friends, made up the first post-war record attempt team.

Despite Viscount Nuffield's wariness in officially supporting the record attempt, Gardner managed to extract one very important concession from Abingdon: he convinced the factory that he needed one of the new MG 'TC' models to show off in front of, he assured them, the combined European press. He would drive the car there, he promised, and use it to test run the route before jumping in EX135. The coverage, he suggested, would be worth a great deal in export sales. Thornley agreed, and on 26th March 1946, a gleaming new black TC was delivered, registered in Gardner's name and displaying the apt numberplate, 'MG6963'. A few upgrades had been specified by Gardner: an oil pressure light where the 30 miles-per-hour light usually sat, engine upgrades and a pair of chrome Lucas 'Windtone' horns that were mounted on the front bar onto which he quickly attached his usual collection of badges.[308]

It was a ragtag bunch who met at Dover ready to board the mail boat to Ostend on 21st July 1946. Goldie was travelling alone in his new MG, the seat next to him and rear compartment filled to the brim with his luggage, spare fuel cans, racing kit and other paraphernalia. Rutter-Harbott was driving Goldie's old MG WA with some of his friends, having given the key of his 3-ton Ford truck to Kes and Jacko who would share the driving, EX135 strapped inside as best they could manage. Various other friends travelled in a variety of different cars, parts stashed wherever they could stow them. The result was as far from Campbell's 1935 expedition to Daytona Beach, with its flag-waving crowds and Vice-Presidential receptions as one could possibly imagine and yet it was a very happy affair. The weather was perfect, with

---

308 Royal Artillery Association, his Brooklands 120mph badge, Brooklands Flying Club,
     BRDC badge and RAC badge.

temperatures in the mid-20s Centigrade and no rain, and the journey wasn't rushed; Goldie had given them four days to reach Monte Carlo with stops at St Quentin, Dijon and Avignon followed by a further rest day in the Principality. The hotels along the way were comfortable, and in the evenings, having checked over their cars, the men met together for dinner. They drank, they shared stories of 'their' war, they laughed. Goldie had not been as happy as this in a long time.

The group rose early on Friday 25th July and readied themselves for the last leg of the journey into Italy. In no time they were off, Goldie leading them in column up the winding road to the frontier, rugged cliffs to their left and the sparkling Mediterranean to their right. Finally, a little later than their 8am schedule they pulled up at the border post where a large wooden barrier blocked their path. Goldie immediately spotted Johnny Lurani dressed in dark shirt and trousers, his hair slicked back and a huge smile on his face. With the confidence of aristocracy, the tall Italian strode out past his own disconcerted border guards, across no-man's land and over to Goldie, where he warmly shook his hand and welcomed his old friend. With his help, border crossing formalities were quickly finalised, and the column moved on into Italy, bound for the home of the great driver Achille Varzi on the cliffs at Alassio, about an hour's drive away. On their arrival, Varzi, Lurani and Goldie posed for photographs with the rest of the team before sitting down at a long table shrouded from the hot sun by grapevines and eating a leisurely lunch. Varzi talked about his difficult return to racing a couple of months previously at Indianapolis, and of plans to restore the Mille Miglia 1,000-mile race around northern Italy the following year. He listened intently as Goldie told him of his record plans and offered to help in any way he could.

Varzi's hospitality was very welcome, but Goldie knew they had to push on as they had to reach Brescia that night and they still had 300km left to travel. It was a challenging journey: many bridges had been destroyed during the war and replaced by temporary Bailey bridges that had to be traversed carefully and could often only take traffic in one

direction. Allied troops still occupied the country and their frequent
checkpoints added to the delays. It was late into the night, Goldie peering through his tiny, flat windscreen at the dim pool of light created by
his Lucas headlamps, suddenly noticed a large white line painted in the
middle of the road. He knew that his destination was near; this was the
autostrada where on Sunday he would attempt his record run.

His first impressions of the road were not good. It was much smaller
than he had expected, some 25 feet across and built from large concrete
slabs, the joints of which rumbled against his tyres as he crossed them.
There were no barriers on the verges, just an expanse of scrubland,
and the concrete was regularly patched where it had crumbled or been
damaged during the war. Even in his TC with its relatively soft springs
and dampers, it was an uncomfortable ride but in EX135 with its rock-
hard suspension, this track would be very tricky indeed. Perturbed, he
found his hotel and fell asleep, concerned whether he had made the
wrong decision to come this far. The next morning, accompanied by
the team, George Moore from *The Motor* and the great racing motor-
cyclist Piero Taruffi, Goldie drove down to the autostrada to take a
closer look.

If anything, it was worse than he had feared the previous evening.
Not only was the road surface very uneven but there was a significant
bend in the road about half-way down the 12km strip that Lurani had
identified as the record route. Plus, as he drove down the road in his
MG his heart fell; a mile from the turning point near the village of Ro-
vato there was a humped-back bridge where the road crossed a railway
track. If he hit this at 150 miles-per-hour, EX135 would surely take off.

Nevertheless, he couldn't back out now. That night, aware that they
needed to start very early the next morning, the team made their way
to the now-closed autostrada near the village of Villanuova on the
southern outskirts of Brescia. After a good-natured meal at a local café,
they set up camp next to the road, Goldie choosing to sleep on the grass
verge next to the lorry. Just before dawn, after a fitful sleep, he was wok-
en by the sound of military trucks depositing troops to clear the road

of any locals who may have been tempted to make use of the now-de-
serted track. One man on a bicycle tried to ignore them prompting a
volley of warning shots; these Italians didn't mess about, Goldie mused.

Gingerly, the team unloaded the record car, slowly backing it down
planks from the back of the truck supported by a Heath Robinson
combination of spares crates and wooden blocks. Safely on the tarmac,
Jacko, Syd, Kes and Chris Shorrock got to work on the car, warming
it up and double-checking everything. It wasn't Goldie's favourite time
at all and he went in on himself. 'The old man is having one of his
moments', one of the lads said to the others, and they knew to steer
clear. Gardner knew he needed to do something to take his mind off
the feeling of apprehension that was gnawing at his stomach, so he
climbed back in his MG TC and set off to drive the route one final
time. By 6.25am, he had returned, donned his racing cap and goggles,
wordlessly handed his stick to Syd and slid his way into the familiar
cockpit. The mechanics screwed down the top deck, cocooning him in
place and he took a moment to compose himself. Hi life had changed
a great deal in the seven years since he had last exercised EX135 at
speed and he knew the conditions for this run were far from perfect,
but he did what he always did, steeled himself and got on with it. Syd
Enever caught his eye and smiled; Goldie gave a thumbs-up back. He
was ready. Quickly, the team assembled behind the car, and all pushing
hard, rolled EX135 forwards. Goldie dropped the clutch, the car jerked
into gear, and off he went.

Quickly, the car gathered pace. Syd, Jacko and the rest of the team
had done a superb job, Goldie thought, as he pushed his right foot to
the floor. Quicker and quicker she rolled, the exhaust ports spitting as
the tiny 750cc engine fired her forwards, the joints in the concrete beating an ever-faster rhythm. With no speedometer to guide him, Goldie
was focused on the rev counter; after a couple of miles, he thought
he must be at around 135 miles-per-hour, and all seemed good. Then
came the bend.

In the TC at 50 miles-per-hour the corner had been a sweeping affair, requiring just a tiny correction of the steering wheel to navigate. Now, travelling at around three times that speed in EX135, it seemed much, much tighter. The tyres skittered as they searched for grip on the cold concrete, but Goldie felt himself drifting ever closer to the right-hand verge. Much as he tried, he couldn't hold the car back, and had to lift his foot a little from the accelerator. Quickly, his speed dropped, the car fell back into line, and he pushed his foot down again. He had lifted for maybe a second, but he knew the run was compromised. Annoyed with himself he pushed on anyway, passing through the measured mile and out the other end where he lifted again and gently applied the brake pedal that squeezed the large Alfin brake drum on the rear wheels. Gradually he slowed; as he reached the humpback bridge, he was still travelling at well over 130 miles-per-hour and the car launched itself, all four wheels spinning in clear air for some yards before crashing back down onto the concrete, rattling Goldie around the cockpit like a penny in a tin. Now back in control, he slowed to a stop, and was quickly met by Jacko and Kes who ran over to turn the car around and push him back to start his return run.

Again, the car quickly gained speed. This time, the bridge came about a mile into the run and he braced himself, hoping that the bump wouldn't be as bad this way around, but his optimism was not well founded. The car launched itself into the air once more, but this time it took off at a slightly skewed angle. Goldie immediately sensed the car turning slightly to one side and knew he was in trouble; the four wheels landed in a skitter and sent him snaking down the road. All his racing instincts came flooding back to him and he fought with the bow-shaped steering wheel that was now twisting in his hands. With no seatbelts to hold his body in place, he braced himself against the seat back and for a moment thought he'd lost it, but this time his right foot didn't lift, he didn't slow, and gradually he regained control. Minutes later, he flashed across the timing line and even at that speed registered Johnny Lurani's serious expression. He knew it wasn't good, but at the end he quickly turned around and went for a second run. Slightly better at dealing with the curve and the bridge, his times were quicker, but not enough to threaten the record. The average of the two best runs was just 137 miles-per-hour, four miles-per-hour under the existing record and way short of his 150 miles-per-hour target. He was unhappy, but thought he knew what needed to be done; after a quick chat with Syd, he decided to call off any more runs for the day, adjust the engine and prepare for the following morning.

The next day, he tried again. Syd and Jacko had adjusted the fuel mixture, and the car drove beautifully. He crossed the line grinning, sure he had averaged around 160 miles-per-hour, but Lurani's leaden face puzzled him. With profuse apology, Johnny told him that the timing apparatus had failed; the run had been in vain. Totally disheartened, Goldie called off the rest of the runs that day.

The following day, he made a third attempt. He had asked that the measured mile be moved further away from the curve and told Syd to change the ratio of his back axle, hoping it would give him quicker acceleration. This they completed, but not before a rainstorm washed out any chance of another run that day.

The following day was their last, but Goldie was confident. The car was now running very well, he was very used to the road, and he considered a speed in excess of 150 miles-per-hour to be entirely possible. At 6.15am on the dot, he was pushed off to start his run. His speed built quickly and before long he was at the curve, which he took with very little effect on his speed. On the straight now, he pushed ahead as fast as he could with the engine screaming at 7,000rpm. All looked good as he started the measured mile, but then his trained ear picked up a sudden clattering and he instinctively backed off, aware that something terminal had happened. Soon after he coasted to a halt, his mechanics arrived and quickly diagnosed the problem: the supercharger had seized. Gardner suspected that it was the final act in a very frustrating play but decided to leave the final decision to Jacko and Syd; after all, they had a spare supercharger and the use of the Alfa Romeo factory in

Arese should they need to fix the original. Syd was happy to continue, but Jacko less so, 'What had not been achieved in a week was unlikely to succeed in a fortnight,' he felt.[309] Goldie gave the order to pack up, ready for the move back to England.

Annoyed but undaunted, Goldie ruminated on what had happened on the long drive back to Ostend. The engine was running well, he felt, and he had been clocked running at 160 miles-per-hour at times, so there was easily potential for the car to break the existing record. The supercharger fault was something that Chris Shorrock would have to address, almost an occupational hazard with a newly developed item of something as complex as a supercharger. No, the real problems he faced now would be persuading his backers to stump up more cash and finding a suitable route. Both were significant issues, and even with his legendary powers of persuasion and dogged determination, he wasn't sure he could overcome them. It would take a miracle to find some- where suitable, ideally closer to home, he mused. And yet sometimes, miracles do happen.

---

309 *Maintaining the Breed*, (ibid), p120.

16

JABBEKE

———⟶———

Not long after his dejected return from Italy, a possible solution to one of Goldie's biggest problems fell right into his lap. Jacko excitedly contacted Goldie; their recent foray had been the talk of the Abingdon shop floor and one of Jacko's colleagues had mentioned it back at home. The man's sister, a woman called Margaret Wills, spoke up: 'Why did he go all the way to Italy when there is a perfect road just the other side of the channel?' Intrigued, the man had asked what she meant. She told him that late on in the war, when she was a member of the Mechanical Transport section of the Auxiliary Territorial Service (A.T.S.), she had been posted to a prisoner-of-war camp on the outskirts of Ostend in Belgium. Virtually every day, she had to drive up and down a wonderful, dead-straight twin-lane motorway towards the port, the only other road users a few locals on bikes and the odd errant sheep. Both ends ended in fields, she said, but the road surface was so flat it was like nothing she had ever experienced. It seemed too good to be true. Goldie quickly telegraphed Jean Simons, a Belgian friend who had accompanied him to Italy, who quickly visited the road and excitedly telegraphed back: it was absolutely perfect. This time, Goldie wanted to check for himself and the following weekend he, Jacko and Syd took the ferry from Dover to Ostend.

The road was just as Simons had described it. It had been built as part of a highly optimistic Nazi plan to link the port of Ostend to Istanbul with a fast, modern motorway, its twin lanes snaking across the entire continent of Europe. They hadn't made it far before the tide of the war turned and Allied bombing reduced much of Ostend to rubble, with just a single stretch completed between the outskirts of the port city, past the small town of Jabbeke and ending at the hamlet of Aeltre[310]. Goldie drove the road in his MG TC, a grin spreading across his face. Unlike the Italian autostrada, this road surface was immaculate, flat and unblemished. The entire length, around 14km of which was suitable, had long sweeping bends at the ends but in the middle was an 8-9km stretch of dead-straight, flat road that would be superb for his record runs. He just couldn't believe it; they had driven past here just months previously at the start of their long journey to Italy; the perfect location was right on their doorstep. Quickly, Goldie pulled in all his favours and enlisted his greatest powers of persuasion to make another attempt happen. Just over a month after his reconnaissance with his mechanics, he had everything in place: official timing staff from the RAC, permission from the Royal Automobile Club of Belgium (RACB) to close the road and even his friend Reuben Rutter-Harbott's lorry that would once again transport EX135. The ad-hoc support group met once more, driving down from Abingdon to the port of Dover where they boarded the ferry to Ostend, the *MV Prince Baudouin*.

Goldie peered down from the upper deck, leaning over the rails so that he had a good view of Rutter-Harbott's lorry being hoisted crookedly into the air and Jacko, who was waving his arms in an attempt to guide the crane operator. 'Better try again,' he called down to his mechanic. 'After all, I had the car washed before we started.' Jacko turned, grinned, and indicated to the dockworker that the truck needed

---

310 I am assured by a native of Belgium that the correct pronunciation is 'Ya-Becker'.

to go back onto the Dover quayside.[311] The second attempt was more successful, and the truck and its precious cargo were safely deposited in the hold. A few hours later, they had reached the *Grand Osborne Hotel* in Ostend where they prepared themselves for their first commitment: a cocktail party hosted by a local motor dealership. Goldie walked into the room and was impressed by what he saw. The British press needed something positive to report on in the austere post-war gloom, and it seemed that Goldie's escapades had suddenly sparked their interest. Not only were the big motoring titles represented – *The Motor, Autocar* and *The Light Car* – but also the major national newspapers including *The Star, Daily Express* and *Daily Mail.* Sure, Goldie had called in some favours to get them there, and the fact that Ostend was a quick day trip away from Fleet Street helped no end, but there was a real buzz of excitement, nonetheless.

Unfortunately, the following day, Sunday 27th October 1946, was a washout. Goldie donned his thick, tartan driving coat, his flat cap and leather gloves but they weren't enough to keep him warm during the short trip to the rain-soaked Jabbeke road in his unheated MG TC. Everyone hung around waiting for the skies to clear, the newspapermen pulling their hats down and their collars up to protect themselves against the drizzle, but by the afternoon it was obvious that no run would be possible that day. EX135, still loaded on the back of the truck, was driven back to its temporary Ostend home at the *Auto Garage du Littoral* with everyone else following behind. The following day was equally frustrating; the RACB were new to all this, and although keen were still struggling to get to grips with some of the technical aspects. The timing apparatus couldn't be made to work and by the time it was fixed, the rain had set in again. Dejected, they all retired back to the *Osborne* again.

By Tuesday afternoon, Goldie could sense the impatience in the press group, so despite standing water he had the car unloaded and

---

311 Press report, Oct 1946.

took it on some practice runs along the road. As the photographers snapped away, he pushed the car; not up to its limits but enough to get a feel for how well Jacko and Syd had set it up. He smiled to himself; given the right conditions, it felt superb: the engine was raring to go and when he pushed the car on the drier sections it responded wonderfully. All he needed now was the weather.

The good conditions arrived the next morning at around 10.30. A light mist had risen, exposing the dry surface of the road and although some moisture hung in the air, there was hardly a breeze and the tall trees that flanked most of the course lay silent. Finally, he'd have a chance to see what the car could do. With racing tyres and spark plugs fitted, he set off, quickly building up speed. The road was much flatter than the awful surface he'd experienced on the Italian autostrada and as he flashed across the line at the turning point, he knew that both he and the car had a great deal more to give. He'd been aiming for 150 miles-per-hour on the first run and despite holding back he reckoned he'd hit around 155 miles-per-hour. On the return leg he pushed the car even faster, still holding a little in reserve, but when he crossed the finish line he felt sure he had demolished the old 750cc record of 140.7 miles-per-hour for the mile. He was right; as he climbed from the car, the official results were delivered: 159.15 miles-per-hour for the mile, and international kilometre and 5km records had fallen too. He was happy, but when a *Movietone* newsreel camera was thrust into his face and he was asked for his response, he couldn't hide a slight twinge of disappointment.[312] As MG's John Thornley later mused, 'It was overgeared... Best utilisation of the power available should have yielded speeds of the order of 175 miles-per-hour.'[313]

Content, the British newspapermen returned to London with their photographs and stories, and the team was left in relative quiet. They

---

312 'You affected an air of complete indifference.' Gerry Sanger, Editor, *British Movietone News*, letter to ATGG 22 Nov 1946 (NMM).
313 *Maintaining the Breed*, (ibid), p121.

had one last thing to try and this wasn't something they wanted to share yet with the media: At the suggestion of Chris Shorrock, the supercharger expert, Syd had forged a couple of pistons both with large holes cut in the dome. Once these were used to replace two of the engine's standard pistons and once the corresponding valve gear had been disabled the car was, in the eyes of those responsible for maintaining speed records, a 496cc four-cylinder, with Johnny Lurani's 500cc (Class I) record 106 miles-per-hour firmly in the firing line. The engine conversion completed, on Saturday, November 2nd, Goldie ran again using only third gear, but still managed to clock 102 miles-per-hour. It was all they needed to know; with a few extra modifications, they could easily take the 500cc records on their next attempt. Happy now, they headed back to Ostend.

Goldie had not driven as fast as he knew he could, but his records stood nonetheless and whether he realised it or not, his trip to Belgium had made a huge impact. As the team packed up, he sifted his way through the pile of congratulatory telegrams and letters that had arrived at the hotel. Some were personal – Johnny Lurani, Freddie March and Charles Follett – but others were of a more commercial nature. The companies who made parts of his car asked whether his success could be included in their advertisements and most importantly, the press was full of praise again for this old-fashioned British daredevil, although most irritatingly reported him once again as being 'one-legged'.[314] Goldie's other achievement was to put Jabbeke firmly on the map as *the* post-war location of speed record attempts. Over the next few years, Donald Healey would test run his new 'Healey Hundred' here, proving its top speed lived up to its name, Jaguar legend Norman Dewis pushed their revolutionary XK120 up to an astounding 172 miles-per-hour, Triumph ran their new TR2 and Rover unleashed

---

314 'Every newspaper in the country seemed determined to describe you as the "one-legged driver",' wrote Gerry Sanger of Movietone News. 'I am afraid our commentator put too much faith in the press... I hope you will exonerate him from the amputation of one of your limbs.' Letter Sanger to ATGG dated 22 Nov 1946 (NMM).

the gas turbine-engined *Jet 1*. Even young motor racing star Stirling Moss drove here under the myriad flashbulbs of the British press.[315] As if they could sense this oncoming popularity (and the associated income it would bring) the Belgians treated Goldie and his team with the most generous hospitality, the RACB hosting him, Jacko and Syd for lunch and the Liège Royal Motor Union presenting him with a heavy cut-crystal *Val St Lambert* trophy vase that he packed into his MG[316].

One group of people who seemed not to be particularly impressed with his efforts were the MG Car Company and their parent organisation, the Nuffield Group. Their policy stood firm: no official support was to be made available for the car although they had no objection to Jacko and Syd working on the engine (during their free weekends) at Milne & Russell and agreed to pay their overtime. Goldie bridled but bit his tongue; he knew making an enemy of such a big organisation was not a sensible move. When, in January 1947, he was asked whether the Swiss distributors of Nuffield Group cars could use EX135 on their stand at the Geneva show he agreed, but on the understanding that it would be referred to as the 'Gardner Special'[317] rather being described as an MG. By the time he was ready to attack the 500cc record in July 1947, relations had not thawed; Syd and Jacko were told they were not allowed to attend during Goldie's first week of driving and were made to return home early. Goldie pointedly left his MG TC at home and drove a car from Austin, MG's old rivals,[318] and a car that Milne & Russell had for sale on their forecourt. It was a small score, but an important one for him.

The run proved to be a challenging one. Despite working with Les Kesterton from S.U. Carburettors and Chris Shorrock, Syd's modifications of the 500cc engine didn't get close to the 130 miles-per-hour

---

315 https://www.hagerty.co.uk/articles/the-jabbeke-speed-trials/

316 Back home, Una was not impressed with this imposing trophy, turning it into a lamp stand, which it remained for the next 76 years (Ros Gardner).

317 *Maintaining the Breed*, (ibid), p125.

318 Austin Sixteen.

he had predicted at the bench test and Goldie managed to reach just 118 miles-per-hour, enough to only temporarily take the records from Johnny Lurani, who won them back before the end of the year.[319] Syd and Jacko didn't even make it to Jabbeke before the deed was done, reading about the success in the evening papers on board the boat train from Ostend.[320] There wasn't as much press this time and in September Goldie's records were eclipsed by John Cobb's successful world land speed record attempt on the Bonneville Salt Flats in Utah, America, where his Railton Mobil Special broke the 400 miles-per-hour barrier on one run, the first time a car had reached that milestone. Goldie knew that he had to do something very special in 1948 to keep his momentum up and his name in the papers.

But 1947 was very important to Goldie for another reason. The previous summer, Una had fallen pregnant and on 21st February 1947, at the Reigate Nursing Home, she gave birth to a daughter who they named Rosalind Goldie Gardner, maintaining the family tradition. At 56 years of age, he became a father but although he took a break for the christening at Reigate parish church, with both Freddie Clifford and Sir Malcolm Campbell stepping up to be Godparents, the arrival of his daughter didn't make him waver from his steel-eyed focus on breaking records. While Una dealt with the new baby, Goldie retired to his study, the walls crammed with photographs of his past exploits, and planned his next move. He analysed the official records: the 2-litre speeds were, he thought, easily within reach but he needed an appropriate engine. An enquiry to the MG Car Company received a terse reply: there were no appropriate engines available. Then, as often happened with Goldie, something fell with great fortune into his lap. Visiting the garage where his existing engine was being bench tested, Goldie noticed an engine hidden under a tarpaulin. Even under the

---

319 The problem was initially diagnosed as a loose fuel line union, but even when fixed Goldie was unable to improve on his times. *Maintaining the Breed*, (ibid), p125.

320 *Maintaining the Breed*, (ibid), p125.

sheet, could make out the twin covers that marked it out as an exotic twin-camshaft motor. His interest piqued, he lifted the cover, exposing the gleaming, polished aluminium cam covers of a very smart-looking four-cylinder engine. Excited, he approached the garage owner, who confided that it was a secret experimental engine, property of Jaguar Motor Cars Limited.[321]

Jaguar was at a turning point in its history. They had moved on from their original incarnation as the Swallow Sidecar Company, through their stately SS Cars era and emerged from the second world war re-branded and ready to take on the world. Founder William Lyons had a vision for a British sports car that would challenge the existing norms of motor design and, while working as a firewatchers in Coventry during the war, he and his engineers had secretly been planning the engine that would be the beating heart of this new Jaguar model.[322] This, a four-cylinder version of the XK engine that would power some of the most famous Jaguar models for the next two decades, was what Goldie had discovered. He immediately wrote to Lyons.

Whereas the Nuffield group was huge, unwieldy and stifled by bureaucracy, Jaguar was more like the old Kimber-era MG: smaller, nimble and quick to take any opportunity offered. Lyons knew of Goldie's successes, immediately saw the potential benefit of teaming up with him and replied by return post, telling him to contact his chief engineer, Bill Heynes. Goldie did so and within days, the two were discussing development of both car and motor, and by early September 1948, the *Gardner Special Engine*[323] was installed and the car ready to run again at Jabbeke. This time though, there would be no Jacko or Syd. Lord Nuffield had not taken the news well that Goldie was working with the new upstarts at Jaguar and forbade their involvement. Les Kesterton

---

321 The garage belonged to Harry Westlake. *Magic MPH*, (ibid), p110.

322 Bill Heynes, Wally Hassan and Claude Baily. See *High Performance* (ibid) for more on this fascinating time in Jaguar's life.

323 This was one of the experimental 'XJ' engines of 1996cc that produced 128.8bhp at 5060rpm (www.jaguarheritage.com/jaguar-history/jaguar-engineering/4-cylinder-xk-engine).

had no such constraints, so attended as usual, and Jaguar's Wally Hassan took the engineering lead. The press, too, joined the group in force, the temptation of an all-British record with Jaguar's fascinating new engine offering too much of a story to resist.

At first, the omens weren't good. The crane driver loading EX135 onto the ship at Dover let it spin into a dockside lamp, badly denting the rear bodywork. On arrival in Ostend on 14th September, the panel was hastily repaired but on the first day rain meant that they couldn't start until 5pm. Then, on the first warm-up run, Goldie narrowly missed a dog that had wandered onto the course and on one of his high-speed runs, travelling at over 170 miles-per-hour, a farmer's cart pulled by a donkey sedately trotted past the timing post. The astonished officials, hearing Goldie approaching, shouted at the farmer, panicking the donkey which, obstinately hee-hawing, stood dead centre in the road and refused to budge. With just seconds to spare, the animal was dragged, pushed, and cajoled out the way as the green record car charged past.

Cocooned inside the bowels of the car, Gardner was oblivious to this drama. Hassan had told him to limit the revs of the new engine, but almost immediately he started his run, Goldie realised it had a lot more to give. '[I was] gathering speed in a phenomenal manner,' he recalled. 'When I reached the beginning of the mile [I] was up to 170 miles-per-hour [but] the engine still wanted to climb.'[324] Immediately, his first runs netted him the kilometre and 5km records but the timing apparatus for the mile had failed so he turned around and set off again.[325] In the car, everything seemed to be running perfectly, so Goldie decided to push it a little harder. 'I decided to ignore Wally Hassan's orders and take the revolutions up higher over the mile,' he later wrote. As he darted past the start of the measured mile, he pushed his right foot to the floor and the revs quickly increased. The old top speed of around 177 miles-per-hour was almost instantly eclipsed and

---

324 *Magic MPH*, (ibid), p114.
325 Whether this was due to the panic surrounding the donkey incident is not recorded.

to his delight, Goldie knew that he was easily over 180 miles-per-hour and still accelerating. The car was running like a dream, he thought, but then everything changed.

Half-way through the measured section, the car suddenly shuddered and started to weave violently from one side to another. His heart pounding in his chest, Goldie instinctively fought the steering wheel to regain control and lifted his foot off the accelerator. As quickly as it had started the tremor seemed to disappear, so Goldie slammed his foot down on the throttle again, trying to gain as much speed as he could for the last 100 yards-or-so of the mile before backing off and coasting into the start where a group of people awaited him. He was puzzled; the engine felt absolutely fine, and it was only when he saw one of the crew pointing to the front of his car did he start to realise what had happened. At about 180 miles-per-hour, just as he passed the first group of timing officials, his tyre had begun to delaminate with huge chunks of rubber tread shearing off and smashing into the wheel arch. All that was left was the canvas inner core of the tyre that had somehow not punctured as Goldie completed the run. He had been millimetres away from disaster.

Regardless of how precarious the run had been, Goldie considered it a complete success. All three (1km, 1-mile and 5km) two-litre records had been broken, and by a significant margin. He was extremely impressed with the Jaguar engine and Wally Hassan's meticulous approach to its preparation, and on his return to the UK realised just how important the partnership had been for him. His return on 21ˢᵗ September 1948 coincided with the very first race at Goodwood which had been won by a Jaguar,[326] and within a month, Jaguar had unveiled its ground-breaking XK120 to great acclaim at the London Motor Show at Earl's Court, the first such event since the war. Lyons and his team were suddenly the talk of the town and some of the lustre rubbed off on Goldie. Most importantly, it made Lord Nuffield and Jack Tatlow,

---

326 The race was won by Paul de Ferranti Pycroft driving a streamlined Jaguar SS100.

the General Manager of the MG Car Company, sit up and take notice. Slowly, over the next couple of months, they allowed the relationship to warm again and talks began. Before long, an agreement was made: the following season, the famous MG octagon would once again adorn Gardner's record car and the weight of the Abingdon engineering team would support his efforts.

In the meantime, Goldie's public profile continued to regain the level it reached before the war. At the BRDC annual dinner in December 1948, he was presented with his second Gold Star by HRH The Duke of Edinburgh and was feted by the others at the dinner. Everyone asked the same question: did he intend to try to reclaim his 500cc records, broken just days previously by his old friend Piero Taruffi? Of course, Goldie replied, with a smile. He knew that while he was away in Belgium with the Jaguar crew, Syd's focus had already shifted to the smaller engine and work on a supercharged 500cc engine had already begun; by the autumn of 1949, Goldie would once again pilot an MG-powered EX135. An increase on Taruffi's result would give him five of the ten recognised international speed records and despite nearing his 60th year on the planet, Goldie's thirst for success had not diminished. He went into 1949 a rejuvenated man.

17

10,000 MILES IN 10,000 MINUTES

One morning in late April 1949, a parcel arrived for Goldie at Milne & Russell. Although a director, his visits to the company had become rather rare occasions in recent years, each time prompting the excitement of the staff who were delighted to see their famous record-breaking boss and his inevitable entourage of engineers.[327] He made a point of talking to them then sifted through his mail, quickly spotting the package and carrying it through to his office, his excitement hard to mask.

Under the brown paper wrapping was a black book with its red title emblazoned across the front: *The Motor Yearbook 1949*. Quickly, he thumbed through it, finding what he was looking for on page 43.[328] This was the first edition of the *Yearbook*, an annual publication that was to become the bible of the British motoring world, detailing everyone and everything important in the industry from racing stars to newly released car models. It included a chapter on record breaking and to Goldie's delight his name dominated the section. With Taruffi's 500cc

---

327 Recollection of Edith 'Edie' Jones, who worked at M&R (interview with her son, Mike Jones, 2023).
328 Laurence Pomeroy/ RL de Burgh Walkerley, *The Motor Yearbook 1949*, (Temple Press, 1949), p46.

records still awaiting official confirmation,[329] Goldie was listed as the holder of a clean sweep of flying mile and flying kilometre records in five classes, and a picture of him driving EX135 at speed in Jabbeke was entitled, '177 M.P.H. Unsupercharged.'

It was a ray of sunshine after what had been a bitter winter. Not only had snowstorms ravaged the south of England, but on the last day of December 1948, Goldie had lost his old friend and mentor, when Sir Malcolm Campbell finally succumbed to the latest of a series of strokes that had hit him like a sledgehammer on a shopping trip with his old friend, the mechanic Leo Villa, just before Christmas. Campbell's death struck him hard, and for a moment he let melancholy overtake him. 'This racing game must be a disease in the blood,' he told Malcolm's son Donald, when he visited his father's house of Little Gatton to console him.[330] Maybe to change the subject as they shared the last bottle of whiskey from the sideboard, Goldie noted to Donald that the American Henry Kaiser intended to try to take his father's water speed record.[331] Donald later said it was the spark which lit his own fire for record-breaking.[332]

Back home a few days later, Goldie decided to continue in the same way he'd always done: he threw himself wholeheartedly into preparing for his next record attempt. Although the use of a Jaguar engine had prevented Syd and Jacko from being part of the previous year's record runs, the pair had kept themselves busy building a three-cylinder version of the standard MG engine with under 500cc displacement, meaning Goldie could have a crack at retaking Taruffi's record. He duly booked the Jabbeke road with the RACB for mid-September.

In the meantime, he tried to keep himself busy. He started writing up his memoirs into what became *Magic MPH,* his rather dry but ex-

329 As the timekeeping apparatus was not officially verified, the speeds set by Taruffi on his run of 26th November 1948 were questioned. Undaunted, he ran again on 18th February 1949 and set new, verified international records that beat Gardner.
330 *Surrey Mirror and County Post,* 2 Dec 1955, p9.
331 Kaiser was the money behind the bid, the boat piloted by Canadian Guy Lombardo.
332 David Tremayne, *Donald Campbell: The Man Behind the Mask,* (Bantam, 2005), p86.

ceptionally detailed autobiography.[333] He accepted invitations to show off the car at Silverstone,[334] acted as a steward at the Brighton Speed Trials and visited his old friend Freddie March at his new circuit at Goodwood, an easy run from Reigate. On 10th May, a very impressive envelope dropped through his letterbox, the title proclaiming it to be from the Office of the Prime Minister. It was a formal and rather brief note, informing him that His Majesty the King had decided that Goldie was to be awarded the Order of the British Empire, the OBE. Finally, he would receive the national recognition he had so long desired.

But it was almost by autopilot he took EX135 to Belgium in September. He managed a searing 160 miles-per-hour from his strange three-cylinder engine, beating Taruffi's records by a healthy 30 miles-per-hour, at which point the Italian sent his congratulations, accepted defeat, and proclaimed that he would not challenge the Englishman again. More awards followed for Goldie from both the BRDC (a bar to his silver medal) and from the RACB (who went one better and presented him with two gold medallions).[335] It was another successful season, but he couldn't help feeling that he wanted something more. Then, shortly after his return from Jabbeke, that something arrived in the form of an invitation from the Austin Motor Company. They wanted to prove the worth of their A40 Devon saloon car to American buyers who made up the biggest market on the planet. Their plan was to take a standard A40 from a US dealership and run it around a measured course with the aim of taking various American stock car endurance and speed records including an epic 10,000 miles in 10,000 minutes target. Furthermore, they planned to do it in the Americans' very own backyard: the Bonneville Salt Flats in Utah.

---

333 Published by Motor Racing Publications Ltd in 1951.
334 The *Daily Express* race at Silverstone, at the invitation of Desmond Scannell (Secretary BRDC and Clerk of the Course, Silverstone). MG octagons painted on head fairing by Thompson & Tailor, Abingdon installed XPAG engine and a Wilson pre-select gearbox on 4th July. Enever, Jacko and Hounslow in attendance in white MG overalls. (Letters in Magna Press Archive).
335 Presented at a dinner on 23 Jan 1950 in Brussels.

Goldie leapt at the chance. Although this wasn't likely to be a high-speed affair, it meant travelling back to America, a country that, despite his divorce from Mariel, he still had very fond memories of. Plus, he would get to drive at Bonneville, a place that had almost mythical status with record-breaking drivers of the day. Austin would pay all his bills, including first-class travel on the *Queen Elizabeth* liner. George Eyston, who had owned EX135 in its original body and was a previous land-speed record holder himself, would manage the expedition. For the first time in years, Goldie was truly excited. A minor operation,[336] the display of EX135 at the London Motor Show[337] and a long interview on the BBC's *Calling All Sportsmen*[338] radio show easily filled his time for the rest of 1949.

1950 started gently. He visited Goodwood again and was made an honorary life member of the BARC, now standing for 'British' Automobile Racing Club,[339] its home having moved from the now-silent Brooklands circuit to Freddie March's glorious new track nestled below the Sussex downs. He also spoke frequently to Syd and Jacko who were developing yet another variation of the MG engine for him, this time a 332cc unit that would enable him to try for Class J records, and he duly booked Jabbeke again for the end of July. Otherwise, he spent time with Una and young Rosalind, enjoyed his cars and engaged fully in his other obsession: that of letter writing. Hand-written notes were fired off daily to various recipients, especially John Thornley, General Manager of MG and a close friend, who had agreed to support Goldie's display of EX135 at the New York International Motor Show, an exposition of British automotive excellence that handily coincided with his Austin A40 jaunt. Other letters went further afield: an attempt to procure a complimentary example of the new MG TD Midget that had just been

---

336 'Guy's did a good job and I am now without something that should not have been there in the first place' he wrote to Thornley. Letter dated 20 Oct 49 (Magna Press Archive).

337 28 Sep – 8 Oct, Olympia.

338 Howard Marshall interview with ATGG *BBC Home Service*, Saturday 19th Nov 1949, 7.30pm and Letter ATGG to John Thornley dated 24 Nov 49 (Magna Press Archive).

339 Rodney Walkerley, *Brooklands to Goodwood*, (Foulis, 1961), p164.

created by Jacko and Syd[340] was received with some humour by his old friend Jim Elwes at distributors University Motors. Elwes quickly wrote back. 'I loved your letter... which has cheered me more than anything else on this rather depressing Monday. How exactly I am going to pass a T.D. to you without causing frightful umbrage in other directions, I do not know, but I want you to realise that I am going to do my very best.'[341]

Finally, the departure date arrived, and on 6th April 1950, Goldie carefully made his way up the gangplank of the *Queen Elizabeth* as she sat at berth in Southampton Docks. He was no stranger to the opulence of transatlantic liners, but Cunard's flagship was something else. It wasn't long since her wartime battleship grey had been repainted in her present red, white and black colours and the interior refitted. It would be a comfortable six days until he once again saw the Manhattan skyline hove into view.

The crossing was quite a sociable affair, with many of his friends from the British motor industry on board, all en route to the New York International Motor Show. William Lyons and Sir William Rootes represented Jaguar and Rootes Motors respectively, there was a large contingent from Austin, and Goldie was joined by his old racing friend John Cobb. John Thornley accompanied Goldie onto the ship, carrying a packet of MG club ties brought at the suggestion of his public relations manager, who said he might be able to sell them to supporters.[342] Most of the men brought their wives but Goldie left Una at home with Rosalind preferring, as usual, to travel alone. There was a celebrity on board, too: comedian Tommy Trinder, a household name in Britain, off to play in New York on a bill with Frank Sinatra in what turned out to be a doomed attempt at breaking into the American market.[343]

---

340 'Jacko and Syd Enever took a Y-Type chassis... fitted a widened TC body to it... designed a radiator, bonnet and wings to blend, and submitted the creation ... as the TD. *Mr MG*, (ibid), p74.

341 Letter dated 2 Jan 1950 (Magna Press Archive).

342 Letter dated 1 Feb 1950 RA Bishop to John Thornley (Magna Press Archive).

343 US immigration records, April 1950, (www.ancestry.com).

The International Motor Show was deemed by the British to be a great success. Rootes showed off a 'Ghost' version of its Hillman Minx, complete with see-through panels proudly showing off its independent front suspension, Aston Martin unveiled its new DB2 model and Austin showed a group of cars including their new J40 pedal car, but EX135 made possibly the biggest impact on the visitors. Politics were at play – MG was not supposed to be officially represented, so the information board simply called it 'Lieutenant Colonel Gardner's Record Car' – but the instruction to remove the MG insignia from the head fairings had been ignored and the car proudly displayed the octagon badge, as well as its crossed British and Belgian flags below the BRDC insignia, ready for the next Jabbeke run in a few weeks' time.

But Goldie and the majority of the Austin group were there to break records, not to sell cars, but when they met Eyston on their arrival, he had bad news. A huge storm had raged through Bonneville the previous evening, flooding the salt flats and making a run impossible until June at the earliest. Alan Hess, Austin's publicity manager who had raced with Goldie at Brooklands and was now his co-driver, knew that they couldn't wait that long; not only would Goldie have to return to prepare for his next Jabbeke run, but the cost of keeping such a big group in America for at least another two months would be prohibitive.[344]

They had to find another location, and fast. Quickly, the men spoke to all their American contacts and a possible alternative identified: a racing circuit at the Suffolk County Airport near Eastport, some 70 miles from New York at the eastern end of Long Island. Hess went to look at the site and returned happy; the longer records would be impossible on the octagonal three-mile track, but there were still nearly 50 records possible within a 24-hour timeframe. Calls were made to

---

344 Two other drivers, Ron Jeavons and Jack Walters, were also part of the team but when the location moved to Long Island it was decided that Gardner and Hess could complete the driving as a pair.

the AAA, whose officials quickly descended on the airfield to set up the
necessary apparatus.

Meanwhile, the rest of the group collected the two 'stock' Austins
and moved into the John Duck Eastport Hotel which offered '20 rooms
and 400 seats for banquets, conventions and weddings' and was ap-
parently 'Famous for Duck Dinners.' They ate their fill that night and,
in the morning, took the cars out onto the airfield to run them in. As
Goldie lapped the circuit, he quickly discovered that although the concrete surface was billiard-table flat, the corners were very sharp and the
track sloped off towards the sandy, potholed verge. A mistake would be
easy to make and would inevitably end badly, so the team decided to
make their lives as easy as possible. Striped barrels were placed to mark
each corner and pegs with 'cat's eyes' were pushed into the ground to
mark the turn-in point to every corner. Finally, after hours of prac-
tise, Goldie felt he could go no faster. The record attempt was due to
start the following day but that morning, the team looked out from the
hotel as heavy rain sheeted down the windows and knew that no run
would be possible. But, by 6am the following morning, the rain had
stopped, the track had dried and Hess was behind the wheel of the
Austin, warming the engine. At 6.19am, the timing clock started and
the longest record run that Goldie had ever attempted was underway.

After two hours, Hess came into the pits much earlier than expected, his petrol gauge already showing empty. Soon, the reason for the
extraordinary fuel consumption was identified: as the car lapped the
anti-clockwise circuit, petrol was pouring out of the filler cap on the
right-hand side of the car. The tyres too were suffering on the tight
corners and the front offside tyre had been rubbed down to the canvas,
but after a few hours both crew and drivers had worked themselves
into a rhythm. An average speed of about 67 miles-per-hour was maintained, a remarkable feat considering the flat-out top speed of the car
in a straight line and with no pit stops to contend with was only 72
miles-per-hour.

The pair drove throughout the day, clocking up records as the miles increased. One-hour and three-hour records fell; then six, then twelve. At 9.15pm, Hess once again pulled into the pits and handed over to Goldie. 'It's bloody awful out there,' Hess shouted. 'Enjoy your shift!'

Within a lap, Goldie realised that Hess had not been exaggerating.[345] A thick fog had rolled in from the nearby Atlantic coast, cloaking the final two corners in a mist that reduced visibility to a matter of yards. As the Austin's dim headlamps struggled in vain to break through the gloom, Goldie was forced to use all his racing driver's skill, driving almost blind with the accelerator flat to the floor until he saw the glint of the cat's eyes mark his turn. It was driving by instinct, and twice it almost ended in disaster as he failed to see the cat's eyes in time but, rumbling over the sandy verge, he managed to pull the car back onto the road. After running for more than 15 hours the 1,000-mile record was taken, leaving just two to collect: the 2,000km and the 24-hour record.

But just before midnight, the road conditions as treacherous as before, Hess left the road as Goldie had done earlier, but this time became firmly stuck in the sand and 11 minutes were wasted as a breakdown truck was despatched to pull him out. Then, at 1.25am, with Goldie at the wheel, disaster struck.

Hammering blindly through the fog down a straight at over 70 miles-per-hour, Goldie suddenly glimpsed movement coming from the side of the road. Fifty yards ahead of him, a deer ambled into the road, turned and looked like it was moving off the track again, but at the last moment changed its mind. Goldie could do nothing but brace his arms against the steering wheel, his feet against the floor, and wait for the impact. Fortunately for him, it was no more than a dull thud, but one that proved instantly fatal for the poor animal. The front-left wing had

---

345 'I had a particularly bloody awful drive during the hours of darkness until we stopped at 1.25 am when I hit a 100lbs deer full into (??) broadside to him at 70 miles-per-hour! From 7pm onwards a thick sea fog came down with visibility down to less than 20 yards on each point of the deck!' Letter, ATGG to Thornley, 9 May 1950, (Magna Press Archive).

taken the brunt of the impact, crumpling a mass of metal back onto the tyre, and although this made a dreadful noise, it was the damage to the radiator that was Goldie's undoing. He limped back to the pits, but everyone knew their long night was over. Undaunted, the following day, Goldie and Hess returned in the second car and took another stack of shorter records, taking their total National and US Stock Car Record haul to 48, whilst the Austin team rebuilt the damaged vehicle so that Hess could use it in a fuel economy test by driving it to Canada. Meanwhile, the press team leapt into action, describing how the collision with the unfortunate deer was actually a *good* thing, as it demonstrated the strength of the Austin's construction. [346]

Goldie took his time to return home. At the invitation of Milt Marion, the driver who had won the Daytona Beach race back in 1936, now a racing team owner, he was driven overland to Indianapolis to see track testing for the famous 500-mile race, stopping along the way to see the sights of smalltown America and to drop the odd postcard to Una and Rosalind. Given an all-access pass to the racecourse, he met an old friend in the pits: the movie star Clark Gable. It was a great way to end the adventure, and on the late evening of his birthday, 31st October 1950, he set foot once more on the gangplank of the *Queen Elizabeth* bound home to Southampton, his head swirling with ideas for another American escapade.

Meanwhile though, there was work to be done. EX135 had beaten him back from America and by the time he arrived on British soil, it was in the capable hands of Jacko and Syd. While Goldie was away, they had been working on a two-cylinder version of the MG engine to lower the engine size under 350cc so that he could attack Johnny Lurani's records in yet another area, this time designated Class J. They fitted this supercharged engine, adjusted the axles and prepared the car to run again. MG's change of heart about whether to officially sup-

---

346 'The pressed steel body took the collision without a murmur [and] undoubtedly averted disaster.' (Pressed Steel Company Ltd release, 9 May 1950).

port Gardner again was a dramatic U-turn and almost entirely based on cold hard economic fact: the Nuffield Group publicity department had calculated that Goldie's run with Jaguar had created 92 press reports, each column inch of which was worth £1,560 (around £38,000 in 2023).[347] This was too good to miss, and on 22nd July 1950, the old team of Goldie, Jacko, Syd, Les Kesterton and a host of others met at the Metropole Hotel in Folkestone before setting out once again for Ostend. Goldie's regular companion Freddie Clifford was present, as was Dick Benn, a friend from Brighton who owned an MG Y-Type and had asked Goldie whether he could see what it could do on the speed record course. Goldie reckoned the car, which was described as 'About as sporting in appearance as the average Victorian bathtub'[348] could do 100 miles-per-hour and as if to ensure he wasn't proved wrong, on their rest day Jacko and Syd set about the car, making sure it was as ready as it could be. The final result, which they had started back in Abingdon, was a supercharged and highly tuned engine, a flattened undertray, oversize tyres on the rear and racing tyres on the front.

Compared with the souped-up Y-Type, EX135 seemed a little tame. The car had the smallest engine it had ever run with, less than a quarter of the size of the saloon, but once Goldie rolled off along the motorway and Jacko pulled out the set of *Smiths* stopwatches that he always used to time the runs, it was obvious that the record car was as quick as they had expected. After a few frustrating runs left unrecorded due to the old gremlin of timing equipment failure, Goldie set a host of new records, all tantalisingly close to the 200kph mark. He went again to see if he could improve but a dense cloud of white smoke suddenly filled the cockpit and called a halt to proceedings. Dick Benn ran up with the results: three new records, all substantially higher than Lurani's. It was a good day at the office.

347 Letter, Central Publicity Department to John Thornley dated 13 Oct 49 (Magna Press Archive).
348 Wilson McComb, *The Story of the MG Sports Car*, (Dent, 1972), p109.

Now, it was the Y-Type's turn. With very little time left before the road reopened, Goldie hurried back and jumped into the saloon. Syd just had time to explain that the speedo only went up to 100, so if the needle stopped at the end of the gauge, he'd be doing well. Gardner went out, duly pushed the speedo needle off the end of the counter and recorded a top speed of over 107 miles-per-hour and an average of 104.725 miles-per-hour for the mile, making it the fastest 1.5-litre saloon in the world. Goldie was content he'd racked up yet another record, and 'Then, having satisfied his own quiet, unshaken argument, Richard Benn stepped into his closed carriage and motored himself sedately home to Brighton…'[349] Lurani, with tongue firmly in cheek, wired Goldie later that day. 'You pig. Stop.' It read. 'Nevertheless, bitter congratulations from Nibbio.'[350]

That evening, Gardner ruminated. 'What class is there left which we might be able to tackle in this car?' he wrote. 'On the other hand, it is possible to improve on the figures I have already set up in all the six classes! Maybe I shall try to do this…'[351] But to go faster, Goldie knew he needed a longer course. He needed to go back to America.

---

349 Russell Lowry, *Motoring* magazine (in-house magazine of the Nuffield Organisation) date not known.
350 *Nibbio* was the name of Lurani's record vehicle. *Magic MPH,* (ibid), p151.
351 *Magic MPH,* (ibid), p151-152.

18

SPEED ON THE SALT

As the passengers alighted from the London train at Oxford station just before midday on 4th July 1951, they were greeted with the sight of a row of gleaming new MG saloons parked along the Botley Road, their suited drivers standing proudly by each door. Slowly, the cars filled with the journalists who had made their way from Fleet Street for a rare day out of the office. Half an hour later, they arrived at the MG works in Abingdon where they were met by John Thornley who introduced them to Goldie, Syd and Jacko.

A buffet lunch and other refreshments were offered as Goldie and the team explained what they intended: an attempt at improving the Class F (1,100-1,500cc) records using a supercharged version of the standard engine out of their current MG TD road car. This time though, it was not to be just a few quick 1-mile or 1-kilometre runs, but an attempt to break the longer distance records including the hour and 200km targets. For this, Belgium was just too small; they needed to go to the home of the land speed record itself: Bonneville Salt Flats in Utah, USA. Murmurs of interest rippled through the room before Goldie continued, giving more details of the venture. The journalists made polite notes but weren't really that interested. What they wanted to see was the car, and to hear the engine being run up to full speed.[352]

It was all smiles that day, but behind the scenes an aide-mémoire from Thornley had been circulated to the senior staff at MG in case they were asked difficult questions about why this venture was being bankrolled by MG. 'The public may be said to fall into two categories – the technically erudite and the rest,' the memo stated. 'Of these we primarily aim to reach [the latter] through world record attempts… the advertising value is tremendous, especially as world-wide publicity is achieved.' It also explained why they were sticking with Goldie. '[He] is now 60 years of age… to break with him now would undoubtedly invoke a fresh period of adverse publicity, which apart from anything else would be felt very strongly at Abingdon. As an instance of the sort of thing that would happen if support for Goldie were withdrawn at this stage, the car which is due to be exhibited at the Festival of Britain… would unquestionably appear there with its MG monograms removed.'[353]

Thornley should not have worried. The press reports from the day were very gentle and the direction received from those at the top of the Nuffield Organisation was that Goldie was to remain supported. Consequently, the gleaming EX135 took its place as exhibit B801 on the South Bank and was, in the organisers' words, 'An immense attraction to all the visitors to the Exhibition.'[354] The 'advertising value' that Thornley had spoken of was already starting to be repaid: Pathé News even ran a 7½ minute reel of the car, backed with a stirring military brass band soundtrack.[355] But EX135 had another appointment that it needed to keep. In the early morning of Friday, June 15th, the team

---

352 Letter from the Nuffield Organisation central publicity department dated 5 June 1951 (Magna Press Archive).

353 *Lt Col AT Goldie Gardner's Future Projects* letter, June 1951 (Magna Press Archive).

354 Council of Industrial Design letter to Thornley dated 9 June 1951 (Magna Press Archive).

355 https://www.youtube.com/watch?v=dGfbHetdL1U

from MG arrived to remove the car and take it back to Abingdon for final fettling before it was shipped off to America.

Even with the car on its way to Bonneville,[356] the organisational effort required for the record attempt didn't abate. Crossing the channel to Ostend was one thing; shifting the car, crates of spares and a big team of people halfway around the world, organising official record keepers to be in the right place at the right time and even dealing with the vagaries of the weather, were quite another. 'A safari from England to the West-Central USA is a fairly expensive undertaking,' Thornley wrote. 'Car, and possibly fuel, must be shipped and railed 5,000 miles; driver, team manager and mechanics must be transported and maintained; the promoter must foot the bill for the preparation of the course and for the transport and sustenance of the necessary time-keepers and officials… the US dollar being what it is, the whole thing adds up to a pretty penny.'[357]

Planning the event dominated Gardner's life which he expressed in letters to Thornley, with sheaves of them arriving on his desk every day. 'I get about fourteen letters a week from Goldie, and ring him about one a month,' Thornley told his friend 'Bev' Rowntree at Shell-Mex. 'Correspondence between us is severely one-sided.' [358] Gardner sometimes forgot that John Thornley had a major British motor manufacturer to run and that dealing with the record attempt wasn't always his top priority. Nevertheless, his instructions, covering everything from hand-drawn sketches of the car's livery to how the team's bags should be labelled continued to pour in. Gardner treated this like a military operation, trying to plan for every eventuality and even addressed his letters to Thornley with the latter's old Army rank: 'My dear Colonel…' Finally, on 12th August 1951, Goldie, Syd, Jacko and Dick Benn

---

356 It was only after the Flats had been used for various record runs in the 1930s that a Mr Bonneville approached the AAA to tell them that he owned the land. He told them that he should be accorded a 'consideration' for its use and told them that although he wanted no payment, he would like them referred to as the 'Bonneville Salt Flats.' George Eyston, *Speed on Salt* (Batsford, 1936), p78.
357 *Maintaining the Breed,* (ibid), p132.
358 Letter dated 6 July 1951 (Magna Press Archive).

– the Y-Type owner from Brighton whose car Goldie had driven to record speed in Jabbeke and who had decided to accompany the expedition – arrived at Heathrow airport in good time for the 5.15pm BOAC
flight to New York. Thornley breathed a sigh of relief; for a time, the
letters stopped.

The journey to their final destination was a long one. After emerging bleary-eyed onto the tarmac in New York, the small group of men
had a day to kill before departing again that evening and flying into the
night on a United Airlines aircraft, landing at Salt Lake City at 1.20am.
There, they were met by two drivers from MG's local dealership, the
Foreign Motor Co, who handed over two cars, theirs for the duration
of the visit. Then, it was a two-hour drive due west, arriving at their
final destination of Wendover as the dawn broke. The town was a small
dot in the middle of the desert, home to around a thousand people.
Few had heard of the place then, and for good reason: towards the end
of World War Two, the tiny Wendover Air Force Base had been selected due to its remoteness and obscurity for a very special role, hosting
the B-29 Superfortress crews[359] who would later drop the first atomic
bombs. By the time Goldie and his team arrived, most of the USAF
contingent had long since left but the small town remained, including
what was to be the centre of their operations for the next couple of
weeks: the Wendover Service Station. Offering 'cabins, café, lubrication storage and repairing' the square, white buildings squatted in the
lee of some small, scrub-covered hills on the edge of what they called
the Great Salt Lake Desert.

The next morning the men met, eager to get on with the task at
hand. The sun was still low on the horizon, but the temperature was
already climbing, and Goldie felt the sweat prickle on his back as he
squinted into the daylight. The team quickly tracked down the garage
proprietor, but a shock was in store: EX135, expected to have arrived by
rail several weeks previously, was nowhere to be found. Not only that,

---

359 509th Composite Group, USAF.

being the first time they had tried this sort of venture on the other side of the Atlantic, nobody had bothered to note down the number of the freight car that it was tucked away in, somewhere in the 2,300 miles of railroad between themselves and New York.[360] Frantically, Goldie and Dick started contacting everyone they could think of: the American Express staff who had made the transport arrangements, the US railroad staff and even MG's West Coast distributors. It seemed like a hopeless task but after three nerve-wrenching days, a message arrived to say that the car had arrived at the sidings and was ready to be unloaded.

Goldie was relieved but by no means happy. It was now 17th August 1951 and with the first run scheduled for dawn on 20th, the time they had set aside for final preparation of the car had been dramatically cut. They had also already discovered another problem they hadn't bargained for, a lack of local support for Jacko and Syd. Goldie had a war chest of £1,000 to cover expenses on the trip and had assumed that he would easily be able to hire local mechanics, but Enever and Jacko were not at all impressed with the quality of the local workmanship. Wendover mechanics, it seemed, despite being extremely keen and eager to help, lacked the skills needed for a project requiring such fine tolerances, especially when most of them had rarely even seen a British car before, let alone worked on a speed record machine. Goldie recorded the lessons they were learning, making a note to write to Thornley on his return.[361]

Nevertheless, in the two full days they had left, working in daily temperatures that reached close to 100 degrees in their unfamiliar workshop, the two very capable MG mechanics did everything they needed to. Their meticulous preparation back in Abingdon had paid off and the car was ready for the evening of 19th with just a final polish needed on the morning of the first run. The car had even been

---

360 *Maintaining the Breed*, (ibid), p135.
361 He sent this two-page letter to Thornley on 10th September 1951. Gus Perry from Lucas and Cliff Webb from MG were co-opted into lending a hand. (Magna Press Archive).

tested, of sorts, running up and down the street outside the Service Station, one mechanic driving and the other either running alongside or sitting perched on the back deck, listening to make sure everything was working as it should. Goldie had also driven out to the desert and tried the course for himself, lapping it a few times in a road car to get a feel for the circuit. Nevertheless, as the team emerged from the motel at 2.30am the following morning, there was a palpable sense of nervousness. Syd and Jacko made one last check on EX135, now loaded on the back of a trailer, before setting off on the 12-mile journey to the Flats. There, as they pulled up, the two mechanics were astonished; in the middle of nowhere, Gus Backman and his team, working on behalf of the AAA, had spent weeks constructing the perfect location for a speed record attempt. Small wooden timing huts had been built to allow observers an uninterrupted view of the ten-mile circular course which had been scraped flat to a width of 100 feet and a thick black line drawn along the inside or the curve. A few feet inside this line, poles had been erected, the salt so hard that a machine had been needed to drill the holes in which they sat. Between them, twin-strand copper wire had been laid which at each record distance point connected 'light rays' that would time the car to within a hundredth of a second.[362] All of this wasn't cheap: Goldie had agreed a course preparation budget of £2,340 with Thornley (worth around £87,000 in 2023) of which he contributed £350 and sponsorship by oil manufacturer Duckham's, which was trying to break into the American market, that softened the blow by a further £600.[363]

As the team pulled to a halt, Art Pilsbury of the AAA Contest Board, who had flown in from Los Angeles to lead the official delegation, strode out to meet Goldie, a smile wide across his face. For months, the two men had communicated by letter and finally they were here, ready to go. Pilsbury had worked with George Eyston and John

---

362 Letter Pilsbury to Gardner, Jan 1951, (Magna Press Archive).
363 Letter Gardner to Thornley, 28 Feb 1951, (Magna Press Archive).

Cobb and had a soft spot for these rather eccentric British drivers; as Goldie hobbled across to meet him, Pilsbury wasn't disappointed. As the two men exchanged pleasantries, the mechanics quickly unloaded the car and made their final preparations as the dawn started to break on the horizon.

Soon, both car and driver were ready. Surrounded by a gaggle of officials, journalists and Jack Duckham, who had flown over to see where his sponsorship money was going, Goldie pulled on his white windcap and goggles, shook a few hands, then climbed into the car, wriggling down on the familiar green leather padding to make himself as comfortable as was possible, given the situation. It was 7am, and although the sun was still low on the horizon, the air was already hot and with the engine ticking over the temperature in the alloy body of the car was stifling even before Jacko and Syd screwed down the Dzus fasteners of the cockpit lid, cocooning him inside. He watched as Pilsbury came over to the edge of the track, raised the flag, then smartly dropped it. As he'd done a thousand times before, Goldie dropped the clutch, pressed the accelerator and felt the jolt of speed as the spinning tyres gained purchase on the hard rock salt.

Compared with his earlier runs, the experience of driving on salt was a strange one. With none of the barriers, trees or other surrounding paraphernalia present during all of his road record attempts, the course engendered a sense of safety; there was very little to hit out here and if something went wrong, there were miles of flat salt on which to slow down, so large in fact that Goldie noted to himself that he could make out the curvature of the earth across this plain expanse. There was also an absence of the rhythmic thumping of the tyres crossing joins in the road surface, just a smooth rushing as they danced over the salt. The only slight downside was a significant pull on the steering that, in his typically understated way, he described as 'quite noticeable.'[364]

---

364 Published report by ATGG, August 1951 (NMM).

Meanwhile, there was a strange reaction from the team once the car had departed. Jacko and Syd looked at each other; for now, their work was done. All they could do was hope that the car held together, the engine performed as well as expected and that Goldie did his job. They had been around the 'old man' long enough now to know that the last was a given. In fact, all they could do was listen: a gradually fading sound as the car shot off into the distance, reducing to nothing before building again to a crescendo as Goldie passed into the lee of the Silver Island Mountains. Then, as he rounded near the 'beach' leading to Pilot Peak, the sound softened again until the southwest wind caught the exhaust note and the noise increased again, this time building to a climax as the car sped past in a bottle-green blur.[365] Both mechanics strained their ears to hear the slightest murmur of trouble, but none came.

Inside the car, Gardner was really settling into the rhythm. The only thing he didn't like on the first couple of laps was the way the light changed: brilliant rays of daylight emerging from the east, a backdrop of almost pitch darkness in the west and a murky gloom in between. Soon though, daylight had engulfed the whole area in a bath of light. Squinting now, Goldie concentrated on holding the line, watching the marker posts flash by and glancing down at his stopwatch to work out his speed. Every circuit, he became faster; by the 13th lap, his penultimate, he was averaging 146.5 miles-per-hour and was on occasion hitting 160 miles-per-hour. Although he'd hoped for more – he wanted to exceed the 150 miles-per-hour average – it was still a phenomenal achievement for a car with a 1,250cc engine, as it matched the speed achieved at Bonneville (although over 24 hours) by the 21-litre *Speed of the Wind* 15 years previously.[366]

---

365 *Speed on Salt*, (ibid), p55.
366 This car, powered by a Rolls-Royce Kestrel aircraft engine, was created by Ernest Eldridge for George Eyston and driven by him, John Cobb, Albert Denly and Chris Staniland at Bonneville to take 24 (and latterly 48-hour) endurance records in 1935 and 1936. *Speed on Salt* (ibid).

Then, about 45 minutes into his run, something felt wrong to Gardner; Enever and Jacko heard it, too. Knowing he needed to run for another 15 minutes to achieve the hour record, Gardner gently let up the
pressure on the accelerator, slowing gradually until he was lapping at
around 75 miles-per-hour. Finally, just after the hour was over, he coasted into the pits and stopped next to the crowd who awaited him there.
Syd unscrewed the canopy and Goldie clambered out, his legs stiff and
his green shirt wet with perspiration. Jacko ran over to hand him his
stick and was quickly followed by Pilsbury who handed him the results:
despite the slow finish, he had achieved six new international records
and ten American class titles with times that were not quite fast enough
to put them out of reach of any European attempt at Montlhéry but
a significant increase over the existing speeds. Despite the problem,
quickly diagnosed as a broken camshaft oil pipe, it was a fair day's
work and when a smiling Jack Duckham pulled out a magnum of Piper
Heidsieck champagne, the team were very happy to sink a glass while
they posed for photographs with the car in the desert sunshine. Then,
as the light began to fade, they headed back to Wendover, keen to have
a good night's sleep before starting work again on the car to prepare it
for Goldie's high-speed, short duration runs, planned for two days' time
on Thursday, 23rd August. For Syd and Jacko, this was hardly a challenging deadline, and there was plenty of time for Goldie to give it a
160mph test after which he announced that the car was ready to run.[367]

But the following day, things didn't go according to plan from the
off. Due to a miscommunication, a member of staff at the motel woke
every guest at 2.30am rather than just the record team and Goldie was
faced with the disgruntled, bleary-eyed faces of the other guests as he
walked over to the garage. Then, on their arrival at Bonneville, they
learnt that a spectator had driven through the wires linking the tim-

---

367 During this day (22 August 1951), the circuit was used by Dick van Osten, an editor of *Motor Trend* who,
   along with three colleagues, drove a totally stock MG TD to 23 American stock car records over a 12-
   hour period, averaging around 75 miles-per-hour a lap. *Maintaining the Breed*, (ibid), p136.

ing lights, wrecking them. Hour after painful hour they waited as Pilsbury and his team replaced the wires, only to find that the equipment still didn't work. That afternoon, an apologetic Pilsbury confirmed to Goldie what he feared: the apparatus would not be fixed that day. Dejected, the team returned to Wendover.

The next morning, things were not much better. Engineers had identified the problem as static electricity that had built up in the uncovered copper wires and finally, after lunch, they announced that the course was ready. Quickly, Gardner mounted up and carried out a couple of runs which Enever clocked at around 190 miles-per-hour; a good start. But then Pilsbury, his face leaden, waved him back in: the equipment still had not recorded. 'Nerves tautened, tempers became uncertain,' wrote John Thornley.[368] Then, as the AAA engineers finally confirmed that the kit was operational, Gardner looked up at the horizon and saw storm clouds building. That night, to their extreme frustration, the rains came, sheeting off the salt, wrecking the surface and making it quite unusable for speed records until the following year. Despondent, Gardner admitted defeat and called a halt to the proceedings. EX135 and all the spares were packed up and handed over to Kjell Qvale, the impresario importer of MG motor cars who had persuaded Goldie to let him take the car on a tour of American showrooms on the understanding that he'd ship the lot back to Britain at his own expense by the new year. Now unencumbered, the team drove to Salt Lake City then flew back to New York, checking in to the Roosevelt Hotel on Madison Avenue on Sunday 26th where Goldie wrote back to John Thornley, read a sheaf of congratulatory telegrams and went to bed early. Jacko and Syd on the other hand decided to make the most of the opportunity and hit the town.[369]

The following day, Goldie had the press to deal with. As well as being a motor entrepreneur, Qvale seemed to know everyone in the city

---

368 *Maintaining the Breed*, (ibid), p137.
369 Letter, Gardner to Thornley, 26 Aug 1951 (Magna Press Archive).

and had helped to arrange interviews with almost every major news network. Goldie was shuttled between studios and treated like a celebrity wherever he went: he was interviewed by Jimmy Powers of CBS, Nancy Craig of ABC and Bill Slater, whose live radio show was broadcast over lunch at Sardi's Restaurant, a block from Times Square. Then in the afternoon one of the biggest names in US television took their turn: Jinx Falkenburg, queen of the informal chat show joined Goldie on the studio sofa and, as he puffed away on his pipe, she tried to get inside the mind of this extraordinary man. Goldie, true to form despite his sixty-one years, didn't seem to mind the attentions of this woman who *The New Yorker* described as having, 'one of the most photogenic faces… in the western world.'[370]

For once, Goldie enjoyed the press attention at the end of what had been an expedition of mixed fortunes. 'Personally, I know the results achieved are very satisfactory,' he told Thornley, 'although could have been better.' Privately, he was disappointed, and on his return following a leisurely cruise back to Southampton aboard the *Queen Elizabeth*[371], a plinth he had been presented with slipped from his hand, landing painfully on his left ('good') foot.[372] No bones were broken, but it seemed to sum up his summer.

Thornley, on the other hand, was delighted; not only did the records make for good reading, but MG had received more positive press attention in the critical US market than ever before. 'It did not need second thoughts to decide that a return visit should be paid in the late summer [of 1952] to have another go,' he wrote,[373] although this time he had another idea: they would take a second, larger engine and attempt to break two classes of records.[374] Goldie loved the idea and started plan-

370 *The New Yorker*, 13 Jan 1992.
371 The team departed from NY bound for Southampton on 29th August 1951 (www.ancestry.com).
372 Letter ATGG to JWT, 26 Sep 1951, (Magna Press Archive).
373 *Maintaining the Breed*, (ibid), p137.
374 This was the VC22 engine of 2215cc as fitted to the Wolseley 6/80. It would allow them not just to challenge for Class F records as they had done in 1951, but also Class E records.

ning immediately. Surely 1952 was going to be the year he and EX135 returned to their full potential.

19

THE FINAL RUN

The dockside crane groaned as the vast wooden crate lifted off the quayside. The driver paused, waiting for the heavy box to slow its gentle swinging before engaging the engine and pulling it high into the hazy Liverpool air. It was still early morning on 4th July 1952, but the dock worker was already feeling the temperature rise as the sun beat down on the concrete around him.[375] Marked "Lt.Col. A.T.G. Gardner, C/O Foreign Motor Car Co., 425 South Main St, Salt Lake City, Utah", the crate containing his record car was carefully lifted over the side of the *MV Brittanic* and securely deposited deep in the hold of the Cunard liner. 21 smaller crates followed, all marked with the same script, containing all of the spares Goldie thought he would need for his next speed record attempt.[376] It would take nearly a month for the crates to work their way across America via the docks of New York, Chicago and Denver before arriving in the desert heat of Salt Lake City on July 29th, a day before the team met for a send-off party about the Cunard

---

375 Early July saw a mini heatwave in the UK with temperatures of over 33 degrees Centigrade recorded.
376 *Summary of Arrangements for Record Attempts at Utah, August 1952* (MG, 1952).

flagship, the *Queen Elizabeth*, before they too crossed the Atlantic towards the tiny town of Wendover on the edge of the famous Bonneville salt flats. The newly created British Motor Corporation press team had done their work well, and photographers followed the team from the moment they set foot in New York. By the time they reached Wendover, the newspapers were printing a photograph of Goldie showing their United Airlines cabin crew member a model of his record car.[377] All was looking good.

Once again, it had been an epic feat of planning to get to this stage, but at least they had done it all before and knew what to expect. Goldie's flurry of letters arriving in John Thornley's inbox had still been considerable, but not quite on the same level as the previous year and they didn't have the added complication of having to extricate the car from the Festival of Britain. This year, with a supercharged version of the new MG TD engine in the car, Goldie was sure that he could take home even more than the six international and ten national records he'd secured in 1951. Whether he was just being careful or felt uneasy is unclear, but Goldie had also just renewed his will[378] and left instructions that in the event of any 'untoward' incident that John Thornley was to inform Una and the directors at Milne & Russell.[379]

But as they arrived, so did torrential rain. Peering out from the plate glass windows of the Wendover Service Station, the team watched as the once hard-packed earth that the town was built on turned to mud. All they could do was wait. The 12th, the first planned day of running, came and went. By the night of 15th, the ground had mostly dried, and Goldie visited the track to see whether a run was possible the next day. It was still sticky, but he persuaded himself it was safe and decided to go for it. Quickly, Jacko, Syd and the rest of the team set to work in their final preparations.

---

377 Photo, 6 August 1952 (Magna Press Archive).
378 Copy of will, March 1952 (HMCTS).
379 Letter, ATGG to Thornley dated 9 Jul 51, (Magna Press Archive).

As dawn broke the following morning, Goldie's feet crunched on the smooth crust of salt as he hobbled towards the car. Pausing, he turned and held out his cane to Jacko, who took it and pinned it under his arm like a sergeant major's pace stick. As he'd done a hundred times before, Goldie lifted his bad leg onto the side of EX135, shuffled over toward the cockpit, then dropped both feet onto the green leather pad that formed his seat.[380] Although it was still early in the morning, the Utah sun was already hot and he felt the first prickles of perspiration dance across his forehead under his white linen wind cap, the same headgear he'd been wearing for nearly thirty years of driving racing cars. At 62 years of age, with his baggy white trousers and green short-sleeved shirt, BRDC badge proudly sewn onto the left breast pocket, he didn't really look like a land-speed record holder, but looks can be deceptive.

Goldie made himself as comfortable as he could in the familiar cockpit and set about his final checks. George Perry, who had been sent by Lucas to support the record attempt, handed him his bowtie-shaped steering wheel which he clicked into place. Finally, he removed his sunglasses and swapped them for a set of green-tinted 'Panorama' goggles, an improvement from the previous year when he found the glare from the salt flats to be almost unbearable.

Syd and Jacko tinkered, as they always did, making sure the car was ready to go. Then Goldie turned the big switch away from the 'OFF' mark that Syd had drawn in huge letters on the dash, firing up the engine, which quickly barked into life. He checked the gauges, each marked out in white paint to make them stand out when the driver's head was rattling around at 200 miles-per-hour. The rev counter was front and centre, tilted so that the supercharged two-litre engine's peak power as identified on the bench at Abingdon – around 5,400rpm – was at the top. Next to it were the other critical gauges: oil and supercharger pressure. All he had to do was keep the big needle pointing upwards,

---

380 There is a great period newsreel of this at https://www.youtube.com/watch?v=26Fe4xCnAIg

keep the others out of the red, and drive as smoothly as possible around the ten-mile circuit that had been marked on the salt flats.

With a final polish of the bodywork, Syd and Jacko were happy. Jacko nodded, and Goldie smiled and nodded back. They had been doing this a long time: Jacko had first helped Gardner back in 1937 on his first record attempt in Frankfürt, then in his single-seater MG Magnette. Since the creation of EX135 in its present form, both he and Enever had been his almost constant companions. Goldie pulled down his goggles and the Perspex canopy was clipped into place. With a wave from Art Pilsbury, the AAA timekeeper, Goldie knew he was good to go. He pressed his right foot down and released the clutch, feeling a lurch as the engine started to build up the revs. Quickly, he gained speed over the white surface of the salt lake and before long he had pushed up through the gears to top. Now, it was just a case of keeping the gently curving line marker to the right, keeping his concentration, and pushing harder than he had ever pushed before.

Inside the cockpit, Goldie's bare forearms beaded with sweat as the steering wheel jolted in his hands, every tiny bump on the surface transmitted through the thin rubber-clad spoked wheels and amplified through the skeleton frame of EX135, shaking him so much that his head rattled against the cowl of the Perspex hood. He was engulfed in a cacophony of sound: the rattles of the bodywork flexing against the chassis, the roar of the un-silenced engine, the exhaust firing straight out in a deafening wall of noise and heat and the incessant whine of the supercharger. The temperature was almost unbearable now: not only had the sun risen, but insulation on the engine bulkhead had been reduced to almost nothing to save weight. As the laps started to build, the heat pulsated through to his feet, leaving them feeling like they were on fire.

Outside, the wooden marker posts were mesmerising as they flashed past. Every few minutes, Goldie passed the red, wooden timing stand surrounded by the expedition's other cars, and he squinted to read what information was on the board that Dick Benn, his team manager, held up for him. Two, three, four laps… still he kept his foot to the floor, ignored the heat, ignored the noise. Five, six, seven… he looked down at the shaking RPM gauge to his front: needle pointing upwards, all was well.

But all was not well. The salt, usually rock hard at this time of year, had been softened by the unseasonal rainstorm they had experienced on their arrival in Wendover. As Gardner built up the laps, tiny specs of salt had been forced into the thin tyre treads, slowly packing together to fill the voids. Now, his tyres lacked any effective grip and all they needed to lose traction altogether was a slight lateral movement.

When it came, after about 74 miles of driving, it came slowly.[381] Something, possibly the most minute over-correction to the steering wheel, or a tiny rock at just the wrong place at the wrong time, pushed the back tyres just a fraction of an inch out of line and the rear of the car started, very slowly, to slip out to the left. Goldie, his senses honed by over a quarter of a century of racing cars, felt it immediately, edged the wheel gently to the left and tried to correct. But the same problem that had slicked the rear tyres had also rendered the fronts ineffective, and when they didn't bite, Goldie knew he was now just a passenger. At a shade over 165 miles an hour, EX135 gradually turned into the mother of all broadside skids.

Looking on, Jacko, Syd and the rest of the crew knew immediately something was wrong. They saw EX135 start to slide, its tail slipping out before it was engulfed in a cloud of white salt dust. They were already running to their cars as they saw the green hulk of the car career into the infield and hit something that disintegrated into parts that flew high into the air. Before the record car had come to a halt, they were driving frantically down the salt flats towards it. Three agonising minutes later, they reached the scene.

Miraculously, the car had not rolled. Possibly, the lack of grip that had caused the accident in the first place may have saved Goldie and

---

381 *The Works MGs*, (ibid), p135.

Spring 1947. Goldie took his time to start a family. Aged 56, he and godfather Sir Malcolm Campbell look on as Una holds young Rosalind after her christening service.

14th September 1948, Jabbeke. Wally Hassan (hand to ear) and Lofty England (opposite him) listen to their 4-cylinder XJ engine, the forerunner to the famous XK 6-cylinder, as Gardner waits to enter the cockpit.

The only known occasion when Goldie let his wife and daughter accompany him on his adventures was in 1948, when they travelled with him to Belgium.

10th May 1949. Goldie cared little for the attention he received as a 'famous motorist' but Royal acknowledgement of his achievements meant a great deal.

CENTRAL CHANCERY OF
THE ORDERS OF KNIGHTHOOD,
ST. JAMES'S PALACE, S.W.I.

Sir,

I have the honour to send to you herewith the Warrant under The King's Sign Manual granting you the dignity of an Officer of the Civil Division of the Most Excellent Order of the British Empire, and to inform you that the Insignia has been sent to you under separate registered cover.

Would you please be good enough to acknowledge the receipt of these on the attached form.

I have the honour to be, Sir,

Your obedient Servant,

J. De la Bere
Brigadier

Registrar of the
Order of the British Empire.

Lieutenant-Colonel Alfred Thomas Goldie Gardner,
O.B.E., M.C.

April 27th 1950, Long Island. Goldie exits the cockpit of the Austin A40 mid-way through his endurance record run as the team set to work on the car.

Photo: Courtesy Mike Jones Family Archive.

May 1950, Indianapolis. Goldie chats with his old friend Clark Gable in the pits as they watch testing for the Indianapolis 500.

Photo: Courtesy Mike Jones Family Archive.

July 1950. Back in Belgium, Goldie successfully took three Class J records with the smallest engine ever fitted to EX135, displacing just 331.48cc. Between runs, he had time to push his friend Dick Benn's MG Y-Type to 104.725mph, setting a new saloon car record.

Photo: Reg Jackson family archive, courtesy of Tracey Rose.

Goldie packing in his office for yet another adventure. Ros Gardner remembers this place as being a wonderous treasure trove of artifacts, pictures and lists which, even at a young age, she knew were important.

Carl Giles created a few different cartoons for Goldie which he used to illustrate his Christmas cards. This, his card for 1950, shows him, Jacko and Syd setting records, then handing the ball to their great rival, Italian Piero Taruffi.

Along with MG, Duckham's was Goldie's biggest financial sponsors throughout his post-war runs and were keen to use his likeness in their advertisements. He appeared in many different adverts for various companies and his car was created in *Dinky* toy form.

Photo: Courtesy National Motor Museum Trust and Duckhams.

Magic MPH, Goldie's autobiography, was published in 1951. He seemed to enjoy writing when he was not racing and edited various motor racing annuals.

Bonneville. Dawn breaks as EX135 is towed onto the
salt flats for another day of record breaking.

August 20th 1951. Jacko tops up the Duckham's NOL oil in front of the AAA
timing hut. Syd Evener, as ever, is not far away (sunglasses, on left).
Photo: Bill Shipler Photographic Collection, courtesy Utah State Historical Society.

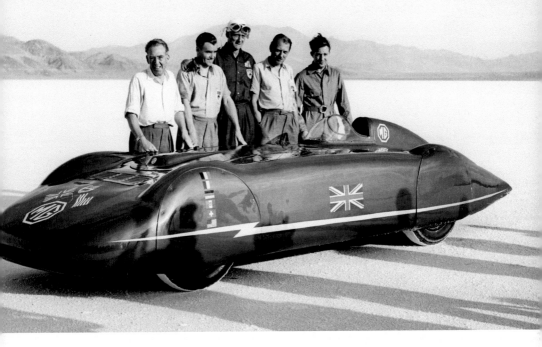

Despite not achieving everything Goldie wanted, the 1951 run at Bonneville was a success, with six international and 16 national records secured. More importantly was the publicity the event generated, helped by high-quality images like this one commissioned from local photographers.

Photo: Bill Shipler Photographic Collection, courtesy Utah State Historical Society.

When he arrived back in New York, Goldie was a sensation. TV and radio broadcasters flocked to interview him, including 'primetime' interviews on various channels including ABC and CBS.

16th August 1952, Bonneville. Tyre treads clogged with damp salt, EX135 slid for a mile before stopping. Syd replaces the Perspex canopy before the team straighten out the rear left wheel arch and reattach the wheel cover.

The slightly battered EX135 sits back in its garage in Wendover, salt still caking the front air intake. Although they didn't realise it, this was the last time either car or driver would break a record.

Photo: Reg Jackson family archive, courtesy of Tracey Rose.

his car: at that speed, as EX135 skidded sideways, the wheels would have only had to catch on a piece of uneven surface or the tyres burst under the extraordinary pressure they were under, and the car and driver would have barrel-rolled into oblivion. As it was, it seemed both had survived remarkably well.

The crew ran over to the car. Facing backwards, it had come to rest outside the circuit, nearly a mile from when the skid started. The Perspex bubble was gone, save a few jagged shards that remained in place around the edge. Goldie was sitting in the cockpit, staring straight ahead, his face red with blood and with a large crimson stain spreading across his white linen wind-cap. One of the Americans was there first. "SIR! COLONEL GARDNER, SIR! ARE YOU OK?"

Goldie Gardner turned his head and looked bewilderingly at his rescuer. Then, as if suddenly aware of where he was, he reached up with both hands and gingerly pulled his goggles off. Jacko had arrived by now carrying a fire extinguisher, but although the car was ticking with heat, it was clear that Goldie had maintained enough awareness to switch the engine off before he had finally come to a halt. 'My head…' Goldie started, but Syd, bandage already unfurled in his hands, cut him off. 'You'll be OK. Here we go…'

In minutes, Goldie was out of the car, his head encased by an over-sized bandage and his pipe clasped back between his teeth. Laughing with the crew, he assured everyone that it was just a minor scrape, a few cuts caused by flying Perspex. They looked at the cause of the damage: a five-foot wooden marker board showing the four-mile point. Hit as the car was still travelling at nearly 200 miles-per-hour, the lightweight sign had smashed the canopy, detached one of the wheel covers and dented a wheel arch. The lack of damage given the speed of the crash was extraordinary.

Gardner was in great spirits and insisted he would be able to run again in a few days' time once yet another engine – this time a supercharged 2.2-litre unit[382] – had been fitted. Jacko and Syd checked over the car and, from a mechanical perspective, agreed that the repairs would take very little time to fix. They quickly hitched it up to their tow car and, Enever now at the wheel, started it on its journey back to their rented garage in Wendover where they would work through the night.

Meanwhile in the hotel, Goldie lay awake. His head ached: not just the sore parts slashed by the shards of Perspex, but a deep throbbing inside. He knew that if the team were aware that he'd been hit hard on the head by the signpost, hard enough for him to black out for a few seconds, they may not let him run again. So, when he sat in the steaming car, gathering his wits, he elected not to tell them. It was a fateful decision, one that was to have terrible consequences for both him and his family. But, four days later, the old racer drove once again.[383]

---

382 Based on the Wolseley VC22 engine.

383 On 20th August 1952 he set Class F 5km and 10km records but the car felt under geared and slipping. After an axle change, he drove again on 21st, setting 1km, 1 mile and 5km US records.

20

SICKNESS

———————➤—————

Rosalind Gardner was starting to worry. Even at just six-and-a-half years old, Ros was a confident little girl and yet the thump she heard from upstairs and silence that followed had unsettled her, especially after she had called out to her father but received no answer. Her mother was not due back to *Rosemount* from her shopping trip for some time so finally, her inquisitiveness becoming so great as to overcome her trepidation, she decided to investigate. Slowly, she climbed up the big staircase, reaching her parent's bedroom, and gently pushed open the door. There, half-dressed and sprawled on the floor, was her father.

Goldie doted on Ros and the feeling was mutual. Despite starting out as a parent at a rather advanced age, he had quickly embraced fatherhood, especially of a child who so obviously inherited his spirit and determination. Whenever she was allowed, she would visit him in his office, clamber up his long legs and sit on his lap. As he smoked his pipe, she would marvel at the pictures on the wall and listen intently as he told her stories of the races he had driven, the princes and film stars he'd met, and the records he'd broken. Although she couldn't fully understand them, she knew the framed lists of numbers were really very important and she felt pride grow in her chest.

She was utterly shocked by finding her father in such a condition, who she thought so powerful and strong. His collapse was so sudden, so unexpected and so hard to deal with, especially as her mother, Una, reacted in the way many parents did in those days and tried to protect her daughter by separating her from what was going on. As her father was taken to hospital, Ros was told very little.

Unknown to them all, Goldie's impact with the wooden marker post at Bonneville the previous summer had left an awful legacy, a tiny bleed that slowly led to a clot in the lining of his brain. Gradually, day-by-day, the clot grew until finally, on that summer's afternoon in late July 1953, the pressure became too much for his body to bear. He was rushed into surgery and a burr hole drilled to relieve the pressure, then kept in a nursing home for observation. In late August, Una made a statement to the press who were keen to know whether a planned record attempt for mid-September at Jabbeke would go ahead, given what they believed was a bout of 'sunstroke'. She confirmed it would not, although he was making steady progress. 'My husband has to have a period of complete rest,' she told them. 'The operation was only a minor one.'[384]

At first, it worked. He returned home, seemingly well again to the young Rosalind, but the old racer knew he had to scale everything back. Any future plans with the record car were shelved, as were his planned responsibilities acting as an official at the Goodwood races. Treatment continued, but the next few months were extremely quiet for him. Goodwill messages flooded in from his friends and the many clubs and societies he was part of, from the Redhill and Reigate (Men's) Swimming Club through to the Croydon Motor Club, where he was president. He also stayed in touch with Syd and Jacko who had already been enlisted to work on other record attempts. He made the odd foray out: the following October, he accepted an invitation from his old

---

384 *Lancashire Echo*, 24 August 1953, p5.

friend John Thornley to a dinner at the Hyde Park Hotel which he accepted, although Una had to drive him there. 'He is still convalescing after his 150 miles-per-hour crash at Utah in 1952 and is not allowed to drive,' the *Evening Standard* reported, '[Although he] hopes to be driving a private car by Christmas. And after that – "more record breaking."'[385]

Goldie was putting on a brave face, but in private he was much more subdued. He wrote to Thornley to thank him, admitting that, 'I thoroughly enjoyed the evening... as it really helped "to get me out of myself" and revive old interests – all <u>very</u> important at this stage of my convalescence.'[386] In reality, Goldie's health was gradually degenerating rather than making any improvement and he and Una soon made the decision to move from *Rosemount* down to Eastbourne to be near her mother who had relocated there from Yorkshire. They found a nice house at 8 Denton Road, close to St Mary's Hospital and a ten-minute walk across some golf links from Una's mother's house, a trip the young Rosalind was allowed to make herself, although they watched her safely cross the fairways. Ros spent a lot of time at her grannie's house as Una tried to keep on top of things at home and she provided a lot of stability, love, and support at a very difficult time. 'She was an artist,' Ros later said. 'She was a lovely, gentle soul, and it was lovely to be with her.'[387]

Goldie's hospital appointments continued, sometimes giving everyone a brief respite from the symptoms. When Sir Malcolm Campbell's six-year-old granddaughter Georgina was admitted to St Mary's to have a swallowed hair grip removed in July 1955, she found her old family friend Goldie in a next-door ward and he was well enough to tell her stories of their racing exploits as she sat on the bed.[388] He remained positive, even telling a journalist that he intended to run again at Bonneville in September 1956,[389] but it was a fantasy: his physical

---

385 *Evening Standard*, 30 October 1954, p5.
386 Letter ATGG to Thornley dated 1 November 1954 (Magna Press Archive).
387 Interview Ros Gardner, Feb 2023.
388 Gina Campbell, *Bluebird*, (Great Northern Books, 2012), p25.
389 *Coventry Evening Telegraph*, 1 Aug 1956 p4.

movement, his coordination and even his speech continued to degenerate and before long they started to fail completely.

The diminutive Una was forced to hire a male nurse to lift the 6'3" Goldie out of his bed, into a wheeled chair and into the bathroom every day. Money too was tight: although Una managed to arrange a few paid displays of EX135, the press had moved on to the new record-breaking exploits of young drivers like Stirling Moss and the old green MG wasn't the draw it once had been, so Una let out a bedroom in the top floor of the house to a single mother to bring in some income. At first, Una received the support of the Christian Science church, dropping Ros off at Sunday School in a ground-floor hall before going upstairs to worship with the other adults, but even that ended badly. One Sunday, she collected Ros in floods of tears. 'My mother *never* cried,' Ros said. 'It just wasn't what you did: you don't cry, you don't show emotion. Something happened there; we never went back.'[390]

As Goldie's physical state deteriorated, so Rosalind was affected. Her mother, unable to cope with looking after both her daughter and her husband and keen for the full extent of her father's condition to be hidden from Ros, arranged for her to board full-time at Ravens Croft School. Ros did not react well; although her teachers knew she was a bright girl, she refused to study, and her behaviour deteriorated. 'I was absolutely foul,' she said. 'My mother spent a great deal of time in the headmaster's office trying to persuade them not to sack me entirely.'[391]

Finally, on Friday 22nd August 1958, a stroke delivered the final blow. Rosalind stood on the parquet floor of their hallway and watched while ambulancemen manhandled her gaunt father down the stairs on a stretcher, placing him on the wooden floor next to her while they backed the ambulance onto their small driveway. She looked down at her father, his face thin and his muscle tone lost from months of inactivity, then watched in silence as the two men lifted the stretcher and took

390 Interview, 11 Feb 2023.
391 Interview, 11 Feb 2023.

him away. In a daze she followed them, saw the ambulance bump off down the drive, then quietly closed the front door. It was the final time she would see her father. He died in hospital three days later.

All at once, the world remembered Goldie Gardner. Hundreds of newspapers around the world, from Ottawa to Oklahoma, announced the death of this old racer and although many fell into the old trap of calling him 'one-legged,' the reports were kind and the memories of him respectful. 'Tall, slim and tough, he personified the popular conception of the adventurous Briton, wrote *The Daily Telegraph*[392] 'He is best remembered for the fantastic speeds he achieved in breaking class records with comparatively small British cars in Germany [and] received the Belgian gold medal for sporting merit in 1956, one of the first non-Belgians to be so honoured.' A long obituary followed in *The Times* the following day. Hundreds turned out for his funeral, leaving such a great swathe of flowers at his graveside in Ocklynge Cemetery that it made an indelible impression on Rosalind's memory when she was allowed to visit with her mother a day after the ceremony.

Three weeks later, the strong turnout (and Rosalind's exclusion) was repeated for Goldie's memorial service at Christ Church in London's Mayfair. Freddie March, The Duke of Richmond and Gordon, drove up from Goodwood, Wilfred Andrews represented the Royal Automobile Club, and Earl Howe and Mike Couper came on behalf of the BRDC along with Lady Guinness, but it was the friends who he'd made along the way of his extraordinary life who packed out the chapel. Dick Benn, whose car he'd driven at Jabbeke in between record runs was there, as was John Thornley who had supported him from MG after the war and probably his greatest friend of them all: his old mate Freddie Clifford. And, amid the crowd, there sat the duo who made it all possible: Reg 'Jacko' Jackson and Syd Enever. George Eyston sent his apologies, but Goldie would have forgiven him, assuming he was preparing for yet another record bid. So, the racing community, his

---

392 *The Daily Telegraph*, 27 August 1958, p8.

friends and family bade a fond farewell to this extraordinary man, and, with Goldie's typical lack of fanfare, his memory began to fade.

21

LEGACY

Today, Stirling Moss remains a household name, my 11-year-old son considers Fangio to be one of the greatest motor racing drivers to have ever lived and most people of middle age and older can picture Donald Campbell's *Bluebird* soaring into the air above Coniston Water on that terrible day in January 1967. Anyone with an interest in motoring will probably know of Malcolm Campbell, Henry Segrave and John Cobb, their names still carrying a magical frisson that combines bravery, glamour, and excitement. And yet one name is missing from the roll call of these men of speed.

My father was in his late teens and a motor-racing fan when Goldie Gardner was breaking records in Jabbeke and Bonneville but even he had a problem remembering much about this extraordinary man. Goldie's problem was that he didn't die in spectacular fashion, nor did he live to tell the tale. His death was grotesque and undignified, played out in private over many years and caused by the most innocuous of injuries. After hundreds of races, hillclimbs and record runs, it was just a flimsy wooden post that caused his downfall, a one-in-a million piece of bad luck after so many near misses. But even before his death,

Goldie Gardner had started to fade in the memories of the public, whose attention was instead focused on a new generation of glamourous, young racing drivers and their exotic Ferrari, Aston Martin and BRM machines.

For his family, too, there was no energy left to try to maintain any sort of immediate legacy following his death. Una, a strong woman who would twice become Eastbourne's mayor in the decades to come, had given everything to look after her husband and continue to raise her daughter. She loved her husband deeply and although his death was in some ways a relief, she felt his loss greatly and she wore black for a year after his death.

His affairs were handled by Eagle-Clarke & Co, Una's father's business, and in November 1959 they reported that his estate was worth £12,119 net, worth around £275,000 in 2023, all left in trust to Una. It was a healthy amount but included the big house and without any income of her own, although not destitute, Una would have to be careful. She quickly distributed some of his things, giving away cups and trophies, and packed up his study. Album after album of photographs, press cuttings, letters and record certificates were carefully stored in boxes. At Milne & Russell, his office was cleared, although the Works Manager Kevin Jones couldn't bear to throw away some of the photos he found and took them home in a shoe box. Once the dust had settled, Una threw herself into a role within the local council.[393]

For Rosalind, an intelligent 11-year-old who already knew her own mind, it was too much to bear. Once the first wave of grief had subsided, it exposed anger: towards her father for leaving her, towards her mother for focusing her efforts on him, and on the world for the injustice of it all. Having already failed all her exams, her mother made her attend a local college to gain formal qualifications in cooking and sewing – subjects she hated – before her grandmother organised a year in Switzerland, ostensibly to learn French. From there, she continued to

---

393 *The Evening Standard*, 6 December 1958, p7.

travel, finally returning home four years later only to find that her old house was now occupied by another family. Bemused, she visited the council office where she knew her mother worked and found her in the middle of a meeting. Una gave her a key and the address to the house she had moved to and told her to go home. It took them both many years to reconnect and to start to talk about what had happened to the man they loved. In the 1980s, they travelled each year together, sometimes to places he had driven: one year, they stayed at Daytona Beach, another Wendover in Utah where they visited the café of the Western Motel where Goldie had stayed, and both burst into tears at the sight of his photo up on the wall.

Meanwhile, Jackson and Enever continued their work creating yet-more streamlined record-breaking vehicles and even before Goldie had died, Syd had designed the new MGA 'at his kitchen table'[394] and went on to develop the MGB in 1962. Jacko, or 'Reggie' as he now preferred to be called, was promoted to oversee quality control, his final role in the company. Neither man lasted long once MG was subsumed into British Leyland in 1968 and Reggie never returned to the MG factory after his retirement, although he was quick to tell any visitors to his home, named *Montlhéry*, how much he hated the rubber bumpers on the MGB.[395]

Looking back at Goldie Gardner's life and the people who surrounded him, it's easy to focus on the stereotypes: the brave, stiff-upper-lipped Englishman, and plucky mechanics whose hard work and ingenuity created engineering masterpieces in oily sheds, with a background cast of rich, daring eccentrics who diced with death and laughed in its face. But below this is a more subtle subtext that seems to link many of these daredevil drivers together, a response to their service during World War One and the aftermath of that terrible campaign. The thrill – and very real danger to life – that motor racing offered in those early days was

---

394 *Sports Car*, January 1975, p20.
395 Interview with Tracey Rose, Feb 2023.

a close match to the exhilaration of combat and the class-dominated structure of the fraternity was not dissimilar to the military rank structure so many of them were comfortable with. At Brooklands, there were (mainly) public school-educated 'officers' supported by the ranks of working-class mechanics and other staff, with 'civilian' onlookers applauding acts of gallantry. It was a comfortable place for many of these men to be.

But look deeper, and there seems to be something else that links many of the most important record-breakers of the era. Both Sir Malcolm Campbell and Sir Henry Segrave served during the war as aircraft delivery pilots, shuttling fighter planes across the channel rather than using them to fight the Germans directly, with Segrave describing himself as 'a rotten pilot.'[396] Cobb was too young to have played any part in the conflict and both John Parry-Thomas and Kenelm Lee Guinness's engineering occupations were considered too valuable for the war effort to risk them taking part in the fighting. Could these men, all with very high personal standards of motivation and pride, have been trying to prove their bravery and their loyalty to their country, if not to the public, then at least to themselves? At first glance, George Eyston and Goldie Gardner seem to have been exceptions. Both were mentioned in dispatches, and both were awarded the Military Cross for conspicuous bravery. Could Eyston have blamed himself for being shot down in 1917 and the resultant injury to his ankle that ended his front-line career?

This may seem like a harsh critique of some very brave men who are not here to defend themselves and I do not mean it to be. After my own time in the British Army, during which I served in Northern Ireland, Iraq and Afghanistan, I worked with various charities that helped veterans of these and other recent wars deal with some of the problems they brought back. Many felt that the mental challenge of being

---

396 https://www.brooklandsmuseum.com/explore/heritage-and-collection/brooklands-stories/brooklands-stories-sir-henry-segrave

wounded was more difficult to deal with than the physical scars. One moment, they had been at the peak of their professional lives, physically fit, confident and with a whole career planned out ahead of them. Then, the random trajectory of a lone bullet or the rasp of a roadside bomb fragment had changed everything. Their support network – the band of brothers who looked after each other and understood what they had been through – was torn away in a flash. Suddenly, they found themselves in hospital back in the UK, their muckers still fighting thousands of miles away in the desert. They were alone, and more importantly, they were now irrelevant to their team. Had a decision they had made led to their injury? Had they let their friends down? Even the most stoic of souls would let these thoughts creep into their heads in the dead of night.

But what of Gardner? Like Eyston, on the battlefield he was trusted by those senior to him, well-liked by those who served with him and undoubtedly very brave. What drove his determination? I believe the answer lies in the air crash that abruptly ended his service in 1917. In those days, flying an aircraft was an exceptionally perilous activity, especially in combat, and usually carried out by young men of more junior officer rank. Gardner, as a 27-year-old Major and one of the most senior members of his Brigade, was an anomaly. Indeed, as I sifted through the meticulously kept records of air casualties during the war, I couldn't find him at all. I enlisted the help of Trevor Henshaw, the historian of First World War combat aviation, who also drew a blank: Gardner wasn't even mentioned in the more general casualty records. Then, on a visit to the Imperial War Museum Reading Room in 2021, I found something that seemed to make sense of it. On page 28 of an obscure pamphlet published by the Royal Artillery Association just after the First World War, I discovered a single sentence that changed everything: 'Major Gardner met with a flying accident while on leave in England.'[397]

397 *A Short History of 72nd Brigade RFA 1914-1919*, (ibid), p28.

The reconnaissance patrol, the enemy action, the crawl across the miles of mud back to the British lines… all of it was suddenly called into question. I read back over all my notes. In his autobiography, Gardner said that he had been 'wounded' in August 1917 but did not elaborate. Everything else that had been written about it was carefully worded, the 'crash' or 'accident' described as being *during* the war but not specifically caused by the conflict.

'Before the Armistice, he had been gassed and hit by a bullet and shrapnel,' wrote the *Sporting Life*.[398] 'His aeroplane also crashed while he was acting as an observer. Each time he recovered, was mentioned in dispatches for gallantry and received the military cross.'

The Segrave Trophy citation told a similar story: 'He was struck by a shell fragment, blown up and buried by a shell explosion and gassed. And he also had a rather bad aeroplane crash in which he fractured his leg.'

Even his own press releases, this one from August 3rd 1952, suggested the crash was in combat, but avoided mentioning enemy action. He had, it said, 'A stiff right leg already broken once before in a World War One flying accident.'

One source of the story about his behind-the-lines exploits is a note that Steve Holter, who knew Una Gardner, read on a leaf from a military *SO Book 130* notepad, and which Una had confirmed accorded with what her husband had told her. The note seemed to have been written in period, but was not in Goldie Gardner's writing and made some other statements that were factually incorrect: it said his Military Cross was awarded as a result of the accident, when it was won for an action the previous year; it reported that he had joined the cavalry on the outbreak of war in 1914, when he had not; and it stated that he was the youngest Major in the British Army at the time. This was also incorrect: he was 26 when promoted to Major and there were 24-year-old Colonels, an even higher rank.

---

398 *Sporting Life*, November 1938.

So, what happened? I believe there are two possibilities. The first is that he managed to arrange a flight over the lines and was shot down as described in the *SO Book 130* note. If this was so against regulations that it could have led to disciplinary action, it could have been hushed up to the extent that James Stirling (who, as Gardner's Commanding Officer, would certainly have known the truth) wrote two years later that it was 'while on leave.' Having served in the British Army during times of conflict I know that rules can often be bent – if not totally broken – during the fog of war and this could be a possibility. However, I would have expected Gardner to have appeared in casualty records as he was being repatriated to England, which he did not.

The second possibility is that he did indeed have a crash whilst on leave in England, as Stirling wrote. It is, after all, a first-person report written shortly after the event by a man who was professionally very close to Gardner. I tried to find out where this reported air accident took place. I searched through the records of his local airfields, including Brooklands, which was dedicated to military flying at the time, but no records mentioning Gardner or the crash emerged.

However, this possibility would make sense of the absence of a military air casualty record and may even account for his absence from a 1932 reunion dinner of officers from 72 Brigade Royal Field Artillery. It could explain his autobiographical one-sentence skimming of the entire Great War, and why he always proudly displayed a *Brooklands Flying Club* badge on the front of his car, despite never having been a pilot. Was he was embarrassed by the way his war ended and did he perceive the racing and record-breaking as a chance to prove himself, to ignore and overcome the wound that he could have perceived as being self-inflicted? If so, it was a secret he carried with him throughout his life.

I am not suggesting for one moment that Goldie Gardner made more of the accident that it was or tried to suggest that it was a combat wound. Everything I have learnt about him from the people who knew him suggested that he was a very proper, very honourable, and genuinely nice man; such a subterfuge just doesn't go with his character. More likely, he was probably embarrassed; when journalists wrote about him, his leg injury was part of what made him stand out. To have to explain, every time, that it was a crash whilst at home on leave rather than in the mud of Ypres, would just have been complicated and scrappy. I know how journalists write and I suspect that given the longing for a British hero in the 1930s and '40s that, even had he told them, they would have written around the subject. It just didn't add anything, and all newspapermen love a good, clean story.

Whatever the truth, and whether this was his impetus to start driving, after World War Two, Gardner returned to record-breaking almost by default. Other than soldiering, he knew of no other profession; other than photography and his late-on experience of fatherhood, he had no other pastime. Driving and racing dominated his life and the thought of retiring because he was advancing in years was anathema to him. Only when he was incapacitated by his injury and subsequent illness did he stop.

So many human advances have been made by those who, when told something was impossible, decided to do it anyway. Gardner was one of those people and, more by fortune of circumstance than by design, surrounded himself with two people with the same mindset: Reg Jackson and Syd Enever. These men were both masters at what they did, with a very rare combination of acute attention to detail and imaginative minds that looked for solutions out of the bounds of normal convention, and the three men seemed to bring out the best in one another. If they were alive today, Syd and Jacko would undoubtedly be working at the very top of British engineering; you may not be surprised to know that Jacko's great grandson, Oli Rose, is a lead engineer in thermal management for the Aston Martin Formula 1 team.

But Goldie's achievements undoubtedly had a major impact outside of his own personal motivations. His successes in Germany during 1938 and 1939 in the face of the state-sponsored might of the German *Rekordmen* gave the British press something to celebrate, as did his postwar runs in Italy, Belgium, and America. His records in Utah certainly

helped raise MG's profile in the country, but how much this contributed to already strong sales under the stewardship of the marketing-mas-
ter Kjell Qvale is debatable. But look at the newsreels of Goldie being
interviewed at the time, and you can see that all that was secondary: he
was breaking records for his own reasons; achieving yet another 'first'
or 'fastest' was the obsession that drove his life.

But today, that legacy stands of its own right: over 150 speed records
collected over the span of 21 years – more than any other person – a
host of 'firsts' including the first 1,100 and 1,500cc runs official exceeding 300kph, the first 750 and 500cc officially exceeding 250kph,
and the extraordinary achievement of holding more than half of all
official speed record titles at once. Plus, according to the FIA, three
of his records, including the run on his birthday at Dessau back in
1939, still stand today.[399] Although he received sporadic official support
from MG, Jaguar, and various other parts suppliers, this was obtained
through his own tenacity and powers of persuasion, and the fact remains that he owned the car and self-funded the vast majority of his
record attempts. As a man without huge personal wealth or family connections, and someone who had to deal with his disability, the level of
his achievement is absolutely extraordinary.

There was another legacy of Goldie Gardner's record attempts.
The people most affected by his sickness and death were his family, especially his only child, Rosalind. Ros admits that his death, and her reaction to it, led directly to her pursuing a career in psychiatric nursing.
Through this, many years later, she worked out why she had reacted
the way she had during her father's illness and death. She had a long
career in the NHS, and as a result directly helped hundreds of people.

But the final word must go to the man himself who, in the BRDC
Silver Jubilee book of 1952 wrote, 'What is the value, if any, of successful attempts at records? I would suggest they are of quite appreciable
value; especially from the angle of British prestige abroad, as well as the

---

399 https://www.fia.com/fia-world-land-speed-records. See 'Class A' records.

fact that they help to emphasise that the British Automobile Industry is second to none. From the personal angle the successful outcome of a project, with which one has been closely bound for months, gives a gratifying feel of having helped to bring to a satisfactory conclusion something worthwhile.'[400]

---

400 Various authors, *BRDC Silver Jubilee Book*, (Trafford Press, 1952), p100.

EPILOGUE

My phone pinged and a message popped up on the lock screen. Absentmindedly, I tapped on the notification, my Google account immediately opening and telling me that one of my saved searches had found something.

This book took me a long time to research, coinciding as it did with the Covid-19 pandemic. It was many months before I could visit the superb archive at the National Motor Museum, run my hand along the flanks of EX135 at the British Motor Museum at Gaydon, or walk across the crumbling concrete of the Members' Banking at Brooklands. In the meantime, I had to make do with what I could find in old books and on the internet. To help me, I'd set alerts for the name *Goldie Gardner* across various platforms that would let me know when someone published something new about him. Most of the time it informed me when another *Dinky* model of 'Gardner's Record Car' came up for sale, or a copy of *Magic MPH* was offered by an antiquarian bookseller. Today though, the alert was different.

It was May 2020. We'd not long emerged from a lockdown here in the UK, and life was slowly returning to a semblance of normality.

In particular, with the weather improving and restrictions easing, the classic car world came back to life. With it came a flurry of live auctions, some of the first since 2019, including a Silverstone Auctions sale at Stoneleigh Park in Warwickshire. Featured in their catalogue was a 1946 MG TC that, according to the description, had been first owned by Lieutenant Colonel A.T. Goldie Gardner, MC, given to him by the factory.

My day job is writing about classic cars, so I know a lot of people in the business. I rang the auctioneer who had consigned the lot, Charles Smalley, and asked if I could come and take a look. If nothing else, he told me that it had a big history file and I may find something of interest, although he didn't think Gardner had actually driven the car much; there was a rumour it had been left with a lady in Scotland. A few days later, I pulled up next to the big hangar in which the cars were stored before the auction. There it was: a tiny, black car with a crinkled patina of ancient paint covering the bonnet, a smart red interior and age-worn instruments looking back from the dash. There was a plastic carrier bag full of papers on the seat and I took a while to go through them. The original buff logbook of ownership was present, signed by Gardner, and sheaves of other fascinating paperwork covering not just this car but also his MG WA that he owned during the War.

Then, I took a closer look at the car. On the outside, it was definitely showing its age, but underneath, someone had taken extraordinary care of it. The chassis was freshly painted, engine clean and grease nipples still oozing. I asked for it to be started, which it did on the button, purring away merrily as I took in the sight. It was my favourite type of car, I found myself thinking, mechanically very sound but not over-restored.

On the journey home, I couldn't help thinking about the little MG. I've owned many classic cars over the years, but they have mostly been much later: vehicles from the 1960s, '70s and '80s. I'd always thought of MGs like this little TC as being an old man's car. But the research I'd already done into Goldie Gardner had taught me that this car had a phenomenal sporting ancestry, from the C-Type that he raced at the Ulster TT and the K3 that he brought home to a podium finish in the BRDC 500-Mile race at Brooklands right through to EX135 which for some of its life was powered by the same engine as this car. As I pulled into my driveway, I'd convinced myself I should bid on it and the following day rang Charles to register my interest.

On the day of the auction, I was at the National Motor Museum at Beaulieu with my family, waiting in a queue to board the monorail when the call from Charles came. I hesitated; what was I going to actually *do* with this car if I bought it? Where was I going to store it? With a very heavy heart, I told him I'd decided not to bid. I thought that was that. A week later, Charles rang me again. 'John,' he said. 'That MG didn't sell… and the previous owner doesn't want it back. Do you want to make an offer?' Now, if you're in the trade and someone says they don't want their car back, there's usually an expensive reason but I'd looked over the car and it seemed to be in great condition. Sure, the lamps and wheels were not original and looked slightly out of place, but the engine ran very well. Plus, since the auction, both of my reasons for *not* buying it had gone away: a good friend had offered me the use of his garage and my 19-year-old son and I had agreed that we would do a hillclimb course at Shelsley Walsh. We could use the MG. So, I moved some money out of an ISA and rang Charles back with an offer. I may or may not have told my wife.

The following day, I was back at Beaulieu, searching through the Gardner archive with the superb archivist, Patrick Collins. Charles rang me as I was looking through a huge photograph album of Gardner's exploits in Jabbeke in 1946. 'The money has gone through, and the car is yours,' he told me. 'Bloody hell' I exclaimed, not to Charles, but in general astonishment. There, looking back to me on the page I had just turned, was the little MG TC I had just bought, its distinctive numberplate crystal clear in the shots. I turned the page; there were more: photos with Gardner, photos of the badges on the front, photos of the car with EX135. On the next page, there were pictures of the car during his record attempt in Italy. 'I love it when this sort of thing happens,' exclaimed Patrick, 'Although that is extraordinary.'

A few days later, I had the car picked up and taken straight to Blue Diamond, the Bicester- based vintage car specialists, for a complete health check. I'd spoken to the previous owner who seemed lovely and very genuine, but I still wondered whether there was something lurking in the car's nether regions that would cost me dearly. Shortly afterwards the workshop manager telephoned me. 'About your car…' he started. My heart froze. 'It's odd… we can't find anything really wrong with it at all. That's very unusual for a car of this age.' I breathed a huge sigh of relief.

The car spent the first couple of months in my friend's garage, but then I brought it home to tinker with and instantly fell in love. I found out a lot more about its history, thanks to the team at the MG Car Club who unearthed its racing records, and I even found a copy of the *Daily Mail* from 1966 showing it being raced at Silverstone. Ros Gardner, Goldie's daughter, who I got to know well during the writing of the book, was delighted when I told her about the car which, we both realised, was the vehicle her father drove when she was brought home from hospital after her birth. Other than replacing the original headlamps, wheels and badges, I've just polished it, greased it and driven it. When my son is back from university and the weather is fair, we always try to take it out and the car never fails to bring a smile to our faces.

Finally, a few weeks ago, at the Goodwood circuit that Goldie's old friend Freddie March established in 1948, I took the MG out onto the track for the first time. With the windscreen folded flat to minimise drag, I hunkered down and did my best to push the little car as fast as it would go, managing a top speed of 72mph on the Lavant Straight. Even with my full race suit, helmet and gloves, and at not much more than a third of the speed that Goldie managed in essentially a streamlined version of the same car with none of my protective clothing, it was still an electrifying experience. I hope that if he's looking down, he'd approve of another old soldier giving his little MG some exercise around a track once more.

The author, in his 1946 MG TC.

Photo: Jonathan Fleetwood/Octane.

ACKNOWLEDGEMENTS

'Don't write a non-fiction book,' my friend and author Toby Harnden warned me. 'They're a huge amount of work and you'll never make any money.' Although he was absolutely correct, I'm glad I didn't listen to him.

Researching Goldie Gardner's life has certainly been an epic undertaking, but it has put me in touch with a group of the most lovely, fascinating and supportive people who otherwise I never would have met. Every person I approached for help went out of their way to do so, and I've been given access to family records, long-stored photos, and sometimes difficult memories. I'm hugely appreciative of it all.

My first port of call was at the superb National Motor Museum archive at Beaulieu. Patrick Collins, the wonderful Research Curator, was a constant support who shared my enthusiasm for the subject and spent hours patiently waiting as I sifted through the archives. Alongside Patrick, Jon Day deciphered my hand-scrawled notes, correctly identifying and scanning all the photographs I needed. Lord Montagu, Jon Murden, Michelle Kirwan and Anna-Marie O'Connor all believed in me and helped me get the text off my laptop and onto the shelves, as did Ian Strathcarron at Unicorn, who so successfully distributed the book. I'm also extremely grateful to The Duke of Richmond, who immediately agreed to my request to write a foreword and provided such an interesting and personal text.

Then there were those whose phenomenal skills helped to create a book that I am very proud to have my name on. I gave what I thought was a finished manuscript to Antony Ingram, who handed it back a few weeks later, having spotted and corrected numerous tiny errors. Thank you to the exceptionally talented Maisie Minett who created my wonderful maps and the superb James Bristow who designed the rest of the book including the cover, which I love. I must also sincerely thank the Michael Sedgewick Trust and the other supporters, without whom this book and the National Motor Museum Publishing brand would not have happened. Thank you too to Richard Noble, who gave me the extraordinary perspective of someone who knows what it is like to risk everything in the pursuit of speed, and his view of just how important Goldie's records were.

In the earliest days of writing, I received some superb advice from Mark Lucas of The Soho Agency. He made me realise that I had to write for a wider audience than the usual petrolheads that my day job caters for. I ripped up the first chapters and started again; I'm very glad I did.

Then, there were all those names that everyone in the MG world knows and respects. Firstly, Malcolm Green, whose knowledge and archive rivals that of any museum. I thoroughly appreciate being given the freedom to search through the papers and photographs and want to also thank Andrea for looking after me so well and keeping me sustained throughout my visit. Thank you also to Jon Pressnell, who took time out from writing his own book about Cecil Kimber to provide me some key parts of the jigsaw, Mike Allison, whose first-hand knowledge of MG was extremely useful in clarifying some of the questions I had and David Knowles, whose insights about Syd Enever were very timely.

Other people spent ages sorting through archives on my behalf: Beatrice Meecham at the Brooklands Museum, Gemma Bray at the MGCC, Trevor Swettenham at BARC and David Moore at the Shelsley Walsh/ MAC archive. Thank you also to the support from Allan Winn at Brooklands, Don Wales, Simon Johnston and to my old friends Gary Axon and Dan Cogger, who helped me rediscover details of some of Gardner's more obscure cars, and Martin Chisholm who trusted me to drive Gardner's racing MG K3 on the snowy Cotswold roads near his wonderful Classic Motor Hub.

To help shed light on Goldie's war records, I must thank the staff at the Imperial War Museum, plus the help I received from Trevor Henshaw, Peter Hodkinson and Siân Mogridge at the Royal Artillery Association, the latter who went out of her way to help me. Jerry Rudman, the archivist at Uppingham School, also provided details of Goldie's early life.

Then there were the families. Keri Beak and Tracey Rose were so kind and helpful in providing me with all they knew about their grandfather, Reg 'Jacko' Jackson, trusting me with their photographs and letting me see so many family treasures. Mike Jones allowed me to sift through the boxes of papers that his father and mother retained, both having worked at Milne & Russell alongside Goldie, and he provided me with first-hand reminiscences about their time there. Robert Gardner gave me some lovely recollections of his uncle and it was a delight sharing some of what I knew with him.

Then, there is Ros Gardner, for whom the last few years have been exceptionally difficult, but who let me ask questions that probably unearthed feelings hidden for many decades. Thank you so much for your honesty and trust, and for helping me bring your father's story to the public after so long.

I must also thank those people who took it upon themselves to record Goldie's life in print, either at the time or in the years that followed. Without Bill Boddy, Barré Lyndon, John Thornley, Wilson McComb and Goldie himself, this would have been a very thin story.

Finally, a huge thank you to Johanna, my wife. She put up with the constant flood of old books arriving on the doorstep, my late nights of working while she put the kids to bed and the days I spent on the road or writing away from home. She overlooked the fact that I bought one of Goldie's cars, gave me encouragement and honest feedback on what I'd written, and pushed me forever forwards. Without her, this book simply would not have been finished. I love you.

LIST OF RACES

DATE	LOCATION	MEETING	RACE	CAR	CAR No.	RESULT	COMMENT
21 Apr 1924	Brooklands	BARC Easter Meeting	Private Competitors' Handicap	Austin Seven GE Special RK1020	14		
21 Apr 1924	Brooklands	BARC Easter Meeting	Small Car Handicap	Austin Seven GE Special RK1020	5		
7 May 1924	Brooklands	JCC Spring Meeting	Race 2	Austin Seven GE Special RK1020			
9 Jun 1924	Brooklands	BARC Whitsun Meeting	Whitsun Private Competitors' Handicap	Austin Seven GE Special RK1020	20		
9 Jun 1924	Brooklands	BARC Whitsun Meeting	75mph Short Handicap	Austin Seven GE Special RK1020	15		
5 Jul 1924	Brooklands	BARC July Meeting	75mph Short Handicap	Austin Seven GE Special RK1020			
4 Aug 1924	Brooklands	BARC Aug BH Meeting		Austin Seven GE Special RK1020		DNF	Holed crankcase.
5 Apr 1926	Brooklands	BARC Easter Meeting		Salmson San Sebastian VB3080			

DATE	LOCATION	MEETING	RACE	CAR	CAR No.	RESULT	COMMENT
12 May 1928	Brooklands	Essex Motor Club 6 Hours	Single race	Salmson 2-seat SC (works)	38	10th Gold Medal	Factory loan.
16 Jun 1928	Brooklands	JCC High Speed Trial	Class B	Salmson San Sebastian VB3080		DNF	Hit railings having pitted with tyre trouble.
25 Aug 1928	Brooklands	New Cycle and Car Club	Novice's Handicap	Salmson San Sebastian VB3080	33	1st	79.68mph.
3-9 Sep 1928	Boulogne Le Touquet	Speed Week		Salmson San Sebastian VB3080		Various awards	
10 May 1929	Brooklands	Double Twelve		Salmson San Sebastian VB3080	81		
12 Jul 1929	Phoenix Park, Dublin	Irish Grand Prix	Saorstát Cup	Amilcar C6 YV91	39	DNF	Pippin Murton Neale as passenger. Would not start at half distance stop.
5 Aug 1929	Brooklands	BARC August Meeting	Gold Star Handicap	Amilcar C6 YV91			
31 Aug 1929	Brooklands	New Cycle Car Club Meeting	Short Handicap	Amilcar C6 YV91	1		
31 Aug 1929	Brooklands	New Cycle Car Club Meeting	Cycle-car Grand Prix	Amilcar C6 YV91	1		
21 Sep 1929	Brooklands	BARC Closing Meeting	100mph Short Handicap	Amilcar C6 YV91	7	1st	85.54mph .
21 Sep 1929	Brooklands	BARC Closing Meeting	Race 6 Mountain Handicap	Amilcar C6 YV91	11		
28 Sep 1929	Lewes Speed Trials	Kent & Sussex LCC	1500cc class	Amilcar C6 YV91	NA		Fastest time of the day 24.4 seconds.
8 Apr 1930	Brooklands	BARC Easter Meeting	Mountain Race 3	Amilcar C6 YV91		DNF?	
8 Apr 1930	Brooklands	BARC Easter Meeting	Mountain Race 6	Amilcar C6 YV91		DNF?	
21 Apr 1930	Brooklands	BARC Easter Meeting	Sussex Short Handicap	Amilcar C6 YV91			

DATE	LOCATION	MEETING	RACE	CAR	CAR No.	RESULT	COMMENT
21 Apr 1930	Brooklands	BARC Easter Meeting	Sussex Long Handicap	Amilcar C6 YV91			
21 Apr 1930	Brooklands	BARC Easter Meeting	Mountain Race	Amilcar C6 YV91		DNF	"New circuit proving hard on cars" (Boddy, p 426).
9-10 May 1930	Brooklands	Double Twelve		Aston Martin S31 VB7976	63	DNF	With Miss D.M Burnett. Valve Spring failed.
9 Jun 1930	Brooklands	BARC Whitsun Meeting	Devon Jnr Short Handicap	Amilcar C6 YV91			
9 Jun 1930	Brooklands	BARC Whitsun Meeting	Devon Jnr Long Handicap	Amilcar C6 YV91		1st	51 sec handicap, winning at 88.81mph.
18 Jul 1930	Phoenix Park, Dublin	Irish Grand Prix	Saorstát Cup	Amilcar C6 YV91	41	18th overall, 2nd 1100cc class	Martin Jameson passenger. Burnt hole in silencer but finished.
26 Jul 1930	Brooklands	LCC Meeting	Long Handicap	Amilcar C6 YV91	11		
26 Jul 1930	Brooklands	LCC Meeting	Light Car Grand Prix Heat 2	Amilcar C6 YV91	11	3rd	
26 Jul 1930	Brooklands	LCC Meeting	Light Car Grand Prix Final	Amilcar C6 YV91	11		
4 Aug 1930	Brooklands	BARC August Meeting	Cornwall Jnr Short Handicap	Amilcar C6 YV91			
4 Aug 1930	Brooklands	BARC August Meeting	Cornwall Jnr Long Handicap	Amilcar C6 YV91		3rd	30 sec.
20 Sep 1930	Brooklands	BARC Autumn Meeting	Middlesex Junior Long Handicap	Amilcar C6 YV91		2nd	34 sec.
20 Sep 1930	Brooklands	BARC Autumn Meeting	Middlesex TT Handicap	Amilcar C6 YV91		2nd	1min 6 sec.
20 Sep 1930	Brooklands	BARC Autumn Meeting	September Mountain Speed Handicap	Amilcar C6 YV91	11?	3rd	1 min 35 sec.
4 Oct 1930	Brooklands	BRDC 500 Miles		Amilcar (works)	12	DNF	With Vernon Balls.

DATE	LOCATION	MEETING	RACE	CAR	CAR No.	RESULT	COMMENT
9-10 May 1931	Brooklands	Double Twelve	JCC 1000 miles	MG C-Type Midget RX8591	70	DNF	Broken piston. Team entry with Murton Neale, Samulson, Horton, Jackson, Humphreys.
25 May 1931	Brooklands	BARC Whitsun Meeting	First Whitsun Mountain Speed Handicap	MG C-Type Midget RX8591	12		
25 May 1931	Brooklands	BARC Whitsun Meeting	Somerset Jnr Short Handicap	MG C-Type Midget RX8591	18		
25 May 1931	Brooklands	BARC Whitsun Meeting	Somerset Jnr Long Handicap	MG C-Type Midget RX8591	17		
5 Jun 1931	Phoenix Park Dublin	Irish Grand Prix	Saorstát Cup	MG C-Type Midget RX8591	34	1st (Team) 3rd (Saorstát Cup) 4th (overall)	Team entry with Horton 2nd (3rd overall) Robin Jackson 10th (16th overall).
25 Jul 1931	Brooklands	LCC Relay Grand Prix		MG C-Type Midget RX8591	4c		Horton, Jackson, Gardner. 70.14mph.
3 Aug 1931	Brooklands	BARC Aug BH Meeting	London Jnr Short Handicap	MG C-Typee Midget RX8591	18	2nd	1 min 20 sec handicap. Humphrey's Amilcar 6 caught Gardner 50 yards from the finish.
3 Aug 1931	Brooklands	BARC Aug BH Meeting	London Jnr Long Handicap	MG C-Type Midget RX8591	19		
22 Aug 1931	Ards Circuit	Ulster Tourist Trophy		MG C-Type Midget RX8591	44		
5 Sep 1931	Brooklands	Brighton Motor Club Meeting		MG C-Type Midget RX8591	26	First Class Award	
26 Sep 1931	Brooklands	MCC High Speed Trials	Race 7: 2 lap scratch race	Rover 20 Speed Special		1st	Did not win final.
26 Sep 1931	Brooklands	MCC High Speed Trials	Race 11	Rover 20 Speed Special			
26 Sep 1931	Brooklands	MCC High Speed Trials	Race 14	Rover 20 Speed Special			

DATE	LOCATION	MEETING	RACE	CAR	CAR No.	RESULT	COMMENT
3 Oct 1931	Brooklands	BRDC 500 Miles		MG C-Type Midget RX8591	10		
17 Oct 1931	Brooklands	BARC Autumn Meeting	Cumberland Junior Short Handicap	MG C-Type Midget RX8591	34		
17 Oct 1931	Brooklands	BARC Autumn Meeting	Cumberland Junior Long Handicap	MG C-Type Midget RX8591	6	1st	92.99mph average, lapping at 100.61mph (1 min 11 sec handicap).
17 Oct 1931	Brooklands	BARC Autumn Meeting	October Mountain Handicap	MG C-Type Midget RX8591	8		
7 Feb 2032	Eynsham	Speed Trial	OUCC Inter-Varsity	MG C-Type Midget RX8591			Possibly 1933.
12 Mar 1932	Brooklands	JCC Rally		Rover 20 Speed Special	93?		
28 Mar 1932	Brooklands	Easter BH BARC Open	Norfolk Senior Short handicap	MG C-Type Midget RX8591	9		
28 Mar 1932	Brooklands	Easter BH BARC Open	Norfolk Senior Long handicap	MG C-Type Midget RX8591	10	4th	
23 Apr 1932	Brooklands	JCC Members'	1 Lap Handicap Race B	Rover 20 Speed Special	23		
23 Apr 1932	Brooklands	JCC Members'	2 Lap Handicap Race B	Rover 20 Speed Special	23	3rd	Second Class Award (Over 1100cc) overall.
23 Apr 1932	Brooklands	JCC Members'	1 Lap Handicap for MG Cars	MG C-Type Midget RX8591	15	DNS?	
30 Apr 1932	Brooklands	British Empire Trophy	Heats	MG C-Type Midget RX8591	11	DNF	Retired, head gasket. Only other competitor in 750cc class was March in an Austin Seven.
30 Apr 1932	Brooklands	JCC High Speed Trial	2 Lap Handicap Race B	Rover 20 Speed Special	10?	3rd	
16 May 1932	Brooklands	BARC Whitsun Meeting	Nottingham Jnr Short Handicap	Rover 20 Speed Special		3rd	37 sec handicap.
16 May 1932	Brooklands	BARC Whitsun Meeting	Nottingham Long Handicap	Rover 20 Speed Special	12		

DATE	LOCATION	MEETING	RACE	CAR	CAR No.	RESULT	COMMENT
3-4 Jun 1932	Brooklands	JCC 1000 Mile Race		MG C-Type Midget RX8591	51	265 laps	With Hugh Hamilton, Class 8.
18 Jun 1932	Brooklands	BARC Inter-Club Meeting	Race 2	Rover 20 Speed Special			
18 Jun 1932	Brooklands	BARC Inter-Club Meeting	Race 6	Rover 20 Speed Special			
18 Jun 1932	Brooklands	BARC Inter-Club Meeting	Race 7	Rover 20 Speed Special			
18 Jun 1932	Brooklands	BARC Inter-Club Meeting	Race 8	Rover 20 Speed Special		1st	Won Stanley Cup representing JCC team with Aldington & Rayson.
16 Jul 1932	Brooklands	LCC International Relay	Handicap	MG C Type Midget RX8591	14A	DNF, 28 min 30	Jeffress, ATGG and D. Cook driving in Aston Martin.
20 Aug 1932	Ards Circuit	Ulster Tourist Trophy		MG C-Type Midget RX8591	32	DNF, crash lap 6	
3 Sep 1932	Brooklands	MCC High Speed Trials	2nd Trial	Talbot 75/90 GO8057	41	DNS	Still in hospital.
9 Sep 1933	Brooklands	Motor Cycling Club	Second One-Hour Trial	Talbot 75/90 GO8057	3		
9 Sep 1933	Brooklands	Motor Cycling Club	One Lap Scratch	Talbot 75/90 GO8057	114		
23 Sep 1933	Brighton	Speed Trials		Alfa Romeo GT6074	20		
12 May 1934	Lewes	Speed Trials	Unlimited Class	Alfa Romeo GT6074		Third in class	
21 May 1934	Brooklands	BARC Whitsun Meeting	Merrow Lightning Short Handicap	MG K3 Magnette K3015	9	Stated 'No glory'	
21 May 1934	Brooklands	BARC Whitsun Meeting	Merrow Senior Long Handicap	MG K3 Magnette K3015	11	Stated 'No glory'	
9 Jun 1934	Shelsley Walsh	June Hillclimb	3000cc sports cars	Alfa Romeo GT6074	53	3rd	50.2 secs.

DATE	LOCATION	MEETING	RACE	CAR	CAR No.	RESULT	COMMENT
6 Aug 1934	Brooklands	BARC Aug Meeting	Esher Senior Short Handicap	MG K3 Magnette K3015	3	3rd	
6 Aug 1934	Brooklands	BARC Aug Meeting	Esher Lightning Long Handicap	MG K3 Magnette K3015	9		
25 Aug 1934	Craigantlet, Belfast	Hillclimb		Alfa Romeo BGO246			With his surgeon, Alec Calder.
15 Sep 1934	Brighton	Speed Trials		Alfa Romeo BGO246	70		
22 Sep 1934	Brooklands	BRDC 500 Miles		MG K3 Magnette K3015	17	3rd (1st in class)	With Benjafield. 5hr 13 ins 15 sec. 162 laps.
29 Sep 1934	Shelsley Walsh	Autumn Hillclimb		2300 Alfa Romeo BGO246		55 secs	"One of the smartest cars at Shelsley," Motor Sport, Nov 3.
13 Oct 1934	Brooklands	BARC Autumn Meeting	First Kingston Senior Long Handicap	MG K3 Magnette K3015	4	3rd	
13 Oct 1934	Brooklands	BARC Autumn Meeting	Second Kingston Senior Long Handicap	MG K3 Magnette K3015	11	1st	
28-29 Dec 1934	London to Exeter Trial			Alfa Romeo BGO246	359		
16 Mar 1935	Brooklands	BARC Opening Meeting	Races 2 & 3	MG Magnette K3007		DNS	Still in USA. DNS.
22 Apr 1935	Brooklands	Easter Meeting	Easter Senior Long Handicap	MG Magnette K3007	7	DNF	Three complete laps.
22 Apr 1935	Brooklands	Easter Meeting	Easter Senior Lightning Long Handicap	MG Magnette K3007		DNF?	
10 Jun 1935	Brooklands	BARC Whitsun Meeting	Whitsun Lightning Short Handicap	MG Magnette K3007	5		31 sec
10 Jun 1935	Brooklands	BARC Whitsun Meeting	Gold Star Handicap	MG Magnette K3007	10		
5 Aug 1935	Brooklands	BARC Aug Meeting	First August Short Handicap	MG Magnette K3007	2		13 sec handicap. Green 1087cc with black wheels.

DATE	LOCATION	MEETING	RACE	CAR	CAR No.	RESULT	COMMENT
5 Aug 1935	Brooklands	BARC Aug Meeting	First August Long Handicap	MG Magnette K3007	3		46 sec handicap.
14 Sep 1935	Brooklands	MCC High Speed Trial		Rover 20 Speed Special		82 miles in 60 mins	
21 Sep 1935	Brooklands	BRDC 500 Miles		MG Magnette K3007	8	7th	With William Everitt.
26 Sep 1935	Brighton	Speed Trials		Mercedes-Benz SS GC4466	102		
19 Oct 1935	Brooklands	BARC October Meeting	First October Long Handicap	MG Magnette K3007			
8 Mar 1936	Daytona Beach	Stock Car Race		Lincoln Zephyr	7	DNF	First ever US stock car race, precursor to Nascar. Only non-US driver. Retired just before end.
1 Jun 1936	Brooklands	BARC Whitsun Meeting	Gold Star Trophy	MG Magnette K3007		DNF	
3 Aug 1936	Brooklands	BARC Aug Meeting	First August Short Handicap	MG Magnette K3007	3	1st	112.35mph 20 sec.
3 Aug 1936	Brooklands	BARC Aug Meeting	Locke-King Trophy	MG Magnette K3007	6	1st	114.27mph 16 sec.
27 Aug 1936	Brooklands	NA		MG Magnette K3007		1100cc Outer lap record	124.40mph .
26 Sep 1937	Brighton	Speed Trials		MG 1287cc	138		
12 Oct 1936	New York	Vanderbilt Cup		Maserati 4CM 1521	48	18th	Programme lists entrant and driver as ATGG but driver on day was Teddy Rayson.
29 Mar 1937	Brooklands	BARC Easter Meeting	Broadcast Trophy Handicap	MG Magnette K3007		DNF	1 min 28 handicap. 'Came adrift and... retired.' (Boddy, p690).

DATE	LOCATION	MEETING	RACE	CAR	CAR No.	RESULT	COMMENT
17 May 1937	Brooklands	BARC Whitsun Meeting	Star Gold Trophy	MG Magnette K3007	10		
25 Sep 1937	Brighton	Speed Trials		Mercedes-Benz SS GC4466	99		
16 Oct 1937	Brooklands	BARC Final Meeting	Second October Short Handicap	MG Magnette K3007	2		
16 Oct 1937	Brooklands	BARC Final Meeting	10-Lap Scratch Mountain	MG Magnette K3007	3		
2 Jul 1938	Brighton	Speed Trials		Mercedes-Benz SS GC4466	78		

Notes:
1. Times are handicaps unless otherwise specified.
2. Contrary to some online reports, Goldie Gardner did not take part in the Le Mans 24-hours in 1935 and 1934, and did not win a VSCC prize at the 1946 Northern Section rally! This was R.P. Gardner (no relation) and a Major Gardiner (sic).

LIST OF RECORDS

DATE	LOCATION	RECORD TYPE	DISTANCE	CLASS	FLYING OR STANDING START	CAR	SPEED (MPH)	COMMENT
17 Oct 1931	Brooklands	Local - Brooklands	Outer Circuit Lap	750cc	FS	MG C-Type C0256	100.61	First 750cc lap over 100mph.
27 Aug 1936	Brooklands	National	Outer Circuit Lap	1100cc	FS	MG Magnette K3007	124.4	Outright hour record unsuccessful.
28 Aug 1936	Brooklands	National	50km	G	SS	MG Magnette K3007	118.96	Thornley notes that this was 'subsequently disallowed'.
28 Aug 1936	Brooklands	National	50 miles	G	SS	MG Magnette K3007	119.664	As above.
27 Aug 1936	Brooklands	Local - Brooklands	Outer Circuit Lap	1100cc	FS	MG Magnette K3007	124.4	Outright hour record unsuccessful.
28 Aug 1936	Brooklands	Local - Brooklands	50km	G	SS	MG Magnette K3007	118.96	Thornley notes that this was 'subsequently disallowed'.
28 Aug 1936	Brooklands	Local - Brooklands	50 miles	G	SS	MG Magnette K3007	119.664	As above.

DATE	LOCATION	RECORD TYPE	DISTANCE	CLASS	FLYING OR STANDING START	CAR	SPEED (MPH)	COMMENT
15 Jun 1937	Frankfürt, Germany	International	1km	G	FS	MG Magnette K3007	142.2	
15 Jun 1937	Frankfürt, Germany	International	1 mile	G	FS	MG Magnette K3007	148.5	
23 Jun 1937	Montlhéry, France	International	5km	G	FS	MG Magnette K3007	130.5	
23 Jun 1937	Montlhéry, France	International	5 miles	G	FS	MG Magnette K3007	130	
23 Jun 1937	Montlhéry, France	International	10km	G	FS	MG Magnette K3007	129.8	
23 Jun 1937	Montlhéry, France	International	10 miles	G	FS	MG Magnette K3007	129.4	
23 Jun 1937	Montlhéry, France	International	50km	G	FS	MG Magnette K3007	123.22	
23 Jun 1937	Montlhéry, France	National	5km	G	FS	MG Magnette K3007	130.5	
23 Jun 1937	Montlhéry, France	National	5 miles	G	FS	MG Magnette K3007	130	
23 Jun 1937	Montlhéry, France	National	10km	G	FS	MG Magnette K3007	129.8	
23 Jun 1937	Montlhéry, France	National	10 miles	G	FS	MG Magnette K3007	129.4	
23 Jun 1937	Montlhéry, France	National	50km	G	FS	MG Magnette K3007	123.22	
23 Jun 1937	Montlhéry, France	Local - Montlhéry	5km	G	FS	MG Magnette K3007	130.5	
23 Jun 1937	Montlhéry, France	Local - Montlhéry	5 miles	G	FS	MG Magnette K3007	130	
23 Jun 1937	Montlhéry, France	Local - Montlhéry	10km	G	FS	MG Magnette K3007	129.8	
23 Jun 1937	Montlhéry, France	Local - Montlhéry	10 miles	G	FS	MG Magnette K3007	129.4	
23 Jun 1937	Montlhéry, France	Local - Montlhéry	50km	G	FS	MG Magnette K3007	123.22	

DATE	LOCATION	RECORD TYPE	DISTANCE	CLASS	FLYING OR STANDING START	CAR	SPEED (MPH)	COMMENT
25 Oct 1937	Frankfürt, Germany	International	1km	G	FS	MG Magnette K3007	148.8	
25 Oct 1937	Frankfürt, Germany	International	1 mile	G	FS	MG Magnette K3007	148.7	
25 Oct 1937	Frankfürt, Germany	International	5km	G	FS	MG Magnette K3007	143.6	
25 Oct 1937	Frankfürt, Germany	International	5miles	G	FS	MG Magnette K3007	144.6	
25 Oct 1937	Frankfürt, Germany	National	1km	G	FS	MG Magnette K3007	148.8	
25 Oct 1937	Frankfürt, Germany	National	1 mile	G	FS	MG Magnette K3007	148.7	
25 Oct 1937	Frankfürt, Germany	National	5km	G	FS	MG Magnette K3007	143.6	
25 Oct 1937	Frankfürt, Germany	National	5miles	G	FS	MG Magnette K3007	144.6	
9 Nov 1938	Frankfürt, Germany	International	1km	G	FS	EX135	186.6	
9 Nov 1938	Frankfürt, Germany	International	1 mile	G	FS	EX135	186.5	
9 Nov 1938	Frankfürt, Germany	National	1km	G	FS	EX135	186.567	
9 Nov 1938	Frankfürt, Germany	National	1 mile	G	FS	EX135	186.582	
31 May 1939	Dessau, Germany	International	1km	G	FS	EX135	203.54	Highest speed one way was 206mph.
31 May 1939	Dessau, Germany	International	1 mile	G	FS	EX135	203.16	
31 May 1939	Dessau, Germany	International	5km	G	FS	EX135	197.54	
31 May 1939	Dessau, Germany	National	1km	G	FS	EX135	203.5	

DATE	LOCATION	RECORD TYPE	DISTANCE	CLASS	FLYING OR STANDING START	CAR	SPEED (MPH)	COMMENT
31 May 1939	Dessau, Germany	National	1 mile	G	FS	EX135	203.2	
31 May 1939	Dessau, Germany	National	5km	G	FS	EX135	197.5	
2 Jun 1939	Dessau, Germany	International	1km	F	FS	EX135	204.28	
2 Jun 1939	Dessau, Germany	International	1 mile	F	FS	EX135	203.85	
2 Jun 1939	Dessau, Germany	International	5km	F	FS	EX135	200.6	
2 Jun 1939	Dessau, Germany	National	1km	F	FS	EX135	204.2	Highest speed one way was 207.4mph.
2 Jun 1939	Dessau, Germany	National	1 mile	F	FS	EX135	203.9	
2 Jun 1939	Dessau, Germany	National	5km	F	FS	EX135	200.6	
3 Oct 1946	Jabbeke, Belgium	International	1km	H	FS	EX135	159.1	Highest speed one way was 164.72mph.
3 Oct 1946	Jabbeke, Belgium	International	1 mile	H	FS	EX135	159.2	
3 Oct 1946	Jabbeke, Belgium	International	5km	H	FS	EX135	150.5	
3 Oct 1946	Jabbeke, Belgium	National	1km	H	FS	EX135	159.1	
3 Oct 1946	Jabbeke, Belgium	National	1 mile	H	FS	EX135	159.2	
3 Oct 1946	Jabbeke, Belgium	National	5km	H	FS	EX135	150.5	
24 Jul 1947	Jabbeke, Belgium	International	1km	I	FS	EX135	118.043	
24 Jul 1947	Jabbeke, Belgium	International	1 mile	I	FS	EX135	117.493	

DATE	LOCATION	RECORD TYPE	DISTANCE	CLASS	FLYING OR STANDING START	CAR	SPEED (MPH)	COMMENT
24 Jul 1947	Jabbeke, Belgium	International	5km	I	FS	EX135	114.105	
24 Jul 1947	Jabbeke, Belgium	International	5 miles	I	FS	EX135	110.531	
14 Sep 1948	Jabbeke, Belgium	International	1km	E	FS	EX135 'Gardner Jaguar Special'	176.76	Highest speed one way was 178mph.
14 Sep 1948	Jabbeke, Belgium	International	1 mile	E	FS	EX135 'Gardner Jaguar Special'	173.66	
14 Sep 1948	Jabbeke, Belgium	International	5km	E	FS	EX135 'Gardner Jaguar Special'	170.52	
14 Sep 1948	Jabbeke, Belgium	National	1km	E	FS	EX135 'Gardner Jaguar Special'	176.76	Highest speed one way was 178mph.
14 Sep 1948	Jabbeke, Belgium	National	1 mile	E	FS	EX135 'Gardner Jaguar Special'	173.66	
14 Sep 1948	Jabbeke, Belgium	National	5km	E	FS	EX135 'Gardner Jaguar Special'	170.52	
14 Sep 1948	Jabbeke, Belgium	International	1km	I	FS	EX135	154.8	Highest speed one way was 159.32mph.
15 Sep 1949	Jabbeke, Belgium	International	1 mile	I	FS	EX135	154.2	
15 Sep 1949	Jabbeke, Belgium	International	5km	I	FS	EX135	150.5	
27 Apr 1950	Long Island, USA	National Stock	1000km	F	FS	Austin A40 Devon Saloon	64.83	With Alan Hess.
27 Apr 1950	Long Island, USA	National Stock	1000 miles	F	FS	Austin A40 Devon Saloon	64.84	With Alan Hess.
27 Apr 1950	Long Island, USA	National Stock	6 hours	F	FS	Austin A40 Devon Saloon	65.69	With Alan Hess.
27 Apr 1950	Long Island, USA	National Stock	12 hours	F	FS	Austin A40 Devon Saloon	65.08	With Alan Hess.
27 Apr 1950	Long Island, USA	National Stock	250 miles	F	FS	Austin A40 Devon Saloon	65.6	With Alan Hess.

DATE	LOCATION	RECORD TYPE	DISTANCE	CLASS	FLYING OR STANDING START	CAR	SPEED (MPH)	COMMENT
27 Apr 1950	Long Island, USA	National Stock	300 miles	F	FS	Austin A40 Devon Saloon	65.94	With Alan Hess.
27 Apr 1950	Long Island, USA	National Stock	400km	F	FS	Austin A40 Devon Saloon	65.59	With Alan Hess.
27 Apr 1950	Long Island, USA	National Stock	400 miles	F	FS	Austin A40 Devon Saloon	65.7	With Alan Hess.
27 Apr 1950	Long Island, USA	National Stock	500km	F	FS	Austin A40 Devon Saloon	65.99	With Alan Hess.
27 Apr 1950	Long Island, USA	National Stock	500 miles	F	FS	Austin A40 Devon Saloon	64.67	With Alan Hess.
27 Apr 1950	Long Island, USA	National Stock	1km	F	SS	Austin A40 Devon Saloon	47.51	With Alan Hess.
27 Apr 1950	Long Island, USA	National Stock	1 mile	F	SS	Austin A40 Devon Saloon	55.13	With Alan Hess.
27 Apr 1950	Long Island, USA	National Stock	5km	F	SS	Austin A40 Devon Saloon	61.36	With Alan Hess.
27 Apr 1950	Long Island, USA	National Stock	5 miles	F	SS	Austin A40 Devon Saloon	61.99	With Alan Hess.
27 Apr 1950	Long Island, USA	National Stock	10km	F	SS	Austin A40 Devon Saloon	62.5	With Alan Hess.
28 Apr 1950	Long Island, USA	National Stock	10 miles	F	SS	Austin A40 Devon Saloon	62.8	With Alan Hess.
28 Apr 1950	Long Island, USA	National Stock	1km	F	FS	Austin A40 Devon Saloon	68.1	With Alan Hess.
28 Apr 1950	Long Island, USA	National Stock	1 mile	F	FS	Austin A40 Devon Saloon	65.67	With Alan Hess.
28 Apr 1950	Long Island, USA	National Stock	5km	F	FS	Austin A40 Devon Saloon	66.55	With Alan Hess.
28 Apr 1950	Long Island, USA	National Stock	5 miles	F	FS	Austin A40 Devon Saloon	66.26	With Alan Hess.
28 Apr 1950	Long Island, USA	National Stock	10km	F	FS	Austin A40 Devon Saloon	65.79	With Alan Hess.
28 Apr 1950	Long Island, USA	National Stock	10 miles	F	FS	Austin A40 Devon Saloon	64.95	With Alan Hess.

DATE	LOCATION	RECORD TYPE	DISTANCE	CLASS	FLYING OR STANDING START	CAR	SPEED (MPH)	COMMENT
28 Apr 1950	Long Island, USA	National	1km	F	SS	Austin A40 Devon Saloon	47.51	With Alan Hess.
28 Apr 1950	Long Island, USA	National	1 mile	F	SS	Austin A40 Devon Saloon	55.13	With Alan Hess.
28 Apr 1950	Long Island, USA	National	5km	F	SS	Austin A40 Devon Saloon	61.36	With Alan Hess.
28 Apr 1950	Long Island, USA	National	5 miles	F	SS	Austin A40 Devon Saloon	61.99	With Alan Hess.
28 Apr 1950	Long Island, USA	National	10km	F	SS	Austin A40 Devon Saloon	62.5	With Alan Hess.
28 Apr 1950	Long Island, USA	National	10 miles	F	SS	Austin A40 Devon Saloon	62.8	With Alan Hess.
28 Apr 1950	Long Island, USA	National	1km	F	FS	Austin A40 Devon Saloon	68.1	With Alan Hess.
28 Apr 1950	Long Island, USA	National	1 mile	F	FS	Austin A40 Devon Saloon	65.67	With Alan Hess.
28 Apr 1950	Long Island, USA	National	5km	F	FS	Austin A40 Devon Saloon	66.55	With Alan Hess.
28 Apr 1950	Long Island, USA	National	5 miles	F	FS	Austin A40 Devon Saloon	66.26	With Alan Hess.
28 Apr 1950	Long Island, USA	National	10km	F	FS	Austin A40 Devon Saloon	65.79	With Alan Hess.
28 Apr 1950	Long Island, USA	National	10 miles	F	FS	Austin A40 Devon Saloon	64.95	With Alan Hess.
24 Jul 1950	Jabbeke, Belgium	International	1km	J	FS	EX135	120.394	
24 Jul 1950	Jabbeke, Belgium	International	1km	J	FS	EX135	121.048	
24 Jul 1950	Jabbeke, Belgium	International	1km	J	FS	EX135	117.51	
24 Jul 1950	Jabbeke, Belgium	National	1km	J	FS	EX135	120.394	
24 Jul 1950	Jabbeke, Belgium	National	1km	J	FS	EX135	121.048	

DATE	LOCATION	RECORD TYPE	DISTANCE	CLASS	FLYING OR STANDING START	CAR	SPEED (MPH)	COMMENT
24 Jul 1950	Jabbeke, Belgium	National	1km	J	FS	EX135	117.51	
24 Jul 1950	Jabbeke, Belgium	International	1 mile	F (Saloon)	FS	MG Y-Type KCD698	104.725	Belonging to Dick Benn.
20 Aug 1951	Bonneville, USA	International	50km	F	SS	EX135	127.81	
20 Aug 1951	Bonneville, USA	International	50 miles	F	SS	EX135	130.6	
20 Aug 1951	Bonneville, USA	International	100km	F	SS	EX135	132.06	
20 Aug 1951	Bonneville, USA	International	100 miles	F	SS	EX135	135.1	
20 Aug 1951	Bonneville, USA	International	200km	F	SS	EX135	136.69	
20 Aug 1951	Bonneville, USA	International	1 hour	F	SS	EX135	137.48	
20 Aug 1951	Bonneville, USA	National	25km	F	FS	EX135	132.5226	
20 Aug 1951	Bonneville, USA	National	25 miles	F	FS	EX135	133.037	
20 Aug 1951	Bonneville, USA	National	50km	F	FS	EX135	133.4729	
20 Aug 1951	Bonneville, USA	National	50 miles	F	FS	EX135	134.7507	
20 Aug 1951	Bonneville, USA	National	75km	F	FS	EX135	134.5178	
20 Aug 1951	Bonneville, USA	National	100km	F	FS	EX135	135.8037	
20 Aug 1951	Bonneville, USA	National	75 miles	F	FS	EX135	136.5188	
20 Aug 1951	Bonneville, USA	National	100 miles	F	FS	EX135	137.6485	
20 Aug 1951	Bonneville, USA	National	200km	F	FS	EX135	139.0699	

DATE	LOCATION	RECORD TYPE	DISTANCE	CLASS	FLYING OR STANDING START	CAR	SPEED (MPH)	COMMENT
20 Aug 1951	Bonneville, USA	National	1 hour	F	FS	EX135	139.2875	
20 Aug 1951	Bonneville, USA	National	50km	F	SS	EX135	127.81	
20 Aug 1951	Bonneville, USA	National	50 miles	F	SS	EX135	130.6	
20 Aug 1951	Bonneville, USA	National	100km	F	SS	EX135	132.06	
20 Aug 1951	Bonneville, USA	National	100 miles	F	SS	EX135	135.1	
20 Aug 1951	Bonneville, USA	National	200km	F	SS	EX135	136.69	
20 Aug 1951	Bonneville, USA	National	1 hour	F	SS	EX135	137.48	
16 Aug 1952	Bonneville, USA	National	25km	E	SS	EX135	133.29	
16 Aug 1952	Bonneville, USA	National	25 miles	E	SS	EX135	140.825	
16 Aug 1952	Bonneville, USA	National	50km	E	SS	EX135	143.23	
16 Aug 1952	Bonneville, USA	National	50 miles	E	SS	EX135	147.4	
16 Aug 1952	Bonneville, USA	National	75km	E	SS	EX135	146.88	
16 Aug 1952	Bonneville, USA	National	100km	E	SS	EX135	148.725	
16 Aug 1952	Bonneville, USA	National	25km	E	FS	EX135	155.7	
16 Aug 1952	Bonneville, USA	National	25 miles	E	FS	EX135	155.17	
16 Aug 1952	Bonneville, USA	National	50km	E	FS	EX135	155.07	
16 Aug 1952	Bonneville, USA	National	50 miles	E	FS	EX135	154.955	

DATE	LOCATION	RECORD TYPE	DISTANCE	CLASS	FLYING OR STANDING START	CAR	SPEED (MPH)	COMMENT
16 Aug 1952	Bonneville, USA	National	75km	E	FS	EX135	154.98	
20 Aug 1952	Bonneville, USA	International	50km	E	SS	EX135	143.23	
20 Aug 1952	Bonneville, USA	International	50 miles	E	SS	EX135	147.4	
20 Aug 1952	Bonneville, USA	International	100km	E	SS	EX135	148.725	
21 Aug 1952	Bonneville, USA	National	1km	F	FS	EX135	202.14	
21 Aug 1952	Bonneville, USA	National	1 mile	F	FS	EX135	202.02	
21 Aug 1952	Bonneville, USA	National	5km	F	FS	EX135	200.2	
21 Aug 1952	Bonneville, USA	National	5 miles	F	FS	EX135	189.506	
21 Aug 1952	Bonneville, USA	National	10km	F	FS	EX135	182.8	
21 Aug 1952	Bonneville, USA	International	5 miles	F	FS	EX135	189.51	
21 Aug 1952	Bonneville, USA	International	10km	F	FS	EX135	182.85	

Notes:

1. Some record sheets give slightly different (rounded) speeds.
In this case, official record sheets (if available) have taken priority.

LIST OF CARS

MAKE	MODEL	YEAR OF CAR	VIN	REGISTRATION	COMMENT
Austin	Seven Gordon England Special	1924		RK1020	One of the first Gordon England Brooklands specials.
Salmson	San Sebastian	1928		N/A	Narrow two-seater Unsupercharged. Factory loan in 1928.
Salmson	Supercharged	1928		VB3080	Collected various awards in speed trials.
Amilcar*	C6	1929		YV91	Bought by Gardner in 1929 from Beris Harcourt-Wood. Later raced by Harry Clayton. Reregistered MPC702.
Aston Martin	International	1930	S31	VB7976	Driven in Double Twelve but owned by Miss D.M. Burnett.
MG*	C-Type Midget	1931	C0256	RX8591	Car 32 1932 Ards TT crashed by ATGG. Still raced today.
MG*	C-Type Midget	1931	C0253	RX8623	Car 31 1932 Ards TT (owned Randolph Jeffress).
MG*	C-Type Midget	1931	C0279	GT679	Initially Car 30 1932 Ards TT crashed by Hammy.

MAKE	MODEL	YEAR OF CAR	VIN	REGISTRATION	COMMENT
MG*	C-Type Midget	1931	C0257	RX8586	Replacement Car 30 1932 Ards TT driven by Barnes. Known as Hoodoo.
Talbot*	A075/90	1931	29518	GO8057	Ordered at 1930 Motor Show, modified by Fox & Nichol with body by KC bodies: extra fuel tank and faired running boards.
Talbot	AV105	1931		GO51	Pictured with Gardner in 1939 in Coats Mission photograph (NMMT).
Alfa Romeo*	8C 2300 Zagato Spider	1932	2111016 / SF31	BGO246	Owned by Gardner 1934. Zagato two-seater Spider, Scuderia Ferrari. Una recalled he picked it up from Maranello.
Rover	Speed 20	1932		GP3338	One of the very first Rover 'Twenty' Speed Models and used for publicity photographs.
MG*	K3 Magnette	1933	K3007	N/A	Offset single seater record car. Engine used in EX135 and original car rebodied.
MG*	EX135	1933	K3023	N/A	Original 'Humbug' commissioned by George Eyston. Adapted for record-breaking with body by Reid Railton in 1938. Currently located at the British Motor Museum.
Alfa Romeo*	8C 2300 long chassis 4-seater	1933	2111011	GT6074	Owned by Gardner 1933 and '34. Now green.
MG*	K3 Magnette	1934	K3015	JB3180	Factory loan. Now two different cars (one rebodied with new chassis 1937, the other registered CAS696).
Mercedes-Benz	SS	1934		GC4466	Owned 1935 to 1938. Crashed in Battersea, 22 April 1937.
Maserati	4CM	1936	1521	N/A	Now known as 'The Sulman car', it was later owned by Roy Salvadori.
MG	WA Saloon	1937		BBL793	Lent by Cecil Kimber. Used to prove route in Frankfurt 1938.
MG*	WA Drophead Coupe	1939		EOY672	Given by factory, registered 17th July 1939. Various mods including twin spare wheels mounted on front wings.
MG	TB	1939		CBL191	Photos NMM archive showing Una (1939/'40) Tickford adaptations. Lent to Una?
MG	VA	1942		MO5594	Pictured in Magic MPH.

MAKE	MODEL	YEAR OF CAR	VIN	REGISTRATION	COMMENT
MG*	TC	1946	TC/0498	MG6963	Given by factory, registered 23 March 1946, sold 23 Feb 1948. Used to prove route in Italy and first Jabbeke run.
Austin	Sixteen	1947		N/K	Mentioned in Magic MPH.
Talbot Lago*	T26 Grand Sport	1948	110106	726214	Third Talbot-Lago T26 bought from the factory in August 1948. Vanden Plas body, shown at 1948 Brussels Motor Show. Belgian registered. Kept for 18 months.
Healey	Sportsmobile	1949		GVB24	Possibly bought after seeing Donald Healey run the Elliott at Jabbeke in 1947. Sourced a close-ratio box from Abingdon (letters to JWT 1950, Magna Press).
Riley		1950		HVC199	Mentioned on insurance doc for 1950 Belgian run. (Magna Press).
Austin	A40	1950		N/K	Mentioned letter Jun 50 to JWT. 'If you can't lend me a car I can take the A40 over.' (Magna Press).
MG	TD	1950		FRX839	Lent to Gardner by John Thornley. Letter, 30 Jun 50 (Magna Press).
Jaguar	Mk VII	1953		KBY467	Prix d'Honneur at Coronation Concours, Brighton & Hove Motor Club.

Notes:

1. Listed in order of year of manufacture rather than when owned/driven by Gardner.
2. Those cars marked '*' are still known to exist in 2023.

1946, Jabbeke, MG TC.
*Photo: Taken from Goldie's own albums
(courtesy NMMT).*

... the

Automobile Associat...

that

AN AUSTIN DEVON SEDAN, MODEL A40, OF STRICTLY STOCK STATUS,
USING STRICTLY STOCK FUEL AND CRANKCASE OIL, ON A TEMPORARY COURSE
LAID OUT ON THE SUFFOLK COUNTY AIRPORT, WESTHAMPTON, LONG ISLAND, NEW YORK,
APRIL 27, 1950, ESTABLISHED NEW NATIONAL CLASS "F" SPEED RECORDS:
FROM A FLYING START FOR THE FOLLOWING RECOGNIZED PERIODS:

TIME	DRIVERS	DISTANCE	AVERAGE M.P.H.
1 HOUR	HESS	66.04	66.04
3 HOURS	"	197.45	65.82
6 "	HESS, GARDNER	394.14	65.69
12 "	"	780.95	65.08

Sanction No.

18TH

To my old Friend "Goldie"
Wishing him all the luck in the World from

Photos taken from Goldie's own albums.

Syd Ern
o S.O.
al Entrans
to his
Salt Beds

Bill Back
Flats

BIBLIOGRAPHY

AUTHOR	TITLE	PUBLISHING HOUSE	YEAR
Allison & Browning	The Works MGs, 2nd Ed	Veloce	2010
Boddy, William	Brooklands Vol 1-3	Grenville	1948
Campbell, Malcolm	My Thirty Years of Speed	Hutchinson & Co	1935
Clausager, Anders Ditlev	Factory-Original MG T-Series	Herridge & Sons	2019
d'Amico & Tabucchi	Alfa Romeo Production Cars 1910 - 1962	Nada	1996
Davis, S.C.H.	A Racing Motorist	Chapel River Press	1949
Drackett, Phil	Like Father Like Son	Clifton Books	1969
Eyston & Bradley	Speed on Salt	Batsford	1936
Fleischman, Bill & Pierce, Al	The Unauthorized NASCAR Fan Guide	Visible Ink	1999
Galpin, Darren	A Record of Motorsport, 1919-1950	http://www.dlg.speedfreaks.org/archive/book/beyond_1918.pdf	2012
Gibson, John Eason	Motor Racing 1946	Motor Racing Publications Ltd	1948
Goff, Leonard	Magnette-ised	Biddles	2007
Goldie Gardner, Alfred Thomas	Magic MPH	Motor Racing Publications	1951

AUTHOR	TITLE	PUBLISHING HOUSE	YEAR
Goldie Gardner, Alfred Thomas	Motor Cycle and Motor Racing 1951	Country & Sporting	1951
Goldie Gardner, Alfred Thomas	Car Racing 1953	Country & Sporting	1953
Green, Malcolm	Enjoying MG 'MG Hero'	MGOC	Feb 2013
Green, Malcolm	MG Sports Cars	CLB International	1997
Green, Malcolm	The MG Story	Herridge	2020
Grimsdale, Peter	Racing in the Dark	Simon & Schuster	2021
Grimsdale, Peter	High Performance	Simon & Schuster	2020
Henshaw, Trevor	The Sky Their Battlefield	Grub Street	1995
Kimber, Cecil	The Luck of the Game	Morris-Oxford Press	1932
Knudson, Richard	MG Competition Cars & Drivers	Iconografix	2006
Ludvigsen, Karl	Reid Railton: Man of Speed	EVRO	2018
Lyndon, Barré	Combat	The Windmill Press	1933
Lyndon, Barré	Circuit Dust	John Miles	1934
Lyndon, Barré	Grand Prix	John Miles	1935
May, C.A.N.	Shelsley Walsh	Foulis	1946
McComb, F. Wilson	Story of the MG Sports Car	Littlehampton Book Services	1972
McComb, F. Wilson	Reg Jackson, MG's Golden Boy	Safety Fast!	Oct/Nov 1987
McLellan, John	The Art of Abingdon	Motor Racing Publications Ltd	1982
MGCC	C0256 Chassis File	MGCC	1980
Montgomery, Bob	The Irish International Grand Prix 1929 - 1931	Dreolín	2019
Moore, Simon	The Legendary 2.3 Alfa Romeo	Parkside	2000
Mortimer, Charles	Brooklands: Behind the Scenes	Haynes	1980
Odgers, Major Paul	A Tac Chronicle	IWM	1945
Percy, Richard James	Scarborough's War Years	Sutton	1992
Pidgeon, Trevor	The Tanks at Flers	Fairmile	1995
Pomeroy, Laurence & de Burgh Walkerley, R.L.	The Motor Year Book 1949	Temple Press	1949

AUTHOR	TITLE	PUBLISHING HOUSE	YEAR
Poole, Alec	A Life by the Poole	Self-published	2021
Propert, George	MG Wartime Activities	MGCC	2018
Spurring, Quentin	Le Mans 1930-39	Evro	2017
Stirling & Richie	A Short History of 72nd Brigade RFA 1914-1919	Royal Artillery Association	1920
Thompson, Neal	Driving with the Devil	Crown	2007
Thornley, John	Maintaining the Breed (Revised edition)	Motor Racing Publications Ltd	1956
Thornley, Peter	Mr MG	Magna Press	2003
Tremayne, David	Donald Campbell: The Man Behind the Mask	Bantam	2005
Various	MG Cars 1940-1947	Brooklands Book Company	1947
Various	BRDC Silver Jubilee Book	Trafford Press	1952
Villa, Leo	The Record Breakers	Paul Hamlyn	1969
Walkerley, Rodney	Brooklands to Goodwood	GT Foulis & Co	1961
Walsh, Mick	Alfa Romeo Monza	Porter Press	2018
Weissmann, Karl-Joachim	The Hawke History of MMM Competition Cars	Self-published	2015
Wood, Jeremy	Speed on the Downs	JWFA Books	2005
Yates, Brock	Vanderbilt Cup Race	Iconografix	1997

Notes:

Newspaper and magazine articles have been credited in the footnotes. In particular, the following publications have been extensively used:

Motor Sport
The Motor
Autocar
Safety Fast!
The Brooklands Gazette Magazine
The Light Car & Cyclecar

The Daily Mail
The Express
The Times
The Telegraph

WILL'S CIGARETTES

M.G. MAGNETTE (MAJOR A. T. G. GARDNER)

L-R
with Ben
Arroga brother of
Hutheen (Eng)
Clarence McLeod
(the reputed of
his brother-in-law
Stirling) Ant
Pulling (Sir AAA
supervisor)

Telegramm

Deutsche Reichspost

56 LONDON 14222 16 1 1259 =

Dessau

aufgenommen
Jahr Zeit
38 15 — 52
durch
M

MAJOR GARDENER BRITISH RACING
MOTIRIST LZG =

Tag

Befördert
Zeit

an

durch

HEARTIEST CONGRATULATIONS OLD SPORTSMAN ON YOUR MARVELOUS
ACHIEVEMENT = MALCOLM CAMPBELL +

ISE DESSAU +

C 187 b Dia 4A

on at it's best!

GOLDIE GARDNER (holder of the
'Fastest Ever' in 6 International Car
Classes) SAYS . . . . .

"Use NOL Engine Oil. I do for the
arduous engine test of breaking International Speed Records. YOU can
rely on NOL and other Duckham's
Lubricants for trouble-free motoring."

Lt.-Col. A. T. Goldie Gardner, holder
of 26 International Speed Records
since 1939, consistently used

INDEX

NATIONAL
MOTOR MUSEUM

National Motor Museum Publishing

Goldie is the first title by the National Motor Museum Publishing (NMMP), established as part of the National Motor Museum group in 2023.

The NMMP has been set up to support the publication of high-quality, well-researched books that share the stories of motoring to a wide audience. It exists to give a low-cost outlet to those who want their detailed historical research to reach other enthusiasts, and to encourage engaging book-form storytelling that shares the personal, social and cultural tales of motoring with a non-specialist audience. The NMMP especially seeks to encourage talented young motoring writers and photographers into book authorship, providing them with guidance, design advice and practical help. It also aims to support the sharing of the National Motor Museum's extensive archive with a national and international audience.

A percentage of all net profits from each copy sold will directly support the National Motor Museum, helping to protect, share and expand our nation's motoring heritage. For more information, please visit: **www.nationalmotormuseum.org.uk**

1946, Jabbeke, MG TC.

Photo: Taken from Goldie's own albums (courtesy NMMT).